C000283808

THE SOUTH WALES
DIRECT LINE

Westerleigh West Junction circa 1962. In the background, above the farmhouse roof, can be seen the formation of the east curve. The branch to Yate curves away to the left of the photo. In the foreground is the viaduct over the Midland main line. WILF STANLEY

THE SOUTH WALES DIRECT LINE

History and Working

P.D. RENDALL

THE CROWOOD PRESS

First published in 2014 by
The Crowood Press Ltd
Ramsbury, Marlborough
Wiltshire SN8 2HR

www.crowood.com

© Peter Rendall 2014

All rights reserved. No part of this publication may be reproduced or
transmitted in any form or by any means, electronic or mechanical,
including photocopy, recording, or any information storage and
retrieval system, without permission in writing from the publishers.

British Library Cataloguing-in-Publication Data
A catalogue record for this book is available from the British Library.

ISBN 978 1 84797 707 6

Acknowledgements
Thanks are due to: the staff of the Wiltshire Records Office, in
particular Claire Skinner and Gill Neale; to Bristol Records Office
for permission to reproduce the plan of Wapley depot. I am grateful
to retired signalmen and one-time work colleagues Malcolm
Eggelton, Dave Dart and Wilf Stanley; the late Eric Holwell, driver,
Bristol Bath Road shed, and the late Chilston Frampton, signalman,
Bristol District, for sharing their memories of working the line.
Thanks are also due to Chris Goodman for keeping me up to date
on current developments and to Wilf Stanley and my brother,
Tim Rendall, for allowing me access to their photo collections.

Typeset by Bookcraft Ltd, Stroud, Gloucestershire
Printed and bound in India by Replika Press Pvt Ltd

Contents

Introduction

It is often said that the twentieth century was the greatest in terms of technological advances: early wood, wire and fabric aeroplanes developed into supersonic passenger aircraft; slow, coal-fired ships developed into fast, ocean-going luxury liners; slow, outdated trains of gas-lit wooden carriages hauled by steam locomotives developed into sleek, air-conditioned trains of comfortable carriages, pulled by modern electric locomotives equipped with radio-signalling and capable of speeds in excess of 125mph (200km/h).

But, in reality, the great Victorian industrial age of the nineteenth century gave birth to technological advances that were just as ground-breaking in their time. The nineteenth century saw the British Isles covered with railway lines almost as fast as the mid-twentieth century saw many of these lines closed and ripped up.

Almost all the great main lines in the UK were built in the Victorian age and even that great Victorian achievement, the Severn Railway Tunnel, had transformed train services to and from South Wales by the time the Queen and Empress died. However, as yet there was still one thing missing: a *direct* rail route to South Wales, to enable a faster journey into the Principality from the capital city of London.

Planned at the end of the Victorian age and built at the beginning of the Edwardian era, the South Wales Direct Railway was the answer. Running from a junction with the existing London–Bristol Railway (via Bath) at Wootton Bassett in Wiltshire, to two new junctions with the existing Bristol and South Wales Union Railway (B&SWUR) at Filton and Patchway in Gloucestershire, the Direct line gave the Great Western Railway (GWR) its fast line into South Wales.

Although the line lost its stations in the early 1960s, it survived Dr Beeching's cuts, gained a new station, Bristol Parkway, in 1972 and went on to become upgraded to the first dedicated High Speed 125mph rail line in 1975. Today, the Direct line is again undergoing upgrading to take the latest high-speed electric trains, which will collect 25kV current from overhead wires. The route will once more be in the vanguard of modern railway technological advances and will become a route fit for the twenty-first century and beyond.

Previous books have concentrated on just the section of line opened in 1903, known as the South Wales Direct line, or the 'Badminton line'. However, from the time the line opened and provided a direct and shorter route from London to South Wales, the section of line between Filton Junction and Patchway, once part of the Bristol and South Wales Union Railway, became somewhat of a 'little brother' to the London–South Wales services. The 1903 survey of the line was taken from Wootton Bassett (inclusive) to the Severn Tunnel (exclusive). Therefore to provide continuity I have included all stations and junctions between Patchway and the Severn Tunnel that were affected by the opening of the new Direct line and without which the descriptions of operating the line would be somewhat lacking.

This book is not a historical survey of the line; it is about how the line was worked and includes the duties (and some names) of those men and women who staffed the stations, signal boxes and goods yards.

CHAPTER I

A Brief History of the Line

In 1841, the Great Western Railway opened the line between London and Bristol in its entirety. The lucrative market of South Wales and its coal-fields was still to be tapped and with the opening up of South Wales it was hoped that the opportunity would be created to seek traffic from the Irish markets and beyond via the development of ports in Wales. To attract this valuable traffic could only sensibly be done by means of a railway, but the River Severn stood as a watery and seemingly insurmountable barrier between England and Wales. Unless the Severn could be crossed in some way, it would seem that the way by rail into England from the Principality of Wales could only be via Gloucester. To go by rail to Bristol and London via Gloucester was not only a long way round, but the Midland Railway was already making inroads into that area. There was little option for the GWR but to look at ways of crossing the River Severn.

However, a river was but a small problem to surmount for a company that could boast none other than the famous Isambard Kingdom Brunel amongst its founders. To this end, various ideas for the river crossing were sought and an abortive scheme for a rail-connected ferry boat crossing was proposed in 1845. In 1856, a new scheme was put forwards: to build a railway line from Bristol to a place on the east bank of the river at New Passage, near Pilning in Gloucestershire. This proposal was more successful and an Act of Parliament was passed bringing into being the Bristol and South Wales Union Railway.

The new, single line was to run from a junction just outside Bristol Temple Meads (close to what is today Dr Day's Junction) and run through the outskirts of Bristol to the east bank of the River Severn at New Passage. To do so, it would have to climb steeply out of the city to Filton and Patchway. From Patchway, the new line would descend through a tunnel and steadily down to its terminus. It would involve serious engineering works to dig a deep cutting at Horfield and to create embankments between Patchway and Pilning. The new tunnel would be 1,246yd (1,139m) long. A new timber landing stage would need to be built at New Passage to enable steamers to dock. The whole new line would be 11½ (18.5km) miles long. Corresponding works would be carried out on the Welsh side.

From its opening in 1863, the line was operated by the Great Western Railway. Steamers were worked by a contractor, John Bland, on behalf of the GWR. However, whilst providing a much-needed link between London and South Wales via Bristol, the river crossing had its limitations; there was mainly only passenger traffic and some small freight. The service was not reliable, as the treacherous high rise and fall of tides in the Severn (40ft [12m] and the second highest rise and fall of tide in the world) proved difficult for ships and provided uncomfortable journeys for passengers. It was obvious that a different method of crossing the river was needed. Voices clamoured for a railway tunnel and an Act of Parliament was passed in 1872, granting authority for work to commence on a tunnel.

Work started on the Severn Railway Tunnel in 1873, a year after work had commenced on another river crossing, the Severn Railway Bridge, further up the river towards Gloucester. This bridge was backed by the Midland Railway and was intended to link the Midland's interests in Gloucestershire with the Severn and Wye Valley Railway, the latter having a junction at Lydney with the Great Western line from Gloucester. However, it was only a single track and as the new Severn Tunnel would be double track, the bridge was not seen as any threat to the GWR's ambitions in South Wales.

The rail bridge was completed in 1879 and was followed in September 1885 by the official opening of the 4-mile, 628yd-long (7km) Severn Tunnel. With the opening of the tunnel, the B&SWUR line, which had been single, was now doubled throughout with a new, 1-mile-long (1.6km) tunnel at Patchway for what was now the Up line between the Severn Tunnel and Patchway. The Up line was also constructed on easier gradients to that of the old line, resulting in the new line running at a different, lower, level between Pilning and Patchway.

Trains were soon running between the developing South Wales ports and Bristol, then onwards to London. The line from the Severn Tunnel to Bristol soon became busy with passenger traffic and large volumes of coal traffic, as well as traffic from other industries. The result was that although the building of the tunnel had speeded up services between Wales and the capital, the extra traffic soon became a problem on the line between Bristol and Swindon. With the increasing need for express trains to run between South Wales and London, the main line was soon operating to capacity. It was realized that there was now a need for a more direct route to the Severn Tunnel; one that would avoid Bath and Bristol.

Plans were drawn up for a shorter, more direct route with easier gradients. This line was to leave the existing Swindon to Bristol line at Wootton Bassett, then join up with the original Bristol and South Wales Union line at Patchway, near Bristol. From Patchway, the line would continue as before to the Severn Tunnel. There would also be a spur to the B&SWUR at Filton, creating a triangle and allowing trains using the new line to run to Bristol as well as South Wales.

There were to be new stations along the route, serving local communities. The line would descend at a gradient of 1 in 300 from Wootton Bassett to Little Somerford, and then rise at 1 in 300 from the Avon Valley up to Badminton. From Badminton, the line would drop at 1 in 300 to Stoke Gifford, where there would be the triangular junction to Filton and Patchway. A small marshalling yard for freight traffic was to be constructed at Stoke Gifford.

Two tunnels would be required to take the new line through the Cotswold Hills: one at Alderton, between Hullavington and Badminton; and one between Badminton and Chipping Sodbury. There was to be a triangular junction at Westerleigh, between Chipping Sodbury and Coalpit Heath, and this would connect the new line to the Midland Railway at Yate, enabling trains to run to and from the Bristol–Gloucester line, over which the GWR had running powers.

The new direct line would cut 10 miles (16km) off the journey to South Wales, relieve the congested line through Bath and speed up services when the line was opened.

Accordingly, the Great Western Railway company laid a bill before Parliament, in which it proposed to construct the new railway line from a junction with the Swindon–Bristol line at Wootton Bassett, near Swindon, to Patchway, just outside Bristol. The new line was to have seven new stations; additionally, three existing stations would be rebuilt. Services between London and South Wales would be made quicker and the bottleneck at Bristol avoided.

The bill received assent and work began on construction of the new railway. The Dowager Duchess of Beaufort performed the ceremony of 'cutting the first sod' in a field near Old Sodbury in

The embankment that so upset Mr Robinson. A BR Standard Class 5 4-6-0 heads west from Coalpit Heath with a train of empty fuel tankers for Avonmouth Docks. WILF STANLEY

1897, which signified that work on the new line had commenced.

In spite of difficulties, which included bad weather and unexpected geological problems, the earthworks, bridges and new station buildings were completed in time to be inspected by the Directors of the Great Western in July 1901. Two years later, on 1 January 1903, the GWR started running freight trains between Wootton Bassett and Badminton and, on 1 May 1903, between Badminton and Patchway. Although the works were complete, passenger trains could not use the line until it had been inspected by the Board of Trade. On 26 June 1903, the Board's Inspector, Col. Yorke, inspected all the stations and signalling works on the line. He found all to be in order and the line was opened to passenger traffic on 1 July 1903.

Most people in the districts through which the new works of the line passed seemed contented enough with the new railway; after all, it provided some jobs and people could use the stations to travel to other places. They could also send and receive their goods and livestock. Not everyone was happy though; Bristol writer W.J. Robinson, who

wrote for the *Bristol Times and Mirror* mostly on local history and ecclesiastical buildings, chose a series of articles in which to vent his spleen upon the new railway. These articles were published in 1914 as a series of books entitled *West Country Churches.*[1] In the article on Coalpit Heath and its church, Robinson wrote:

> It [Coalpit Heath] is noted for the cultivation of plums, and in early spring the plum trees, when clothed in their snowy blossoms, produce a very beautiful effect, giving a special charm to the place, which resembles on a small scale the celebrated Vale of Evesham.
>
> Though the original beauty of parts of the parish has been marred by the unsightly embankment of the railway, and many of its rich meadows have been converted into a stiff and monotonous mound of considerable height which completely shuts off the view …

It is interesting to note that whilst painting a picture of pastoral bliss about Coalpit Heath, Robinson completely fails to make reference to how the village got its name and makes no mention of the various collieries scattered in and around the district that can hardly have enhanced its appearance.

The South Wales Direct line also gets a further taste of Mr Robinson's dislike for it in his description of the parish of Stoke Gifford: 'The picturesque little village of Stoke Gifford, about four miles from Bristol … unmolested in its peaceful repose, save that the railway, with its attendant noise and clatter, has come within its boundaries … '

Although the above was written in the years preceding the publication of *West Country Churches*, and therefore around seven or eight years after the railway had been opened, Robinson's distaste is clear; he could almost, in 2014, be writing about the proposed HS2 line.

The new line brought jobs to the areas through which it passed and gave promotional advantages to people currently employed by the Great Western elsewhere on its network. It also brought changes and business opportunities to the various communities upon which it had an impact. Owned and operated by the Great Western Railway from its opening to nationalization in 1948, the line swiftly proved its worth and saw many famous trains during the days of steam operation – the 'Red Dragon', 'The Bristolian', 'South Wales Pullman' and 'Capitals United Express' were among them. With its junction to Filton and thence to Bristol, the line also became a diversionary route for the other main line via Bath. Later, in 1910, a further junction, that to Avonmouth, was added at Stoke Gifford, linking the South Wales Direct line to Avonmouth Docks.

World War II saw many of the line's facilities expanded and a new marshalling yard with signal boxes built between Chipping Sodbury and Westerleigh. Post-war, the line was part of the route for many expresses between London and the Principality, but local services were little used even before the age of the car. The pendulum of the swinging sixties only swung towards closures of stations and withdrawal of the local trains, even before Richard Beeching got his hands on British Railways (BR).

However, the line did not die and in the 1970s was upgraded to become the first dedicated High Speed 125mph line in the country; it even got a new station – Bristol Parkway. Steam- and diesel-hauled excursions now use the line and the twenty-first century has seen the commencement of works for electrification of the line all the way to South Wales.

The new line was one of the first twentieth-century railways to be built and is still in use today as the high-speed line to the West and South Wales. During its 110-year life to date it has undergone a few modifications here and there and has been bridged by the M4 motorway (both over and under) in several places. Once staffed by many men (and women), the line today employs few regular staff, mostly at Bristol Parkway station and Stoke Gifford Civil Engineering sidings, but it was, for many, the place where they had not so much a job as a way of life. In order to illustrate how the line used to be worked, we need to look at some of the people who actually worked on the line, those whose jobs, whilst sometimes small, kept the whole together.

CHAPTER 2

The People who Worked the Line

The Superintendent of the Line

From the start, the line came under the jurisdiction of the Great Western Railway's Superintendent of the Line, Charles Kislingbury. Mr Kislingbury had come to live in the Cotham area of Bristol, having been previously living in Pontypool, Monmouthshire. His son, John, was Assistant Locomotive Superintendent of the Great Western. Kislingbury was responsible for setting out the duties of the men he was employing to man the stations, goods yards and signal boxes. The following duties are mostly taken from documents written by Charles Kislingbury and issued to each new station at the time of the line's opening in 1903.

The Station Master

The station master was responsible for everything that happened at his station. The duties of porters, booking and other clerical staff, signalling and goods yard staff all fell under his supervision, as did those of wagon drivers and, latterly, motor drivers. He had to know the various timetables, both passenger and freight (where appropriate) and regulations appertaining to the safe and proper working of his station. To him fell the duty of taking command of emergency working arrangements in the event of derailment or other problems, so he also had to know the requisite signalling regulations.

Additionally, the station master had to know the various rates for carriage of goods and parcels and be acquainted with all the local locations where the railway company's posters and timetables were displayed (*see* page 12).

The Porter

The Direct line employed three types of porter at most stations. There was the passenger porter, the goods porter and one or two lad porters. In later years, some stations employed a parcels porter. As with the station master's duties, Mr Kislingbury wrote out the duties of these staff in each Station Log Book.

The Passenger Porter

The turns of duty for the passenger porter were as follows:

- Week One: 06.30–17.30. Breakfast break: 08.40–09.10; Dinner: 12.10–12.40.
- Week Two: 10.50–21.50. Dinner: 12.45–13.15; Tea: 16.30–17.30.
- Saturday: 13.00–Midnight. Tea: 16.30–17.30.

DUTIES OF THE STATION MASTER

The duties of a station master on the South Wales Direct line were laid out in the individual Station Log Books, personally handwritten by Charles Kislingbury, the Superintendent of the Line, and issued to each station:[2]

To see that each member of the staff fully understands the whole of the duties allotted to him, that each man is capable of performing such duties, that a list of such duties is from time to time posted so as to be easy of access and that the men may have such list continually before them. To visit daily each signal box under his supervision and see that all current notices and instructions are on hand and properly preserved, understood and carried out by the staff, and to examine and sign the 'Line Clear' book at each cabin at the time of such visit. To meet all passenger trains during the time he is registered on duty.

To inspect, not less than once daily, all rooms, offices, water closets and urinals and see that they are in every respect clean and that the latter are kept flushed during the day. To see that all legal notices, time tables etc. are carefully and conspicuously exhibited and renewed from time to time as required and that no other notice than that authorized by the Company is exhibited at the station. To see that the distribution of gratuitous time books and time tables is duly and properly made at the various hotels, public and private offices etc. in accordance with the registered list and, by personal visits, satisfy himself that the Company's Regulations are carried out in this respect. To see that the Company's arrangements for the conveyance of passengers, parcels and goods are properly announced and that the Company's business is in every respect carried out satisfactorily both in regard to the dealing with the goods and parcels and the various advertisements of the Company's arrangements. To pay special attention to the receipt and despatch of goods and parcels and their delivery to the public and see that all unclaimed goods and luggage are dealt with promptly, in accordance with the regulations of the Company.

To personally receive all cash and deal with the same in accordance with Company's regulations. To attend, personally, to all correspondence with the public and Chief Officers and deal with the same and the general correspondence promptly.

To prepare all returns and accounts and despatch same to the various offices on the appointed dates. To be responsible for the safe custody of all cash received at the station and see that none is left in insecure places, and on no account, except on special authority, must cash be held over from one day to another.

To see that all circulars and advices are duly and properly noted by all concerned, posted in the guard book and indexed for reference. To enter into Goods Received Book and Inwards and Outwards Abstracts Books. Check change on Inwards invoices.

An additional duty on Sundays was to: 'Make up cash and look round premises once on each Sunday.'

Specifically for Chipping Sodbury station, although no doubt similar arrangements applied to the other stations, was the following instruction to the station master dated 16 June 1903:

When station master leaves Duty he will leave with the Porter who is on duty for Booking Purposes Ten shillings in change and this with the takings for bookings must at close of day's work be made up in a Bag with a memo shewing the total amount of such cash and deposited in the signal cabin for the night. When the early turn man comes on duty he will take the cash from the cabin and on arrival of station master will pay same over to him with the amount of bookings during the early morning – The station master to keep a close check upon the issue of tickets to prevent errors etc.

The spelling and grammar are as written by Mr Kislingbury on 1 May 1903. The 'Line Clear Book' referred to is the signal box Train Register, which the station master had to sign each time he visited the box.

- Sundays: 08.30–17.00, alternate weeks. No breaks recorded. (Perhaps Sunday duties were light enough to enable staff to take breaks when needed.)

The passenger porter's duties were:

- To post all bills and take down any out-of-date ones.

- To do general duties at passenger station.
- Light fires in offices and waiting rooms.
- Clean water closets and urinals and flush same during the day.
- Attend all passenger trains while on duty.
- To label all luggage.
- To load all milk and unload empty milk churns.
- To enter up wagon books and reference off same.
- To assist with parcels traffic, checking the same

in and out, booking up as required.

- To collect tickets and cancel same at once, making out return for station master's signature.
- To sweep platforms and overbridge daily, also to clean windows of station building.
- To trim and clean signal lamps, carry out and bring in the same as instructed by station master. [This latter duty being later incorporated into the lampman's duty.]

Inevitably there were occasions when the porter on duty was unable to be in two places at once, such as when two trains arrived at the same time. When this happened and one or the other train was late away as a result, or goods were not put on the train, the station master was required to address the problem. One such occasion occurred in November 1950, when Chipping Sodbury station master Reg Newcombe wrote to the signalmen at that station:

November 30th 1950

5.45pm Bristol and 5.30pm Swindon

On several occasions when above trains arrive here at the same time one of these trains has left without parcels and letters.

It has now been arranged for the porter to deal with the Down train (5.30pm Swindon) first. So will signalman please hold Up train in platform by signals until Down train has left and porter has had time to return to Up platform.

The Goods Porter

The turns of duty for the goods porter were as follows:

- Week One: 09.15–21.15. Dinner: 12.15–13.15; Tea: 16.30–17.30.
- Week Two: 06.50–18.50. Breakfast break: 08.50–09.20; Dinner: 12.15–13.15.
- Saturday: 13.00–Midnight. Tea: 16.30–7.30.
- Sundays: 11.45–21.45, alternate weeks. No breaks recorded again.

The goods porter's duties were:

- To assist generally with goods traffic.
- Fold (wagon) sheets.
- Take all wagon numbers in and out and record same, making return for signature.
- Clean horse boxes, cattle trucks and pens.
- See all trucks are properly sheeted before despatch.
- To meet all goods trains and assist with shunting.
- Keep weighbridge clean.

As this post was designated an 'Outdoor' job, the porter was issued with a mackintosh as well as his usual porter's uniform.

The Lad Porter

The lad porter generally helped where required. He worked 06.00–18.00 Monday–Saturday and his meal breaks were to be taken 'as convenient'. On alternate Sundays, he would work 08.00–20.00. Again, no Sunday meal breaks were recorded.

The Checker

The checker was involved with goods duties. His turns of duty were:

- Week One: Monday to Saturday, 09.15–21.15. Dinner: 12.30–13.30; Tea: 17.00–17.45.
- Week Two: Monday to Saturday, 07.00–19.00. Breakfast 09.15–09.45; Dinner 13.30–14.30.
- Sundays: 11.45–21.45, alternate weeks.

The checker's duties were:

- To check all goods inwards and outwards.
- Register and report all discrepancies.
- Load and unload all tonnage goods.
- See that signatures are obtained for each consignment before going away.
- Fold all (wagon) sheets and see to despatch of same. Enter up all goods received un-entered and report same at once. See all trucks are properly sheeted before despatch of same.

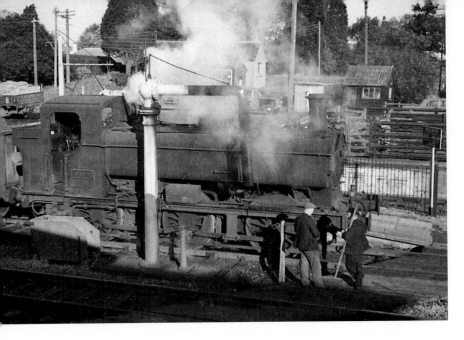

The shunter and checker find time for a chat during shunting operations at Chipping Sodbury in the early 1960s.
WILF STANLEY

- To see that all cattle trucks are properly cleaned before use. Assist generally at station as instructed by station master.
- To book passengers for trains on early or late turns of duty and carry out the instructions as to disposal of cash laid down.

Clerical Staff

Booking clerks were employed and their duties need little description. There were also lad clerks. The duties of the lad clerk at Chipping Sodbury in particular were as follows:

- Week One: 07.00–19.00. Breakfast: 08.40–09.30. Dinner: 13.00–14.00.
- Week Two: 09.15–21.15. Dinner: 13.00–14.00; Tea: 17.00–18.00.
- These hours were worked Monday to Saturday and there were no Sunday duties required.

The lad clerk's duties were:

- To book all trains while on duty.
- Enter up train book and make proof.
- Keep inwards and outwards books.
- To enter up Goods Received book and keep Abstract book up to date.

- To carry out the invoicing and also to check the charges on inwards invoices.
- To help station master in making up accounts and assist generally at the station as instructed.

The Signalman

The signalman's job was, obviously, to signal trains, using the block signalling equipment and the levers in the lever frame to control points and signals. To be based at a station meant that there would be regular visits from the station master, who would check to see that everything in the box was in order and that the rules and regulations were being adhered to. Once satisfied that all was in order, the station master would sign his name and the time in the Train Register.

Aside from the station master, a station box would have visits from the porters on occasions, to check train times. If there was shunting to be carried out, the guard or shunter would at some stage inevitably come up into the box for information or to fill their tea can with boiling water. Every other day the permanent way ganger would pass by on his patrol and sometimes come up to see the signalman to report a problem, or just to have a cuppa and pass the time of day. The job of signalman could be either an insular, lonely position, or a very busy

'Signal boxes must be kept clean …'
A spotless Pilning Station box with
signalman Harry Rose. WILF STANLEY

job with constant contact with other staff, depending on where a man worked. The rules stated that: 'Signal boxes must be kept Private' and this was usually adhered to in the early days.

The furnishings of a signal box were minimal. A desk was provided on which the Train Register was kept. The desk had a lifting lid and inside it books of rules and regulations were kept, along with other books and paperwork appertaining to the job, such as Wrong Line orders and Single Line working forms. A brass-cased clock often sat on top of the booking desk (as it was known). Some boxes had a larger clock on the wall. There was a small cupboard, also with a lid; this cupboard contained things like soap and blacklead in the top and rags, metal polish and other cleaning equipment in the bottom. There would also be a block of lockers in which each regular signalman based at the box could keep his belongings.

The signalmen were required to keep the floor swept and to polish the lino weekly. They had to polish the brass lever plates and the metal lever tops, as well as the brass lever release plungers and other brass and metalwork. The stove, if fitted, required regular polishing with blacklead. It was a military-style regime and was generally treated as such by signalmen and management alike, even up to the 1994 privatization of the railways.

Moving 'Up the Ladder'

As regards signalmen's promotion, it was relatively easy to get 'up the ladder' from Class 5 (the lowest and usually easiest job) to Class 4 or 3 boxes. Beyond that, it was 'dead men's shoes', with the chance of getting a Class 2, 1 or Special Class job being fairly remote. Class 4 boxes usually had Sunday turns, but many Class 3s did not. Promotion could, therefore, sometimes mean loss of earnings. It was not unusual for a man to apply for, and get, a Class 3 vacancy at the same time as applying for a Class 2 job. If he was successful in getting the 3, he was in line of seniority for the 2 and it was possible to make this move up to Class 2 without ever taking up the Class 3 vacancy.

As is mentioned in the section on Stoke Gifford yard below, yard boxes were very busy jobs. Frequently they were unable to carry out full booking of every move and train owing to pressure of work. In such instances, the box would either be provided with a 'booking boy', or be allowed to carry out only 'skeleton booking', for example just the train descriptions and passing times. The booking boy was usually a lad aged between fourteen to eighteen years. Those under eighteen were not allowed to work night shifts and usually a relief signalman was rostered to cover the booking on nights. Filton Junction, Stoke Gifford West and Pilning Junction boxes all had booking boys.

Relief signalman Malcolm Eggleton started his railway career with the Great Western Railway in 1946 as 'telegraphist' (the official title for 'booking boy') at Filton Junction. Malcolm stayed as booking boy for about a year, before moving to Stoke Gifford West for night turns – still as booking boy. Next, he became relief booking boy, before National Service in the Gloucestershire Regiment during the Korean War. Luckily, one of the Filton Junction signalmen, Ted Hart, kept him informed of vacancies and when Malcolm returned from Korea he applied for and got a vacancy at Hallen Marsh box, in Avonmouth.

As with any young apprentice, a booking boy was subject to practical jokes. Whilst booking at Filton Junction, young Malcolm was once told by signalman Frank Gainsford that the ' rails outside needed polishing' and that he should get the Brasso and get to work. Malcolm did not take the bait.

To start one's signalling career as a booking boy was considered a good first step on the ladder. It was the best way to learn the job and the signalman would frequently teach the 'boy' how to work the job, so that when the boy came of age and applied for a vacancy in a signal box, he would be well placed to get a job. Signalman Baden Lanman at Filton Junction was a Jehovah's Witness and once he had a lad 'trained', he would spend hours writing up a sermon for his next church service, leaving the booking lad to work the frame.

Classification of Signal Boxes

Signal boxes were graded for pay and promotional purposes. Gradings were worked out usually by the District Signalling Inspector on behalf of the Company's headquarters and were based on the number of trains handled by the box, the number of signal and point lever moves, how many telephone messages were dealt with per shift and so on. Each of these procedures was given a mark. All this was then subjected to a mathematical formula and the result was the box grade. The higher the grade, the

more important and busy was the box and hence attracted better pay. The highest graded boxes were 'Specials'.

On the opening of the Direct line, Brinkworth signal box was graded as Class 5, having achieved fifty-one marks per hour. Little Somerford was also a Class 5 box, with sixty-five marks per hour. Hullavington, too, made Class 5, but Badminton and Chipping Sodbury made Class 4, along with Westerleigh West Junction. Westerleigh East and North boxes, being little used, were unclassified at the time.

Coalpit Heath and Winterbourne were two of the smaller stations, but achieved Class 4 grading, mainly due to the amount of shunting moves required for goods trains. Patchway Station box was a Class 3, as were Pilning Junction and station boxes. Cattybrook Siding and Severn Tunnel East boxes were Class 4, as was Patchway Tunnel box when it opened in 1918.

At the yard boxes, the grades of Stoke Gifford East and West were 3 and 2 respectively.

Over the years, the box grades were reviewed, after which some went up and some went down, according to whether traffic levels increased or decreased. For instance, after a 1926 review, Brinkworth box was reclassified as a Class 4 with eighty-one marks per hour. Stoke Gifford West box, which had started off with 218 marks per hour, was reassessed as 260 marks per hour in a review of 1928, but remained a Class 2. After World War II, it became a Special Class box.

Filton Junction started off as a Class 2 with 239 marks per hour, but later achieved 257 marks after a 1926 reassessment.[3]

Staffing of Signal Boxes

Signalmen's jobs initially fell into two categories: regular staff who worked turn and turn about at the same signal box; or reliefmen, who, as the name suggests, worked at any signal box on their district to cover annual leave, sickness and vacancies. Until the 1950s, signalmen worked forty-eight hours per week, Monday to Saturday, with a rostered Sunday duty according to the particular box. When the forty-hour week was agreed, an extra signalman's post was required; that of district rest day relief. This man had the task of covering the rostered rest days, which were taken once a fortnight.

The rest day relief signalman covered the rest days of all signal boxes on his allocated 'patch', according to his grade. For example, a Class 2 Bristol East District rest day relief signalman's job on the South Wales Direct line in 1953 covered only the Coalpit Heath box. The others in his district were: Holesmouth, Hallen Marsh, Gloucester Rd, Filton West and Henbury, which were all on the Avonmouth line. However, there were so many vacancies in the district that the rest day roster was soon put aside, as many signalmen worked their rest days and the rest day relief signalmen went to many more boxes covering vacancies. The other signal boxes were classed as higher grade and thus their rest days were covered by higher-grade reliefmen.

Although often in isolated positions, country signal boxes were only lonely jobs if they were not at stations or yards. The lonely country junction did have its merits, though. During quiet times it was possible to leave the box and pick blackberries if there were bushes near enough to the box to permit this. When ownership of a motor car came within the reach of railway staff, most relief signalmen bought a car to enable them to reach the farthest signal boxes at which they had to work. During quiet periods, it now became possible to clean one's car if blackberrying was not your forte. This is what relief signalman Eddy Mann was doing at Badminton box one quiet Sunday; his car was parked behind the signal box and, having left the box door open, Eddy was busy with soap and

water when a keen manager arrived on the scene and told him off for leaving the signal box without permission.

The Signal Lampman

This man was usually known as the 'lampy'. The duties of the lampy were to clean and trim all signal lamps – which were long-burning paraffin lamps (one reservoir of paraffin would last nine days) – then to refill and relight them. He had to clean all spectacle glasses on the signal arms and clean the bullseye lens on the lamps themselves. This involved carrying out the work of cleaning and trimming a set of lamps in the lamp hut, which was a shed made from corrugated sheet metal that stood (usually) close to the signal box and which contained a 45gal (200ltr) drum of paraffin and spare lamps.

Once a set had been prepared, the lampy would carry them to the part of the layout where he intended to work, using a wooden bar with hooks on to carry the lamps. He would then climb the signal pole and

Although GWR/BR Western Region signals were not often as high as those of the MR/LMS, it was still quite a climb to the lamp platform, as this view shows. Note the height of the signal in relation to the locomotive; Badminton 1968. R. CUFF/AUTHOR'S COLLECTION

remove the lamps in place. Back on the ground, he would light the replacement lamp and climb the signal once more, replacing the lamp in the case. It was could be treacherous work, climbing a tall signal post, especially in wet and/or windy weather, lamp in one hand, other hand clinging on to the steel ladder for dear life. If it was a bracket signal, that is, a post that carried two or more posts for signal arms, there would be a wooden platform at the top of the ladder. If it was wet weather, this platform would be slippery with rain. In the wind, the whole structure swayed. It was a precarious occupation and today's Health & Safety would be up in arms.

However, to the lampy this was his day-to-day job and he simply got on with it. He would repeat this operation for all signals and ground signals controlled by that signal box. Before leaving duty, he would go to the signal box to check that all of that box's signal lamp indicators were showing 'Lamp In', meaning that the lamps were lit and burning correctly.

The lampy often wore an old coat that was stained and smelt strongly of paraffin. He would seldom stand very close to the signal box stove for obvious reasons.

During World War II, problems arose with the long-burning lamps – they kept going out. Whether the GWR was using poor-grade wartime paraffin, or whether they suspected that anti-railway fifth-columnists were at work, sabotaging signal lamps is not recorded. What is recorded is a circular from the Divisional Superintendent's Office dated 27 September 1943:

Long-Burning Lamp Failure

Owing to the large number of failures of long-burning lamps which have occurred recently, it is of the utmost importance that Form 5030 should be completed and sent to the Superintendent of the Line, Stores Superintendent and Divisional Superintendent's Office without delay in all cases of lamp failures. All lamps which fail must be kept on hand and not in any way tampered with, pending inspection by the Lamp Inspector.

A SAMPLE LAMPMAN'S WEEKLY ROTA

The lampy had a weekly rota and would have a different station/junction to work at each day. The following is the Chipping Sodbury signal lampman's rota for 1933:

District Inspector's Office, Bristol, August 24th 1933

HOURS and DUTIES of DISTRICT LAMPMAN, CHIPPING SODBURY

Commencing Monday, 28th August 1933 until further notice.

- **Monday**: Little Somerford 07.10am to 3.10pm:
  Clean, trim and light all lamps at Little Somerford including Distant signal lamps for Kingsmead Crossing (on the Malmesbury branch) and also take oil to the Crossing for the Crossing gate lamps.

- **Tuesday**: Chipping Sodbury and Hullavington 07.10am to 3.10pm:
  Clean, trim and light all lamps at Hullavington and also all lamps at Chipping Sodbury on the London side of the signal box.

- **Wednesday**: Badminton 07.10am to 3.10pm:
  Clean, trim and light all lamps at Badminton.

- **Thursday**: Chipping Sodbury and Westerleigh West 07.10am to 3.10pm:
  Clean, trim and light all lamps at Chipping Sodbury on the Bristol side of the signal box and all lamps at Westerleigh West.

- **Friday**: Wootton Bassett and Incline 07.10am to 3.10pm:
  Clean, trim and light all lamps at Wootton Bassett West and Wootton Bassett Incline (this latter on the line to Bath).

- **Saturday**: Wootton Bassett and Brinkworth 07.10am to 3.10pm:
  Clean, trim and light all lamps at Wootton Bassett East and Brinkworth.

All spectacle glasses to be cleaned on each visit.

Private and not for Publication.

> Copies of this Form must be supplied to every Lampman dealing with Long Burning Lamps, and to every Station Master and Signalman at whose Station these Lamps are in use.

GREAT WESTERN RAILWAY.

Failure of Long Burning Signal Lamps.

In the event of any Long Burning Signal Lamp going out, or failing in any way, this form must be properly filled up by the District Lampman or Signalman, as the case may be, who discovers the failure, and must be handed to the Station Master, who must, **immediately** send copies to the Divisional Superintendent, the Superintendent of the Line, and the Stores Superintendent, Swindon, so that prompt steps may be taken to investigate the cause of failure. The lamp or lamps that have failed must be taken charge of by the Station Master who must retain them in his possession in the same condition as when lamp or lamps failed until they have been inspected by the representative of the Superintendent of the Line or the Stores Superintendent.

	ANSWERS
Station or Signal Box	
Description of Signal from which Lamp that failed was taken	
Time and date at which failure occurred	
Date last trimmed and container filled prior to failure	
Whether oil container of Lamp was dry or had oil in it	
Description of oil in use at the time of failure	
Firm from whom oil was received	
Date barrel was received	
Number on barrel	
Remarks	

_____(Signature)

_____(Station)

To_____   _____(Date)

5,000. 1/46. (8) S.

Form 5030. This was to be filled in whenever there was a case of lamp failure. Did the GWR believe saboteurs were at work? AUTHOR'S COLLECTION

By 1948, with the inclusion of Wapley Common box into the Chipping Sodbury man's duties, the Patchway lampman's district had taken over the lamping duties at Westerleigh West and Westerleigh East Junctions and ran to Pilning station, including the Down Distant signal and Up Starting signal for Filton West Junction and the lamp on the sidings stop blocks at Filton West. At Pilning station, there was an invisible 'demarcation line' at the booking office, where the signal lamps from there to the Severn Tunnel were serviced by the Avonmouth district lampman.

The lamps at Filton Junction and on the Up Home signal from Filton and the Down Starting signal to Patchway, both at Stoke Gifford West, were covered by the Lawrence Hill lampman.

In the event of a lampman being off work through illness or leave, his duty was often covered by a signalman or relief signalman, on overtime.

The Signal and Telegraph Linemen

As the name suggests, these men, known as 'linemen', were responsible for maintaining and repairing all the equipment used by the signalling department. In later days, the word 'telegraph' was changed to 'telecommunications'.

At nationalization in 1948, the Bristol Signal & Telegraph Department covered the Direct line between Badminton and Pilning station, Newport department taking over from Pilning (exclusive) through the Severn Tunnel. Swindon men looked after the equipment as far as Hullavington, but were responsible for the telegraph wires as far as Badminton.

Signal and telegraph men were based at Chipping Sodbury and Patchway and in the days before road motor transport was provided, used trains to get to and from locations of work. One frequently used service was the 06.10am Bristol to Swindon via Badminton stopping train. Lineman Ray Baker and his assistant often used this service on an early shift to travel to a job.

Brian Thompson started his career on the Direct line at Chipping Sodbury after World War II and in May 1956 moved to Patchway as an assistant lineman. Ray Baker moved from North Somerset Junction, Bristol, to Patchway in October 1957, as assistant lineman class 2. In March 1959, C.J. Wilks, previously assistant lineman class 2, moved from

Signal technicians at work. Ray Baker (studying plans) and his son, Dave Baker; Westerleigh Junction 1988.
P.D. RENDALL

Patchway to Bristol West as assistant lineman class 1. Don Parker and Perce Starkey were two more men who worked on the Direct line in the fifties and sixties. Brian Thompson ended up in the panel box at Bristol as a senior technician, whilst cricket-loving Ray Baker became a senior technician at Stoke Gifford. Ray Baker had two sons, Andy and Dave, who both became signal technicians at Bristol.

In March 1959, Harold Fricker was promoted to the position of lineman Special Class at Chipping Sodbury.

As well as maintaining signals and signalling equipment, the lineman was always present when the permanent way gang wanted to work on or near points and work was likely to affect signal wires or point rodding. Disconnections were done by the lineman where necessary to permit the engineers to work on points.

The lineman would be present when signals were renewed, or where alterations were to take place, for example when stages of a resignalling scheme took place. Stage 7(a) of the 1970 Bristol resignalling took place over the weekend of 6–7 June 1970 and involved the closure of Winterbourne box, with multiple-aspect colour-light signalling and continuous track-circuiting being installed in its stead between Westerleigh West and Stoke Gifford East signal boxes. During the weeks

leading up to the weekend that would see Stage 7(a) brought in, the signal engineer's department erected the new signals on their concrete bases and connected them to the cables that were laid in lineside concrete troughing. The work also entailed alterations in the two manual signal boxes concerned. Both boxes would require new, illuminated track diagrams and a bank of telephones, one for each new signal under its jurisdiction.

Towards the end of the 14.00–22.00 shift on Saturday, 6 June, vans of technicians arrived at both Stoke Gifford East, Winterbourne and Westerleigh West boxes, armed with piles of wiring diagrams (known as 'the prints'), boxes of tools and reels of wire. At Westerleigh West, the locking linemen and the permanent way gang also arrived. Their services would be required, as the safety point in the Up branch, lever no. 12, was to be taken out of use. Other than that one alteration, there were to be no other permanent way changes at these two boxes, the remainder of the work being purely signalling.

The hour of 22.00 arrived and Winterbourne signal box switched out of circuit for the last time. The technicians and linemen moved in and the crossover was clipped out of use and disconnected from the box, to be recovered later. All the semaphore signal arms were taken down, along with the

Replacing Westerleigh West Up Starting signal. The renewals men look on as the old post is pulled down.
WILF STANLEY

Technicians George Matthews (left) and Maurice Sperring (right) attending to the elbows at Westerleigh Junction in 1985. WILF STANLEY

existing three-aspect colour light Down Main Home signal. Out at Coalpit Heath, the existing two-aspect colour-light Distant signals for both Winterbourne and Westerleigh West boxes were unceremoniously cut down.

At Stoke Gifford East box, men climbed the new signal posts and the covers were taken off the new four-aspect Up Main Home (sited opposite the box) and Up Main Starting signals. At Stoke Gifford East, as at Winterbourne, gangs of workmen removed the redundant semaphore arms from their tubular steel posts, then cut the posts themselves down, using oxyacetylene torches. In the box itself the technicians removed the block switch and modified the wiring circuit as they had done at Westerleigh West, as these boxes would, from now on, be open continuously. The handle of Stoke Gifford East's lever no. 3 was shortened by 4in (100mm), as it would now fulfil the function of an electric switch; this was done with a hacksaw. A new illuminated track diagram was hung above the block shelf in both boxes. The occupation of a track circuit illuminated a bulb behind a lozenge-shaped red plastic cover, one for each track circuit, which fitted in holes in the diagram, corresponding with the track circuit's position in the layout. These diagrams had to be wired in and tested.

At Westerleigh West, the Up Main Distant, no. 23, was replaced by a previously installed three-aspect colour-light signal, designated WW23. This was now designated Up Main Outer Home signal. In the box, the lever was painted red and had its handle shortened. The redundant safety point lever, no. 12, had its catch handle disconnected and the lever was painted white, to indicate that it was now 'spare'. The interlocking was removed.

As the Bristol Area resignalling took place in stages between June 1970 and May 1971, the signal boxes along the Direct line were closed and the line came under the control of Bristol and Swindon signalling centres (those manual boxes between Swindon and Hullavington having been closed during 1968 as part of the Swindon resignalling); Signal and telegraph staff were gradually transferred to work on the new equipment and staff from other parts of the area were drafted in as men moved to other places, or even left the railways.

Signals and points were operated from Bristol via remote interlocking equipment in lineside relay rooms built at junctions and other places where there was a concentration of points and signals. Each relay room was, in effect, an electronic signal box. Relay rooms were built – one at Westerleigh, which was provided with a standby generator in case of power failures, and two at Stoke Gifford, one at the east end, one at the west end, the latter having a permanent staff of signal technicians and also containing a standby generator. There was a relay room at Wootton Bassett, the latter being part of Swindon Panel signal box area.

CHAPTER 3

The 1903 Stations: Wootton Bassett to Badminton

Concurrent with the opening of the Direct line in 1903 came the opening of seven new stations on the line. These were: Brinkworth, Little Somerford, Hullavington, Badminton, Chipping Sodbury, Coalpit Heath and Winterbourne. In addition, there were three existing stations that were affected in one way or another by the opening of the Direct line and were consequently rebuilt or altered: Wootton Bassett, where the new line diverged from the existing Swindon–Bristol line, and Patchway and Pilning on the stretch of the Bristol & South Wales Union Line between Stoke Gifford and the Severn Tunnel. Each new station was of similar build and design and most were noted for the Scots pine trees planted by the GWR.

Wootton Bassett

Wootton Bassett's first station, known as Wootton Bassett Road, was a temporary platform situated a couple of miles towards Swindon and therefore nowhere near the small town of Wootton Bassett. The first 'proper' station was opened in the town on 30 July 1841. With the building of the South Wales Direct line and the construction of a junction with the Bristol line, the station was rebuilt and facilities expanded. There were still two platforms, but two new signal boxes, East and West, were constructed, plus an Up goods loop and sidings coming off the

Direct line and additional sidings on the Down side.

By 1907, the town was a thriving market town. A cattle market was held on the first Wednesday of each month and the town population was over 2,000. The Beaufort Hotel, run by Charles Fielder, was the nearest to the station, being in the station approach road on the Up side of the line. Not far away, in Station Road, stood the Railway Inn. Nearby were stables, a coal office and wharf, weighbridge and stores. All of the main offices and waiting rooms were on the Up platform, with smaller buildings for the waiting room, urinals and the ladies' waiting room on the Down platform. Both Up and Down buildings had substantial canopies. Both platforms were lined by a covered footbridge, no. 219, and the Marlborough Road crossed the lines via a three-arched brick bridge immediately to the east of the station.

In 1907, the local carrier was J.C. Wall. In 1915, the coal merchant who was based in the station yard was William Frederick Cannon.

The first station master of the new junction station was George Tett. Tett had joined the Great Western Railway in 1883 at the age of fourteen as passenger clerk at Bridport in Dorset. In 1891, he took the same post at Warminster station, before being promoted to station master at Cheddar in September 1899. He was appointed station master to Wootton Bassett in February 1903. In March

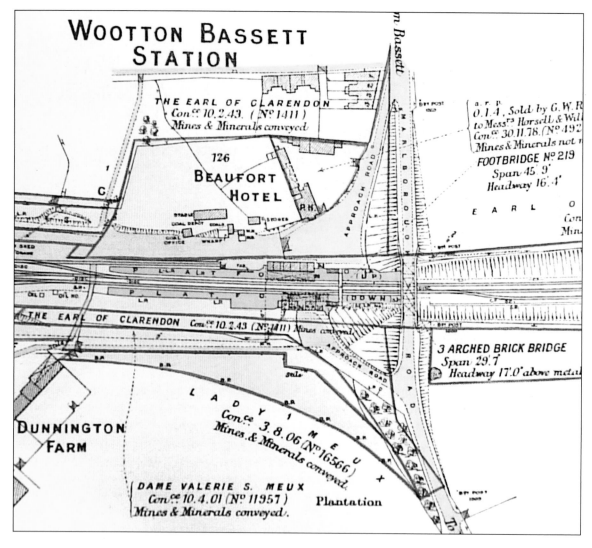

Wootton Bassett Junction; 1903. WILTSHIRE HISTORY CENTRE

1910, he left 'Bassett' to take up the post of station master at Shepton Mallet (GWR) and was replaced by Arthur George Campfield, who had been a clerk at Wootton Bassett station and was promoted to station master on the instructions of the Superintendent of the Line, Charles Kislingbury. Mr Campfield had been succeeded by 1927 by George Barry Humphries, JP. Later station masters included Mr Bull in 1945, Mr W.J. Reynolds in 1960 and Mr R. Biggs in 1962.[4]

Porters at Wootton Bassett after its rebuilding in 1903 included: A. Edwards, who soon after left and took up a porter's post at Chippenham station; J.H. Fowler, who moved to Badminton in May 1903; and W.H. Mann, who moved to Badminton in 1904. Lad porter T.T. Harris had come to Wootton Bassett from Keynsham in January 1899. Rupert Rawe was parcels porter in 1913, but by August 1914 was recorded by the GWR as being 'with the colours', that is, fighting in World War I.

Wootton Bassett station, looking towards Swindon in BR days. AUTHOR'S COLLECTION

In 1903, H.G. Miller was appointed signalman at Wootton Bassett, as was E.J. Hillier, who went there from Westbury (Wilts) in April of that year, replacing G. Brock, who had worked there on a temporary basis; Brock moved to Hullavington box.

During the tenure of station master Humphries, station staff increased to include a man employed for cleaning out the cattle pens. A lorry delivery and collection service was started, serving the surrounding country areas. Local freight by this time was not only coal and timber, but also agricultural commodities such as fertilizer and cattle feed. Cattle and sheep were also transported by rail from Wootton Bassett.

As late as 1963, a private siding was opened on the Brinkworth side of the Wootton Bassett to Lyneham road (A3102) overbridge. This siding, opened on 31 July 1963, served a new factory opened at Whiteshill Lane, Wootton Bassett, by Blanch-Lely Ltd. Blanch-Lely was a manufacturer of agricultural equipment such as balers and

binders and had a main factory at Crudwell, a small town midway between Malmesbury and Kemble. The new factory was where farming machinery produced at the Crudwell factory was assembled. There was a drawing office and development office on the new site. Machinery finished there was mostly for export. The company also owned several farms in the area where new machinery was tested.

The siding was accessed via a ground frame from the Up Badminton line. The ground frame was released by Wootton Bassett West signal box. As the siding was within station limits, that is, between the Up Home signal and the Up Starting signal, its operation came within shunting moves from Wootton Bassett, or it could be accessed by Up freight trains. It was also designated as a siding where 'slower freight trains could be shunted to enable more important trains to pass'.[5]

Control of Blanch-Lely's siding ground frame was transferred to Swindon Panel signal box on

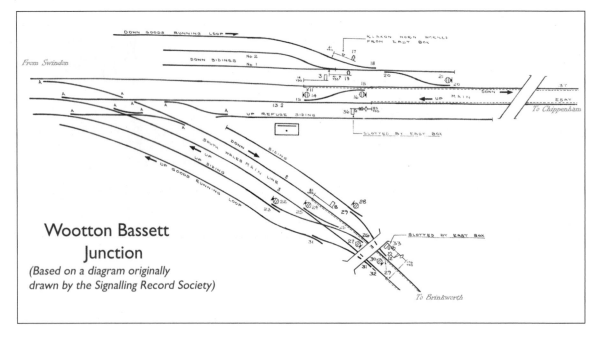

Wootton Bassett junction plan, BR days. Blanch-Lely siding was just off the plan to the bottom right.

24 March 1968, when Wootton Bassett West box was closed.

In 1969, Blanch-Lely sold its business and Wootton Bassett factory to Rigid Containers Ltd, which had little use for the siding and it fell into disuse, being officially closed on 5 May 1975, when it was recovered during the upgrading of the line for high-speed trains.

During March 1941, T.W. Ashley transferred from Yeovil Pen Mill to Wootton Bassett as a goods shunter, taking the place of W.C. Fry, who moved to Corsham. In October 1955, E.A.C. Ayres moved from Wootton Bassett permanent way gang to Little Somerford, where he took over as ganger, and in September 1955, J.G. Alstowe left the post of porter at Wootton Bassett and joined the Civil Engineering Department.

Wootton Bassett closed as a passenger station on 4 January 1965 and closed to public goods traffic on 4 October 1965.

Brinkworth

Brinkworth station was the first on the new line west of Wootton Bassett. Although the directors of the Great Western had envisaged the new line as a main line that would bring much traffic from and to South Wales, the Kelly's local directory for 1901 took a different view, stating: ' the branch line of the GWR from Swindon via Wootton Bassett and the Severn Tunnel has a station south of the village for passenger traffic'.

The station stood some 4 miles (6.4km) north of that of Dauntsey, on the line to Bath, and was 5 miles (8km) west of Wootton Bassett by road. The parish consisted of just over 6,000 acres of land, which was mostly pasture, and the village population (with that of the hamlet of Grittenham) was 1,099 in 1901.

Opened to passengers in 1903 with the other stations, Brinkworth stood a short distance from the

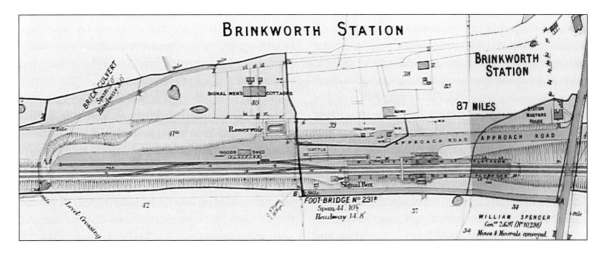

Brinkworth station; 1903. WILTSHIRE HISTORY CENTRE

collection of homesteads and farms that straggled along the Wootton Bassett to Malmesbury road and which led to the village being later described as the 'longest village in England'. It was a small, two-road station with platforms facing the Up and Down main lines.

The station buildings were constructed of red brick with corners of a dark blue Staffordshire brick. The main buildings carried quite substantial canopies and the platforms were joined by a metal, roofed footbridge (numbered 231B). This was the standard construction for all the new stations on the Direct line.

Access to the Up side station buildings and goods facilities was by a short approach road that led down from School Hill and which crossed the line by means of a girder bridge of 27ft (8.2m) skew span. The station master's red brick house stood on the village side of the corner of the approach road, adjacent to the lane.

The Up side station buildings contained the main facilities for passengers and goods. They housed

Brinkworth station just after closure. Note the platform coping stones in the process of being lifted.
WILF STANLEY

the porters' room, the station master's office, a booking office and general waiting room, ladies' waiting room and a gents' urinal. In later years, the general waiting room sported a large framed print of a GWR scene on the wall. Measuring about 6 × 3ft (2 × 1m), it was still there when the station closed to passengers in April 1961. One railway-man considered taking the poster, in its wooden frame, as a souvenir, but found it too big to take down by himself, so left it. The Down side building was smaller and housed a general waiting room and a gents' urinal.

Platform lighting was initially by gas lamps, but in later years illumination of the platforms and approach road was by Tilley paraffin lamps, these being lit and winched to the top of concrete stand-ards. I can speak from experience, having used Tilley lamps during my time as a signalman, that these lamps seemed to be the quickest way to self-immolation ever designed. To start with, one had

to pump them up, much like a blowlamp. Then, when the pressure was reached (and the lamp was oozing paraffin under pressure from various leaks) a small, kidney-shaped 'thing' was produced from a jar of meths (it looked rather like an item from a pathology lab). This 'thing' had a short wire handle – more of a grip – and had to be lit. Then it had to be clipped around the Tilley just below the mantle. By now, the pressure had dropped, so more pumping was necessary. If one was lucky, the mantle heated up quickly and then the valve could be slowly opened and pressurized paraffin would enter the mantle and the lamp was alight. If luck was not with the signalman, paraffin sprayed all over the place and *he* was alight!

Tilley lamps were used many times during night-time engineering works and nobody was more pleased than me when they were scrapped and replaced by battery lamps. How the porters at small wayside stations coped is hard to say;

Tilley lamp winder: Brinkworth station approach road; December 2012. P.D. RENDALL

Tilley lamp standard: Brinkworth station approach road; December 2012. P.D. RENDALL

perhaps the Tilleys were easier to use when in new condition.

At Brinkworth, a single siding was provided on the Up side, immediately west of the platform, accessing a loading dock with cattle pens. A brick goods shed also stood alongside the siding; this shed was built in similar style to the station buildings, but had no canopy. There was a short loading platform outside, which was provided with a 1½-ton crane.

The west end of the siding could hold thirteen wagons; the cattle dock eight wagons. A short distance behind the goods shed stood a short terrace of three houses for the signalmen.

On the Down side, opposite the cattle dock, stood the small brick signal box. This had a lever frame of twenty-one levers length with two spaces.

It was to this small station that the first station master, Alfred Barrington, was appointed in May 1903. Barrington had joined the GWR as a lad porter at Congresbury, Somerset, in 1884, aged fifteen years. He acted as relief porter to various local stations including Portishead and Clevedon and was promoted to parcels foreman at Weston-super-Mare station in October 1891. It was from here that he was further promoted to Brinkworth as Class 3 station master.

Mr Barrington stayed at Brinkworth for just over four years before he was found guilty of fraudulently altering wage sheets and was dismissed from the railway company for 'making false entries through the Brinkworth Pay Bill for ... wages which did not exist'.[6] The crime was all the more poignant when one considered that Barrington was the son of a local police constable in his home village of Woodborough, near Winscombe, Somerset. Barrington was succeeded by Edward George Axe, who had started on the GWR as a lad clerk at Lawrence Hill station, Bristol, and came to Brinkworth from the post of station master at Freshford, on the Bath to Westbury line. In 1922, Axe moved on and his place was taken by Albert Ham, who had previously been station master of the tiny halt of Great Somerford on the Malmesbury branch. Alfred

Barrington later found employment as a ledger clerk in a Bristol soap factory.

Station staff during 1903–05 included: A. Barrington, station master; porters W. Williams, W. Bondo and F.W. Malpas. O.J. Smith and W.H. Hendy were lad porters. Signalmen H.G. Millar, W.H. Parsons, H. Davis, J. Taylor and A. Plumley were all employed at Brinkworth during this short period. Millar came there from Wootton Bassett in May 1903 and returned to Bassett in September; Parsons came from Clevedon to replace him, but left shortly afterwards to go to Ashley Hill, Bristol, in January 1904; this was probably a mutual exchange of duties as Davis came from Ashley Hill to take Parsons' place at Brinkworth. J. Taylor was another signalman who 'passed through', leaving Patchway to work for a few months at Brinkworth, before moving to Westbury, Wilts. Lastly, Plumley had come from Flax Bourton, west of Bristol, to make up the pair of regular signalmen who would work the box round the clock.

Never well used, Brinkworth station was soon under consideration for rationalization after British Railways took over. By the beginning of 1952, the staffing levels had been reduced and the station closed at 15.00 Monday to Friday and by 12.30 on Saturdays. The station was considered an 'unstaffed halt' during the times it was unmanned. Guards of trains that called at Brinkworth after those times were instructed to collect the tickets of any passengers alighting and hand these tickets to the person in charge of the next station the train stopped at. In like manner, the guard had to note the persons who joined the train at Brinkworth and advise these to the next station, in order that their fares could be collected. Parcels traffic was to be picked up or dropped off at Little Somerford and that station would forward any parcels to Brinkworth station by the first stopping train the next day. In 1953, Brinkworth signal box was open between 07.20 and 22.00, Monday to Saturday.

Brinkworth station became an early victim of modernization and its attendant rationalization, when, in May 1958, the west end connection to the Up siding was removed, along with the main-line

Brinkworth. The new ground frame is seen centre left of the photo. The signal box is now closed. WILF STANLEY

crossover. In March the following year, the signal box was closed. New colour-light intermediate block signals were installed between Little Somerford and Wootton Bassett; those on the Up line were controlled by Little Somerford box, with those on the Down line being controlled by Wootton Bassett West box.

Access to the Up siding was now controlled by a ground frame of one lever, which stood just off the west end of the Up platform. This was released electrically from Little Somerford signal box. Trains could now only use this siding in the Up direction, going on to Wootton Bassett after completing work at Brinkworth siding. Brinkworth station closed to passengers and all goods traffic on 3 April 1961.

Little Somerford

Little Somerford, the Great Pretender: just what was the Great Western thinking of when it built a four-track station with a spacious layout in the middle of nowhere? True, it was not unusual for a station to be built some distance from the community it was named after, but considering that the nearest villages to the new station, Great and Little Somerford, were very small communities in 1903 (combined

BRITISH RAILWAYS SECTIONAL APPENDIX TO THE BOOKS OF RULES AND REGULATIONS, 1960

Brinkworth: Instructions for Working Ground Frame

The siding connection is situated in the Up Main Line at 87m 110yds, and is 1,413yds on the Little Somerford side of Brinkworth Up I.B.S signal, controlled by a Ground Frame known as Brinkworth Ground Frame electrically interlocked from Little Somerford Station signal box.

The Ground Frame is worked in accordance with the "Instructions for Working Ground frames operated by Key Control Instrument at Signal Box and Key Release Instrument at Ground Frame."

Telephone communication is provided between Little Somerford signal box and the Ground Frame, and the Telephone Box can be opened with a Goods Brake Van key.

When it is necessary for an Up Freight train to call at Brinkworth Ground Frame to do work, the Guard must inform the signalman at Little Somerford advising him the approximate time required at the siding.

Traffic to or from the siding should, if practicable, be formed next to the engine and detached or attached in one shunt.

Care must be taken to ensure that the rear portion of a freight train left on the Up Main Line during shunting operations, is properly secured.

When the work at the siding has been completed the Guard or person in charge must place the lever in the normal position, lock the Ground Frame and advise the signalman at Little Somerford Signal Box that this has been done and the train is about to leave.

population was just over 800 people and in 1911 it was down to 772) and that the nearest town of any reasonable size, Malmesbury, was already served by a branch line from Dauntsey on the Swindon–Bristol line via Bath, Little Somerford station had an air of status about it which it did not seem to deserve.

The station buildings, constructed in a similar manner to those of the other stations on the line, stood either side of four tracks, being served by platform lines, loops off the main lines. As at Brinkworth, the station buildings housed a porter's room, a station master's office, general waiting room and booking office, ladies' waiting room and gents' lavatory. The smaller Down platform building housed the gents' lavatory and a general waiting room. A telegraph office was opened at the station and was available for use between 8am and 7pm daily, Monday to Friday, for the despatch of telegrams.

The four tracks were spanned by a covered footbridge, no. 239B, with a span of 74ft (23m). Just west of the station, the line crossed the road from Chippenham to Malmesbury by means of an overbridge and the station approach road led from this road up a slope to the Up side station buildings.

The initial layout at Little Somerford was similar to that at Chipping Sodbury. Each platform, as noted above, stood adjacent to a platform line; this allowed passenger trains to call at the station whilst other, more important, trains passed through on the main lines. These platform lines also served as goods loops. The loops were lengthened in 1941 in connection with the huge increase in traffic as a result of the war; the Up platform line could hold thirty-seven wagons, a locomotive and brake van, while the Up goods loop could hold ninety-two wagons, an engine and van. The Down platform line could hold ninety-two wagons, an engine and van.

A siding on the Up side at the Brinkworth end of the station served a dock and cattle pens adjacent to the Up platform. The siding also served a loading platform and brick goods shed identical to that at Brinkworth. Beyond the shed a connection led from a 'mileage' siding. The small 'yard' was equipped with a 6-ton crane. The first business to occupy this yard was that of Samuel Fisher; Fisher's business was that of 'coal and manure merchant' and was managed by Daniel Barnes. In the 1920s, coal merchant A.L. Curtis rented space in the yard for his coal business. Curtis was based in an office at

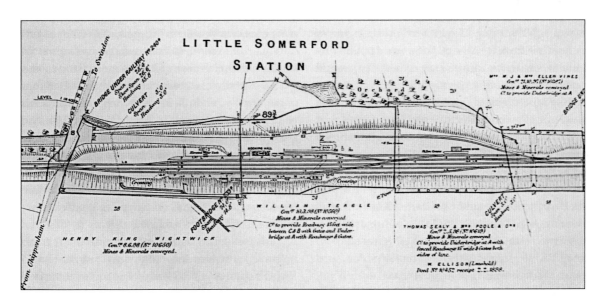

Little Somerford station plan; 1903. WILTSHIRE HISTORY CENTRE

Little Somerford Up platform around 1959. Note the platform 'furniture' of milk churns, buckets and rope. There's a push bike just behind what appears to be a BSA motorcycle, ?YHY644. There are lots of typical GWR platform signs in the canopy and not a passenger in sight as a tank engine and two GW brake vans set off for Swindon. WILF STANLEY

Malmesbury station and traded as a Colliery Agent, also having a site at Hullavington.

At the Swindon end of the Down platform stood a substantial signal box, equipped with a frame holding seventy-eight levers. The frame had thirteen spaces and sixty-five working levers. Oddly enough, unlike that at Brinkworth and out of context with the promise of better things to come displayed by the size of the layout, this signal box was constructed of wood to a standard GWR design.

The line through the station was on a falling gradient of 1 in 400 towards Brinkworth, so station staff

and train crews had to be especially aware of this when carrying out shunting operations. Passenger vehicles with handbrakes fitted had to have these applied and any vehicle not fitted with a handbrake had to be secured by a wheel scotch and, if possible, a brake stick would also be pushed through the spokes of a wheel to act as a stop.

Water columns were provided at each end of the station for the purpose of replenishing locomotive tanks and a tall water tank stood just behind the Up platform at the west end of the station.

A pair of semi-detached cottages were built by the side of a short dead-end track west of the station

Little Somerford station looking west in around 1959. WILF STANLEY

and on the south side of the line. Next to these cottages was the station master's house, which stood in a good-sized plot of land. There was a quarter of a mile walk to the station from here.

The first station master to be appointed at Little Somerford was Thomas Sorrell. He was born in Basingstoke, Hampshire, in 1860. His father, Charles Sorrell, had been a porter at Basingstoke GW station. After leaving school, Thomas joined the GWR and soon was rising through the ranks. By 1901, he was station master at Whitchurch on the GWR Didcot, Newbury and Southampton line. Eager to 'get on', he was soon promoted, in May 1903, to station master at Lavington, on the Berks & Hants main line between Hungerford and Westbury, Wilts. In September 1905, he took the post of station master at Little Somerford. However, after a few years at Little Somerford, Sorrell moved to Pilning as station master; still on the same line but with a busier job.

During the 1920s, Little Somerford's station master was Henry Jefferies. He was succeeded by Albert Plant and in 1945 it was Mr Hunt.

The first station staff in 1903–04 were: A. Edwards, who came from Wootton Bassett in May 1903 as a porter. He moved to Chippenham as a

porter in August of the same year. His place was taken by S.J. Bricker, a lad porter from Box. Bricker moved on in November of 1904 and was replaced by W.G. Poolman, who stayed for at least the next couple of years. He was joined by W.J. Clift, another lad porter.

The Malmesbury Branch

Initially, the Malmesbury branch railway left the Swindon to Bath main line in 1877 from a junction at Dauntsey. It was built north-west and south-east across the parish of Somerford close to the River Avon, with a station called Somerford west of the road near Great Somerford village. It was a single line that terminated at Malmesbury, a short distance from the town centre. A goods depot was opened at Malmesbury station in 1879. In 1880, the line was vested in the GWR.

In 1903, the GWR Direct line from Wootton Bassett to South Wales was constructed on an east–west course south of the village of Little Somerford. It was carried by bridges over the Great Somerford road and the existing Malmesbury branch line and by a viaduct over the low ground near the River Avon. The new station opened south of the village

Dauntsey, 1959. The Malmesbury branch used to curve in from the right. The course of the branch can be determined by the fence line.
WILF STANLEY

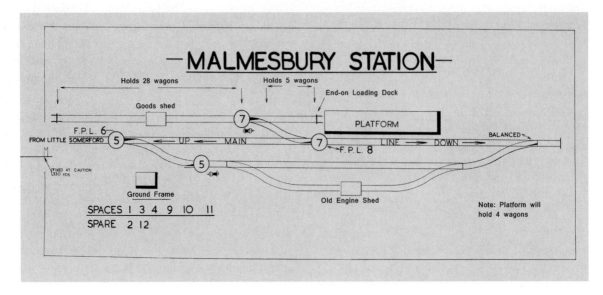

Malmesbury station plan after withdrawal of the passenger service (based on a plan in the Author's Collection).

on the Direct line was named Little Somerford. On the Malmesbury branch, Somerford station was renamed Great Somerford in 1903 and in 1922 became an unstaffed halt. Before closure it had a station master, Mr Albert Ham.

At Malmesbury station it was seemingly the practice for station masters to have distinctive names – in 1903, the station master at Malmesbury was Mr Edgar Harry Doswell, later succeeded by the equally noble-sounding Arthur Wynn Lloyd. Station master in 1923 was G.J. Dinham.

In 1933, a short stretch of new line was built across the fields from a new junction west of Little Somerford on the South Wales Direct line, to a new junction with the Dauntsey–Malmesbury line near Kingsmead Mill, thus linking it to the original branch from Dauntsey. At the same time, the single line from Kingsmead Crossing to Dauntsey was closed, apart from a short stretch at the Little Somerford end, which was used for the storage of condemned wagons and carriages. Great Somerford halt was closed. The branch was now 3 miles 988yd (5.7km) long.

Before the opening of the new cut-off line, there had been a signal box at Malmesbury.

This was reduced to ground frame status in 1933. The line between Little Somerford station and Malmesbury was then worked under the 'one engine in steam' principle, which meant that only one train at a time was permitted on the single line between Little Somerford and Malmesbury. A train staff was provided, which the driver of a branch train had to have in his possession as his authority to be on the single line. No train or shunting move was permitted to enter on to the single line at Little Somerford unless the train staff was present to hand to the driver. This train staff was wooden, round in section and painted white.

As there was now no signal box at Malmesbury and therefore no block working, the rules were that when a train for Malmesbury left Little Somerford, the Somerford signalman would telephone this information to Malmesbury station office and vice versa.

About a quarter of a mile from the main line, the branch was crossed by a minor road that led to a mill. There was a manned, gated level-crossing at this point, known as Kingsmead Crossing. Communication among Malmesbury station, Little Somerford signal box and the crossing keeper's

Looking from the site of the platform, the engine shed now services vehicles of a different kind; June 2011.

P.D. RENDALL

cabin was by telephone. The crossing keeper would be advised of the departure of a train from Little Somerford two minutes before the actual departure. Malmesbury station would advise the crossing keeper when a train left that station.

During the week, the normal position of the crossing gates was across the railway, but obviously the crossing keeper would be present to close the gates to road traffic when a train was due. On Sundays, there was no crossing keeper on duty, so the gates were closed and padlocked across the railway. However, Civil Engineering Department trains were sometimes required to work on the branch on a Sunday, so the Permanent Way Department ganger was issued with a key to enable

him to unlock the crossing gates and close them across the roadway to permit passage of engineering trains. Whilst such moves were in progress, a Permanent Way Department man was stationed at the crossing.

The town of Malmesbury stands mainly on a hill, but the railway station was at the bottom of the hill, the line from Little Somerford descending all the way from the main line to a place just before the town was reached, where the line was carried across a river by a bridge. The steepest part of the descent was between Little Somerford station and Kingsmead Crossing, which was 1 in 90, and from there to the river bridge the gradient was 1 in 500. From the river bridge into the station, it was a

OCCUPATION OF THE MALMESBURY BRANCH BY THE PERMANENT WAY DEPARTMENT.

The instructions under this heading on page 142, amended in Circular S.1562, are amplified as follows :—

Addition to Clause 7.

If the Station Master or person in charge can permit the work to be done he must place 3 detonators 10 yards apart in advance of the train on the running line.

Excerpt from a GWR notice dated December 1934. AUTHOR'S COLLECTION

level run. The line passed through a short tunnel of 105yd (96m) before emerging and curving into the small station.

In the event of a branch train failing or needing assistance, lineside telephones were provided at roughly 1-mile (1.6km) intervals to enable drivers to contact the signal box if they had problems with their train. These phones were sited at 91 miles 10 chains; 91 miles 70 chains and 92 miles 50 chains. These telephones could also be used by the Civil Engineering Department if necessary.

From the Little Somerford signalman's point of view, he had to be careful when using the Up loop at his station because Malmesbury trains had a straight run in off the branch into the Up platform line, which formed part of the Up loop. If a Malmesbury train should run by the branch signal, it could collide with the freight or passenger train standing on the loop. In turn, all drivers of branch trains understood that, on returning from Malmesbury, they were to approach Little Somerford with caution and be prepared to stop at the branch Home signal protecting the station.

The line from Little Somerford to Malmesbury was closed to passengers in 1951. Local freight continued to use the line and there was a daily (weekdays) workmen's train that ran to Swindon. Coal traffic was the staple business carried to the town. The branch and Little Somerford station closed entirely in 1963. The signal box at Little Somerford stayed open until it was closed as part of the Swindon area resignalling in June 1967.

In 1953, Little Somerford signal box was open continuously except on Sundays when the Severn Tunnel was closed for engineering work, when Little Somerford would close between 09.00 and 14.00.

Hullavington

Hullavington station was opened for goods traffic on 1 January 1903 and for passengers six months later on 1 July of the same year. There were two main lines, a siding with a cattle dock and a small goods shed with an external loading platform, plus

a further short siding provided on the Up side. Refuge sidings were provided on the Up and Down lines, one at either end of the layout. These refuge sidings were originally laid out to accommodate seventy-five wagons, but by 1941 the demands of wartime freight movements compelled the GWR to lengthen these refuge sidings and make them into goods loops.

A signal box stood at the Swindon end of the Down platform. Like that at neighbouring Little Somerford, the wooden signal box, although an example of a standard GWR wooden design, was out of kilter with the rest of the brick-built boxes at stations along the line. The two-road station, however, was, like all the others, built of brick with canopies over the platforms outside the buildings. On the Up side were the gents' urinals, the ladies' waiting room, the general waiting room, the booking office, porters' room and station master's office, whilst on the Down side was just a waiting room. A metal footbridge, no. 254B, linked the platforms. Unlike the pretentious Little Somerford, the facilities were adequate for a station serving a small village with a population of 593 people.

There was a horse-drawn carrier, operated by Henry Salter, serving the station daily to and from Chippenham. Henry Tanner, haulier and coal merchant, was based at the station, as was the coal business of Samuel Fisher, managed in this instance by John Wicks, whilst in the 1920s A.L. Curtis of Malmesbury also set up a coal business in the yard.

The first appointed station master was Mr J.J.M. Bishop. Born in 1852 in East Chelborough, Dorset, James Justinian Margus Bishop was the son of a Dorset woodman. On leaving school he became an agricultural labourer, but soon decided that this was not the life for him. He joined the GWR first as a ticket collector at East Chelborough station and moved to Swindon in 1873, where he became a railway policeman. Six years later, he was a ticket collector at Swindon. In 1885, he became the booking porter at the small station of Hannington on the Swindon to Highworth branch. Hannington was a crossing place on the single line and had a

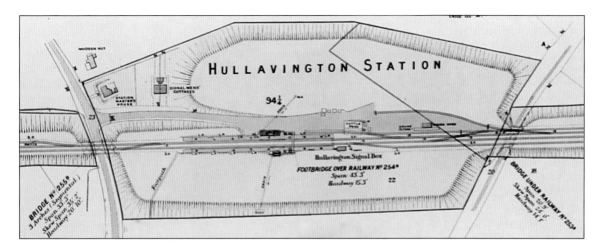

Plan of Hullavington station; 1903. WILTSHIRE HISTORY CENTRE

passing loop and a single siding. In November 1897, Bishop was appointed station master of the one-platform station.

In May 1903, James Bishop was promoted to Class 3 station master at Hullavington. Here was a different set-up altogether. With its main lines and sidings, it was so very different from Hannington. History does not recount if the stress of running a larger station took its toll on Mr Bishop, but by 1910 he was making plans to leave and in November of that year was appointed station master at Edington and Bratton on the Berks & Hants main line near Westbury, Wilts. Whatever his reasons for moving (Edington was also a Class 3 post so it was effectively a sideways move), Bishop was commended by the GWR for his work in August 1911, but in 1913 he was off work with an unspecified illness for three months. He returned to work briefly, but was again off ill between April and September 1914, before resigning so as to enable him to claim his company pension. He died at Westbury in October 1914. James Bishop was replaced at Hullavington by A.J. Jefferies.

In March 1943, the then Hullavington station master, H.J. Tidmarsh, moved to Pilning to fill a vacancy created by the promotion of the Pilning station master, Mr Edwards, to Tidworth, Wilts. Tidmarsh's place at Hullavington was taken by Mr J.R. Lane from Heytesbury on the Westbury (Wilts) to Salisbury line. By 1957, the station master was Mr G. Ludlow, who moved from station master at Hullavington to same post at Shrivenham in October 1957.

The station staff in 1903–4 were: J.J.M. Bishop, station master; porters G. Brook and A.J. Beck; and lad porter H.L. Potter. E.K. Greenman started work as a lad porter in June 1905.

As Hullavington station stood on a gradient of 1 in 300 towards Little Somerford, instructions were laid down that any shunting moves must be carried out with great care; as at Little Somerford and Brinkworth, wheel scotches were to be used and handbrakes applied whenever a vehicle was detached from a train in a platform or siding or on the main lines.

In 1953, Hullavington signal box opened between the hours of 06.00 Monday to 22.00 the following Sunday. On Sundays when the Severn Tunnel was closed for maintenance, Hullavington box would close between 06.00 and 14.00.

Hullavington station was only a mile from the Royal Air Force base of the same name. Mostly used for light aircraft and balloon parachute training, the base would have been expected to be a major user of the railway station; however, this does not seem to have been the case. Certainly,

Hullavington station looking east; 1959. WILF STANLEY

there was some traffic for the base using the GWR station at Hullavington, but the Air Force had its railway warrant office at Chippenham station on the Wootton Bassett–Bath line. Possibly this was the main station for RAF staff, as there were several other air bases in the near vicinity of Chippenham and it was uneconomical to have another RAF office at Hullavington station.

Hullavington station closed to passengers on 3 April 1961 and to goods traffic on 4 October 1965, although a siding remained for use by the Civil Engineering Department.

Badminton

Sited at 100m 1 chain from Paddington and 14 miles (22.5km) from the bottom of the Severn Tunnel, Badminton station opened for goods traffic on 1 January 1903. The new station was constructed just outside the village of Acton Turville, but was named 'Badminton': a title supposedly derived from the nearby villages of Little Badminton and Great Badminton. One suspects, however, that the name was more likely chosen in deference to the Duke of Beaufort, whose ancestral home, Badminton House, was situated less than a mile away from the new station. Two years earlier, the Duke had

signed an agreement with the GWR, in which that company agreed that four passenger trains each way would call at Badminton station every day, and it additionally agreed to stop *any* passenger train at Badminton should a first-class passenger wish to alight.

As at Little Somerford, in order to allow stopping trains to call without delaying faster expresses, the platforms were built against 'loop' or 'platform' lines, the main lines passing between these. The station was equipped with 400ft-long (120m) platforms and a covered footbridge, no. 271B, linking them. Single-storey station buildings were built on each platform and constructed of red brick with bluestone facings. The Up or Badminton village side buildings contained the ticket and booking office, the station master's office, waiting rooms and toilet. A plaque on which was carved the coat of arms of the Duke of Beaufort was mounted on the west end wall of these buildings.

Those on the Down, or Acton Turville, side contained waiting rooms and toilets. Both waiting rooms were equipped with paraffin lighting and coal stoves for the benefit of the travelling public. Platform canopies were provided to protect passengers standing outside from the elements. The cost of providing the station buildings came to the sum

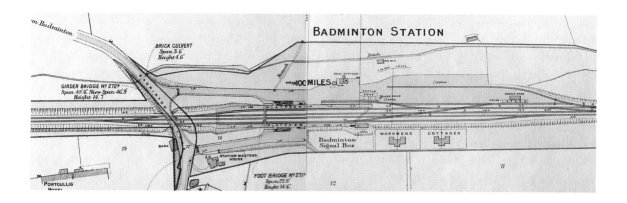

Plan of Badminton station; 1903. WILTSHIRE HISTORY CENTRE

of £1,165 3s 10½d. The station opened for passenger traffic on July 1 1903.

Access to the station was via approach roads built on each side of the bridge (no. 272B) carrying the Acton Turville–Badminton road over the railway at the western end of the layout (originally a steel girder bridge, this was replaced in 2012 by a concrete bridge on the same foundations, but with high metal parapets in preparation for electrification). The Up side approach road, apart from giving access to the station, also gave access to a small yard that contained a weighbridge, coal office, cattle pens and small goods shed with loading platform and crane. There was a loading dock adjacent

to the Up platform. The track into the loading dock had sharp reverse curves, so staff were warned that long carriages or wagons needed to be shunted into the dock with extreme care; coaches over 70ft (21m) in length were prohibited from entering the dock.

To assist with shunting operations, telephone communication was provided at the Hullavington end of the Up goods loop. This allowed communication between the signalman and the shunter or guard carrying out shunting moves in and out of the Up sidings. A code of signals was employed as follows: 'Attend telephone … 1 ring; Set points for yard or vice versa … 2 rings'.[7]

Badminton station looking west from the signal box; 1962. WILF STANLEY

Badminton station stood at the top of a falling gradient of 1 in 300 towards Chipping Sodbury and the tunnel. As with neighbouring stations, shunting operations had to be carried out with great care to ensure that no vehicles ran away.

The Down side approach road gave access to the station buildings and signal box. To control the layout, a brick-built signal box was built near the London end of the Down platform. Equipped with a 61-lever frame, it controlled the signals and points for the main lines, platform loops and small goods yard. The lever frame had thirteen spaces and forty-eight working levers in all. A house for the station master was built near the southern station entrance and two semi-detached signalmen's houses were built behind the signal box.

Nowadays, if one was to ask the average man or woman on the Gloucestershire streets to name the county's 'royal' station, they would most likely tell you 'Kemble'. They would be right, of course; with both the Prince of Wales and the Princess Royal living nearby and the royal train no stranger to its platforms, Kemble station rightly earns its 'royal' tag. But it was not always so. With Badminton House nearby and known in sporting circles as the home of one of the county's major hunts, the Beaufort, whose members dressed in colourful blue and buff coats, the area attracted both gentry and royalty alike, who came from far and wide to take part in the hunts, especially the annual Boxing Day meet. It was not surprising, therefore, that a grand hotel, as befitted a place renowned as the 'headquarters of fox hunting', should be built to accommodate those visitors who were not staying at Badminton House. Named the Portcullis Hotel, the new building was

erected within easy reach of Badminton station and was provided with fifty loose boxes for guests' horses. It was, of course, furnished in such fashion as to afford the maximum comfort and convenience for people from the hunting fraternity.

In the days before road transporters became available, it was natural that the railway station would be of importance to hunting visitors, especially as the Great Western Railway owned two Hound Vans. These were railway carriages built in the 1880s solely for the transportation of hounds and terriers. The Beaufort used to hunt across not only Gloucestershire, but Oxfordshire as well, and one such vehicle was kept at Badminton and used to transport the Beaufort Hunt's dogs to distant meets. The carriage would travel attached to horseboxes containing the Hunt's members' mounts. A note was added by Superintendent of the Line Charles Kislingbury to the station log books at Badminton and Chipping Sodbury stations, to the effect that 'lights need not be provided in Horse boxes requiring to pass through the tunnels' (the tunnels being those of Chipping Sodbury and Alderton).

With the advent, in 1949, of the famous Badminton Horse Trials, held annually in Badminton Great Park and rapidly establishing itself as one of the most important events in the equestrian's calendar, the station became regularly patronized by people attending the event, including members of the royal family.

The coming of the new station not only provided goods and passenger services for the local population, but also gave Badminton village its first running water supply; the contractors building the line needed a regular supply of water and this was provided by the West Gloucestershire Water Company. On completion of the line, this supply was transferred to the village.

With a catchment area that included Tormarton, Acton Turville, the Badmintons, Nettleton, Burton, Luckington and even Castle Combe, Badminton station was well patronized. Villagers and gentry alike used the station and ticket sales were high. As late as 1946, the station boasted an *increase* in passenger and freight traffic. Possibly due to

---

SHUNTING OF VEHICLES DURING HEAVY WINDS AND STORMS

In all cases vehicles, with or without brakes, must be placed in a siding by the train from which they are detached and not left on the Main Line.

Instructions to Staff on the South Wales Direct Line

Badminton: this is the wartime extension to the Up side station building; 1996. P.D. RENDALL

this increase, the Up side station buildings were extended in 1947 to include improved parcels accommodation and extra cycle storage.

Of course, it was not just passengers and the hunting fraternity who used the station's facilities. Apart from the boxes for horses and hounds, public goods facilities were provided at the station. Goods traffic comprised mainly of agricultural foodstuffs and equipment; coal for Silvey's, the local coal merchant, and milk. At one time in the mid-1920s, over 700gal (3,200ltr) of milk per day was taken by rail out of Badminton station. Cattle pens were provided in the small goods yard, but were not exceptionally well used.

Around the time of World War II, a Ministry of Supply buffer depot was built in the goods yard. This depot latterly kept stocks of canned food and other necessities in case of nuclear attack. After the fall of the Soviet bloc and with the threat of attack gone, the depot was closed and the stocks of food disposed of to charities for distribution to the needy.

Badminton station survived both world wars under the Great Western and was taken into national ownership with the advent of British Railways in 1948. The war years had changed the face of country living for ever, though, and in the post-war 'boom' years, people's attitudes were also changing. Hunting was not as popular as it had

been before the war; indeed, the Portcullis Hotel had closed in the 1930s, becoming a private residence. In spite of the extra traffic generated by the annual Horse Trials, fewer people were now using the station. Local folk were finding motor cars and buses more convenient than the sparse railway service. In 1960, the summer timetable provided a well spaced-out service; on weekday mornings there was a Down stopping train that left Swindon for Bristol at 07.15 and called at Badminton 08.02–08.05. An Up morning service left Bristol Temple Meads at 06.10 and called at Badminton 06.58–07.01. In the evening, the 17.45 ex-Bristol called at Badminton 18.33–18.35.

In addition to these local services, which called at 'all stations', Badminton station was served by 1A09, the 03.55 Fishguard–Paddington Express that called at Badminton 08.23–08.28 (and also detached a locomotive that had assisted the train from Severn Tunnel West). 1A21, the Mondays-only Cardiff–Paddington service, called at Badminton 09.29–09.31, as did its Tuesday–Friday variant, which started from Fishguard Harbour instead of Cardiff. 1A11, the 12.05 Milford Haven–Paddington, also called at Badminton 17.10–17.12. There was a further London service that called at Badminton at 23.54–23.59. This was the 15.35 Neyland–Paddington parcels, which stopped to detach an assisting engine.

Badminton: the buffer depot;
December 2012. P.D. RENDALL

Down weekday services from London in 1960 were: 1F46, 13.55 Paddington–Pembroke Dock, which arrived at Badminton 16.08 and departed at 16.10; and the Down 'Capitals United Express', which left Paddington for Neyland at 15.55 and called at Badminton 17.44–17.46.

When local passenger trains on the line were withdrawn in 1962, Badminton was only served by a London–South Wales service in each direction that only stopped there for 'gentry and business-men'. Several chauffeur-driven cars would arrive just before the train was due and disgorge their smartly dressed passengers, the limousines return-ing to collect their owners later that day.

Falling passenger and goods receipts caused BR to consider closing the station as early as 1961, but the Duke of Beaufort objected and the station remained open. Before the notorious Dr Beeching's axe fell on other stations across the UK, falling receipts saw the closure of all other stations on the Direct line; Badminton stayed resolutely open. The loss of public goods facilities occurred at Badminton in November 1966. The station survived another closure attempt in 1967, but was finally to succumb to closure the following year. Although the proposed withdrawal of passenger facilities gave rise to a question in the House of Commons, the station was closed on 3 June 1968. The actual

1F45, a Paddington–Swansea service,
calls at Badminton in the early 1960s.
WILF STANLEY

1A75 pulls into the Badminton Up platform; 31 May 1967. *R. CUFF/ AUTHOR*

CENTRE: *This one is not stopping; the Up 'South Wales Pullman' speeds through Badminton station; 31 May 1967. R. CUFF/AUTHOR'S COLLECTION*

last day of operations was Sunday, 2 June 1968. By that time, there was only one train scheduled to stop at Badminton in the Up direction on Sundays; the 17.00 Cardiff–Paddington, 1A69. However, on 2 June 1A69 was cancelled due to operating problems and so the 'honour' of being the last train to call at Badminton fell to the 16.20 Swansea–Paddington, 1A70, which was given stop orders to call at the station.[8]

Local enthusiasts turned out in large numbers (well over 100 according to the *Railway Magazine*) to see the last train (ironically some twenty-five minutes later than the timetabled service), some having cycled several miles. As was usual with

1982 HST set 253006 passing under the old road bridge – since replaced for the forthcoming electrification of the line. With an HST service to London, what a commuter station this could have been if only it had stayed open for a further eight years until the HST came into service. Close in haste, repent at leisure ... P.D. RENDALL

these closures in the 1960s, if the people who came to witness the station's demise had graced it with their presence more often and used the (by then admittedly meagre) services, then the case against closure could have been strengthened; one passenger was reported to have joined the train and none got off. For the record, the train was hauled by Brush Type 4 (Class 47) diesel D1670.

The first station master appointed to Badminton station was Mr Samuel Joseph Jefford. Jefford had an impressive record, second only to that of the Chipping Sodbury station master. A native of Dorset, he had been born in Bridport in 1852. Shortly after leaving school Jefford joined the Army, serving with a regiment of the Royal Artillery. After Army service as a Gunner, he joined the Great Western Railway as a signalman at Saltford, on the Bristol–Bath line. His next move was as a 'switch man' (points man) at Bristol Joint station, before moving into the clerical grade as a booking clerk at Ashley Hill station. He moved to Dauntsey as booking clerk in 1882 and in 1890 became station master there. Samuel Jefford became station master at Badminton in May 1903, moving into the station house with his wife and children. He stayed at Badminton until he died in February 1912.

Jefford was succeeded as station master by J.E. Randall, who moved there from Chipping Sodbury. By 1929, the incumbent was Mr Bray. Mr Pike was in charge in 1945.

Badminton's first station staff in 1903–04 included porters J.H. Fowler, who moved there from Wootton Bassett in May 1903, B. Button, G.H. Blackford, W.H. Mann and E.J. Marsh. A lad porter,

G. Groom, was also employed. In November 1905, J. Newman, signalman at Dauntsey, on the Swindon–Bath line, got the job of signalman at Badminton

The station was served in its early days by a horse-drawn carrier owned and operated by Thomas Andrews. The service carried people to and from the station and surrounding villages, arriving at the station twice a day, Monday to Friday. In October 1959, A.E.C. Jones became motor driver, Badminton.

After closure, one enterprising railway official made money out of the station's 'royal' connections by selling 'station master' signs from the office doors of various other closed stations and telling purchasers that they came from the 'royal' station.

Although the station had closed, the signal box remained open for a further three years until it too closed in 1971 as modern signalling took over. It had been open continuously since 1953.

Amazingly, over forty years after closure, the majority of the station buildings still stand. At the time of writing, the Down side building is looking quite derelict and the Up side buildings, once used as offices for the coal merchants, are in equally poor condition; the wartime extension has lost its platform canopy. The plaque is no longer on the end wall. High-speed trains tear past the site at 125mph, en route for London or South Wales. Ironically, the Badminton Horse Trials attract crowds every year and many business people now live in the area. It is ironic to think how convenient Badminton station would be if it was open now, with direct links to the capital for commuters; perhaps it would *still* be Gloucestershire's 'royal' station.

CHAPTER 4

Chipping Sodbury to Winterbourne

Chipping Sodbury

Opened for goods traffic on 1 May 1903 and for passengers on 1 July of the same year, the station at Chipping Sodbury was built approximately 104.5 miles (168km) from Paddington and less than a mile from the market town of Chipping Sodbury itself. As with many of the stations along the new line, the platforms were built against loop or platform lines, with the main lines passing between these. Both platform lines doubled as goods loops. The station was equipped with 400ft-long (120m) platforms and a covered footbridge linking them (no. 277B, with a span of 71ft 2in [2.2m]). There was a loading dock adjacent to the Up platform and cattle pens. Access to the station was via an approach road off the Chipping Sodbury to Acton Turville road (later the A432), leading to the station approach, a spacious goods yard with weighbridge, coal office and the largest goods shed on the line.

The single-storey main station building was on the Up (town side) platform and constructed of red brick with bluestone facings in typical late nineteenth-century Great Western fashion. It contained the booking and parcels offices, station master's office, waiting rooms and toilets. The building on

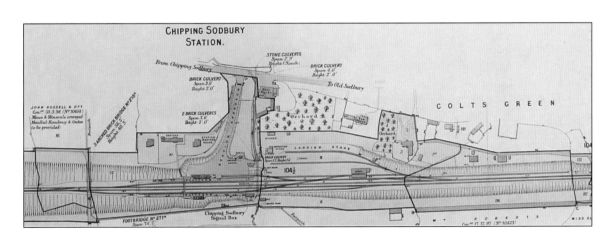

Chipping Sodbury station plan; 1903. WILTSHIRE HISTORY CENTRE

Chipping Sodbury station, 1960. Station master Newcombe can be seen on the Up platform (right) about to enter his office. WILF STANLEY

the Down platform was of less substantial size and construction and was mainly a waiting room. There was no road access to the Down side. Both waiting rooms were equipped with paraffin lighting and coal stoves for the benefit of the travelling public. Platform canopies were provided to give protection from the elements for passengers standing outside.

Although bereft of royal connections, Chipping Sodbury was the only station on the entire line between Swindon and the Severn Tunnel that served a town of any size; where Little Somerford was the pretender, Chipping Sodbury was the true monarch. Of royalty there may have been none, but Chipping Sodbury and its surrounding parishes had more than their fair share of knights of the realm, lords, barons, generals and other assorted gentry. Because of this, it was arguably the most important station and the staff there reflected this. Only Pilning had an allocation of staff larger than that of Chipping Sodbury.

The first station master appointed at Chipping Sodbury was Frederick Savage.[9] A Londoner by birth and the son of a Metropolitan police inspector, Mr Savage was an experienced railwayman, having begun his railway career as a lad clerk in the office of the general manager of the Great Western Railway at Paddington. He served there for six years, before moving to work at the Divisional Superintendent's office in Cardiff. By July 1895, he was working in the Divisional Superintendent's office in Bristol and in October of that year became a booking clerk at Yatton station. Promotion from

there was swift: October 1899, station master at Lawrence Hill, Bristol; May 1900, station master at Bradford on Avon, Wilts; and finally to station master at Chipping Sodbury, when it opened on 1 May 1903.

The station master's house at Chipping Sodbury, like all the others, 'came with the job'. It stood in spacious grounds just to the right-hand side of the station approach road, as one neared the station buildings. There was also a rank of cottages provided for the signalmen. These were built on higher ground above the Up goods loop and access to these was via a lane from nearby Colts Green.

One interesting 'problem' faced by Frederick Savage at the start of his career at Chipping Sodbury, was that of the maintenance of the flower beds on the station approach road. Mr Kislingbury ensured that there was no doubt about who did what, writing to Savage on 4 September 1905 as follows:

Planting of Trees etc. on
South Wales Direct Railway

It has been arranged that you shall attend to the weeding etc. of the lower beds around the approach road. The Engineer's staff will attend to the remainder. Kindly note and confirm.

At the London end of the Down platform stood the brick-built signal box. The box had a 61-lever frame, of which five were spaces. This box was almost

Chipping Sodbury water troughs, 1960. On the skyline above the tunnel, one of the ventilation shafts peeks out of a copse. WILF STANLEY

identical in appearance to that at Badminton. When the Up goods loop was extended in World War II, the new exit points were sited much farther from the signal box; too far for a normal 'pull' on the lever. These points were motorized. A hand-generator for the electricity was provided in the box. In order to move the points, the signalman pulled the lever over halfway. He then wound the hand crank until an indicator showed that the points had responded; then he pulled the lever right over to lock the points in position.

The regular signalmen at Chipping Sodbury in the 1950s were Ted Hawkins, Fred Holley and young signalman Mike Goodrich. Fred Holley was ex-Royal Navy and had a military approach to life; he tended to spurn modern comforts and would work the box with little or no fire in the grate during winter, preferring instead to wear his greatcoat. Goodrich later went to Stoke Gifford East box and moved from there to Patchway Station box, where he was still working when that box closed in 1971 under the Bristol resignalling.

In 1966, the three regular men were Ray Hicks, Ray Williams and Cliff Harris. Hicks had worked at Westerleigh South on the London Midland Region (LMR) until it closed in 1964–65, then took the vacancy at Chipping Sodbury for a while until a vacancy occurred at Westerleigh West, nearer to his home. Cliff Harris had been a guard at Barrow Lane sidings (LMR) at the same time that Wilf

Stanley had been signalman at Bristol St Philips box (also LMR). Harris eventually left the railway, only to return a few years later.

By 1969, Ray Williams was the only regular signalman at Sodbury. He later became a reliefman. In 1970, there were no regular signalmen at the box; all turns were covered by relief staff.

In 1953, Chipping Sodbury box opened between 06.00 Monday to 22.00 Sunday, being closed 09.00–16.20 on Sundays when the Severn Tunnel was closed for engineering work.

Water Troughs

Behind the box, on a higher level, stood the signal lineman's cabin, a pump house and a tall water tank. The pump and tank were there to serve the water troughs that were installed in the Up and Down lines between the station and the tunnel mouth. On the signal box block shelf there was a water level indicator for the tank: this showed 'High' or 'Low'.

The local permanent way ganger was responsible for ensuring that the troughs were clear of ice during the winter. It was up to the ganger to decide when ice had formed to such an extent that its thickness would prevent safe use of the troughs. However, instructions were that if the ice was more than $\frac{1}{8}$in (3mm) thick the troughs must be taken out of use. In addition, if the temperature became low enough to freeze the water as soon as the ice

SODBURY
Water Troughs

TRAIN	FROM	TO	TO TAKE WATER, IF REQUIRED, AT
DOWN—WEEKDAYS			
12.45 a.m.	Paddington	Carmarthen	SWINDON
8.55 a.m. **SX**	Paddington	Pembroke Dock	
9.55 a.m. **SX**	Paddington	Swansea	
10.55 a.m.	Paddington	Pembroke Dock	
11.35 a.m. (Q) **SO**	Paddington	Carmarthen	STOKE GIFFORD*
11.55 a.m.	Paddington	Pembroke Dock	
3.55 p.m.	Paddington	Fishguard Hbr.	
5.50 p.m. **FO**	Paddington	Cardiff	
6.55 p.m.	Paddington	Fishguard Hbr.	
8.30 p.m. **SO**	Paddington	Neyland	SWINDON
9.25 p.m. **SO**	Paddington	Neyland	SWINDON
DOWN—SUNDAYS			
12.50 a.m.	Paddington	Swansea	SWINDON
4.55 p.m.	Paddington	Carmarthen	STOKE GIFFORD*
UP—WEEKDAYS			
3.35 a.m. (Q)	Fishguard Hbr.	Paddington	
3.55 a.m. **WFO**	Fishguard Hbr.	Paddington	
7.45 a.m. (Q)	Cardiff	Paddington	
6.30 a.m.	Swansea	Paddington	
4.55 a.m. **TThSO**	Fishguard Hbr.	Paddington	STOKE GIFFORD*
8.15 a.m. **MWFO**	Cardiff	Paddington	
9.45 a.m. (Q)	Cardiff	Paddington	
7.30 a.m.	Carmarthen	Paddington	
11.45 a.m.	Bristol	Paddington	SWINDON*
7.30 a.m. **SO** (Q)	Pembroke Dock	Paddington	
8. 0 a.m.	Neyland	Paddington	STOKE GIFFORD*
11.10 a.m.	Milford Haven	Paddington	
4.30 p.m. **SX**	Bristol	Paddington	DIDCOT STATION*
12. 5 p.m.	Milford Haven	Paddington	
1. 5 p.m.	Pembroke Dock	Paddington	
4.35 p.m. **SX**	Swansea	Paddington	
2.30 p.m.	Neyland	Paddington	
3.50 p.m. (Milk)	Whitland	Kensington	
5.15 p.m. (Milk)	Whitland	Kensington	STOKE GIFFORD*
5.20 p.m. (Fish)	Milford Haven	Paddington	
6.45 p.m. (Milk)	Carmarthen	Kensington	
4.35 p.m. **SX**	Neyland	Paddington	
8.30 p.m. (Milk)	Whitland	Kensington	
UP—SUNDAYS			
3.55 a.m.	Fishguard Hbr.	Paddington	SWINDON*
10.40 a.m. (Q)	Cardiff	Paddington	
6.45 a.m.	Fishguard Hbr.	Paddington	STOKE GIFFORD*
10.55 a.m.	Swansea	Sheffield	
11.20 a.m.	Carmarthen	Paddington	

* Special Stop.	(continued overleaf)

GENERAL NOTE.
ALL TRAINS BOOKED TO CALL AT SWINDON TO TAKE WATER AT THAT POINT.

10

Excerpts from 1956 BR Instructions to Enginemen etc., showing alternative places to take water when troughs are out of use.
AUTHOR'S COLLECTION

SODBURY—continued
Water Troughs

TRAIN	FROM	TO	TO TAKE WATER, IF REQUIRED, AT
UP—SUNDAYS—cont.			
4.45 p.m.	Cardiff	Paddington	SWINDON*
12.25 p.m.	Milford Haven	Paddington	
4.20 p.m.	Swansea	Paddington	
5.30 p.m.	Swansea	Paddington	
4.10 p.m. (Milk)	Whitland	Kensington	STOKE GIFFORD*
5.25 p.m. (Milk)	Whitland	Kensington	
6.35 p.m. (Milk)	Whitland	Kensington	
9.10 p.m. (Milk)	Carmarthen	Kensington	

was cleared, then again the troughs had to be closed for use. Should any spillage from the troughs into the space between the rails (the 'four-foot way') freeze and ice collect to a depth of 1in (25mm), then closure was necessary.

Should the ganger find it necessary to close the troughs, he had to contact the nearest signal box (either Badminton or Chipping Sodbury, or should either of these boxes be switched out, then the nearest box in circuit) and advise the signalman. The signalman so advised would, in turn, notify the District Operating Controller. The controller would straight away advise the Chief Mechanical and Electrical Engineer's Outdoor Machinery District Mechanical Foreman or Chargeman and the Designated Responsible Water Fitter. He would also advise locomotive depots, HQ Control, the District Motive Power Superintendent and the District Engineer. The ganger would also advise his permanent way Inspector and turn the water supply off to avoid damage to the pipeline. Plans for locomotives to get water at alternative places would now be put into action.

When the thaw set in, then it was the duty of the Chief Mechanical and Electrical Engineer's Outdoor Machinery District Mechanical Foreman or Chargeman and the designated Responsible Water Fitter to consult with the ganger to agree when normal taking of water at the troughs could resume.

Livestock

Horse and livestock traffic was an important source of revenue for the station almost from the start. Cattle travelled in special cattle trucks and, whilst waiting for transport, were temporarily kept in cattle pens adjacent to the loading dock; a practice carried out at most stations. Horses too, had special horseboxes for transit. The problem of shunting horseboxes from the loading dock to be attached to the rear of a Down train without delays being incurred was one that caused the Chipping Sodbury station master to study his rule book and come to the conclusion that he could have the vehicle shunted, by hand, from the dock on the Up side, to stand on the Down main line to await the train to

which it was to be attached. When the train arrived, it would be signalled into the Down loop and when at a stand, the points would be changed and the horsebox (or cattle wagon) pushed on to the rear. Just to be certain though, he decided to write to the Superintendent of the Line, Mr Kislingbury, setting out his thoughts on this move. Mr Kislingbury replied as follows:

Great Western Railway
Divisional Superintendent's Office, Bristol.

March 10th 1905

Dear Sir,

Standing Horse Box on Down M/Line

You have asked whether a horse box may be brought out to stand at B (sketch attached) to be in readiness for picking up.

I do not think a through road ought to be used for standing purposes in this manner and in the case of any vehicles loaded at A the correct thing to do would be to push them back to D in readiness to be pushed over 32, 26 on to the rear of the down train, or for the down train to back from 26, 32 to D on to such vehicle.

Please see that the working is carried out accordingly.[10]

[see drawing on page 50]

Following Frederick Savage's departure in January 1912, a Mr J.E. Randall took the post of station master. By August 1912, Randall had moved to take charge at Badminton and he had been replaced at Sodbury by Mr H.W. Carter, who in turn was replaced by Mr Weeks in 1929. The last station master at Chipping Sodbury was to be Reg Newcombe.

Reginald Ewart Newcombe was born at Plympton St Mary, Devon, in 1897. He was the son of a dockyard engine fitter, who was employed on government work. Reg started his career at Saltash, Cornwall, in 1913, moving to Truro very shortly afterwards. He possibly moved to Bristol sometime

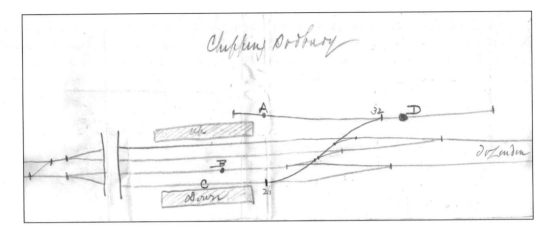

Sketch dated March 1905, sent by Superintendent Kislingbury to the Chipping Sodbury station master, Mr Savage. AUTHOR'S COLLECTION

after World War I, as he met and married Gladys Ellen Coombs in Keynsham, Bristol, in 1926. Gladys was the daughter of Robert and Sarah Coombs. In 1911, Robert Coombs was a railway checker at Keynsham, having previously been a porter at Keynsham station.

Reg Newcombe was appointed station master at Chipping Sodbury in 1943 and he and Gladys moved into the station house. They lived there for many years. Reg Newcombe continued to be employed at Chipping Sodbury even after the station's closure to passengers on 3 April 3 1961. He retired in 1962 and died in 1984, aged eighty-seven.

Signal boxes under the supervision of the Chipping Sodbury master were Chipping Sodbury and the junction boxes further along the line at Westerleigh East, West and North. In later years, when the wartime depot at Wapley Common was built in 1941, the new signal box at Wapley Common came under the supervision of the station master at Chipping Sodbury in addition to new boxes at Westerleigh East and North junctions.

Hours of duty for the station masters were as follows: on duty 08.15; off duty 20.15. Dinner was to be taken between 13.00 and 14.30 and Tea between 17.00 and 18.00.

Another of the duties of the station master was making sure that the station and signal box clocks were kept in working order and sending them for repairs as required. The Chipping Sodbury station master was responsible for the clocks at Chipping Sodbury booking office, goods office and Permanent Way Office, as well as those timepieces at Chipping Sodbury, Westerleigh West, Westerleigh North, Westerleigh East and Wapley Common boxes. One of Reg Newcombe's last duties, recorded in the station book on 9 March 1962, was to send back to the District Traffic Superintendent's office at Bristol for repairs, GWR brass drum timepiece No.0377, from Westerleigh West box. On 14 March 1962, he received a memo from H. Bastin of the DTS office: 'I have today sent you Brass Drum timepiece No.GWR0390 to replace No.GWR0377 received here for repairs. Please amend your records accordingly and acknowledge receipt … ' The memo was glued in as the last entry in that station book.[11]

Early station staff 1903–04: porters included P. House, A. Powell, J.S. Dando, C.H. Sorrell, J. Ledbury, F.H. Thomas and G.S. Hole. A lad porter employed there was C.G. Dewer. This latter was marked in the records as having 'absconded' in December 1903. There was a female porter at Sodbury in the 1950s – Nell Sparkes. She and three male staff ran the station. There were two staff on early turn and two on late turn, plus two booking clerks – one on early shift and one on lates. Their hours of duty were: Week One, 07.00–19.00. Breakfast was between 08.40 and 09.30; Dinner between 13.00 and 14.00. Week Two, the day commenced at 09.15 and ended at 21.15. Dinner break was again 13.00–14.00 and Tea between 17.00 and 18.00.

Additionally, there was yard staff: a shunter and a wagon checker. T.W. Weeks was employed as a wagon checker. There was also a road motor driver (a lorry driver) employed at the station in the 1940s. His name was Heal and he was issued with a denim 'suit' as a uniform.

In 1903, an agreement was entered into between the Great Western Railway and a Mr Beer of Beaufort Mews, Chipping Sodbury, to operate an omnibus service between the railway station and the town. This was dated July 1903. The omibus was then horse-drawn and Mr Beer operated a regular service between the two locations for a number of years.

The advertising of the Great Western's services was an important part of every station's duties. Locally, posters were placed wherever the company could get permission to put them. Free ('gratuitous') train timetables were handed out to local dignitaries and shops, public houses and hotels. Here are a few of the locations where Chipping Sodbury station advertised: the Portcullis Hotel, Grapes Hotel, George Hotel and Royal Oak Hotel in Chipping Sodbury High Street; the Bell Hotel outside the station entrance; the Cross Hands Hotel at Old Sodbury a couple of miles away; the Railway Hotel at Wickwar, about 3 miles (5km) from Chipping Sodbury and on Midland Railway territory; Chipping Sodbury Post Office; Chipping Sodbury Police Station; the National Provincial Bank and the Literary Institution – both in Chipping Sodbury – and the Chipping Sodbury Board of Guardians; J.S. Bees, the local omnibus proprietor; Mr Gerrish, the auctioneer and Mr J. Tranfield, the solicitor. Yate Iron Works' manager Mr Cryer also received a free copy and he agreed to erect a two-sheet poster board, fixed to the buildings at the Works, for which the GWR paid him five shillings per year. This agreement was made in May 1907 and terminated in May 1915. The village of Tytherington was about 7 miles (11km)

from Chipping Sodbury and was on the Midland's branch from Yate to Thornbury, but nevertheless the Great Western gave free timetables to the Swan Hotel in Tytherington and the Tytherington Stone Company's offices at their quarry. Chipping Sodbury Permanent Way Department also had a free copy and the station master got two.

Posters and handbills were also put up in conspicuous places. It was the duty of the station staff to ensure that posters were given to all hotels, shopkeepers and 'places of public resort' in Chipping Sodbury, Old Sodbury and the villages of Westerleigh, Horton, Codrington, Yate and district. The GWR had poster hoardings in local streets: Rouncival Street, Bowling Hill and the Pound. Hoardings were also to be found on 'walls and gates at Chipping Sodbury, Old Sodbury, Yate, Nibley, Westerleigh and Wapley' (*Chipping Sodbury Station Log Book*). Handbills were sent out by post to hotels as far away as Wootton Under Edge, 8 miles (13km) away.

The Goods Yard

There were many farms and other businesses such as animal feed mills associated with farming in and around Chipping Sodbury, so it is of no surprise that these had a presence in the yard; the Alfa-Laval company that manufactured dairy farming equipment and whose local representative was the quaintly named Mr Herring, rented an old box van body in the yard equal to 16sq yd for 9s 2d per month. Local industry provided animal feed mills with business and there was, of course, more than one coal merchant.

Almost from the commencement of freight operations on the line, coal was one of the main commercial products handled, both in bulk (for cities, docks and engine sheds) and locally (for towns and villages). At Chipping Sodbury, three coal merchants rented space in the yard: F. Benjamin rented 60sq yd and an office at a cost of £3 per annum for the 'wharfage' (as it was known) and £1 10s per annum for the office; J.D. Russell rented coal wharfage of 60sq yd for £3 per annum and a smaller office for £1, and the Fishponds Coal

View over the goods yard at Chipping Sodbury. Note that the yard is full. There are two yard cranes.
WILF STANLEY

Company rented wharfage of 60sq yd and an office for £4 per annum inclusive. Francis Wintle rented coal wharfage of 120yd in 1952; it cost him £2 10s per quarter. After closure of the station, Wintle's used the buildings as offices and still rented space in the yard into the twenty-first century.

Locally, stone was quarried and the British Quarrying Company rented an office of 8 × 6ft for £1 10s per annum. In later years, a stone siding and a loading bank (platform) were built in the goods yard and opened on 10 June 1907. There was a small fixed crane in the yard.

Starting in March 1913, a small petroleum storage facility was opened in the yard by British Petroleum (BP) acting as distributing agents for the Asiatic Petroleum Co.; this contract was transferred to the Shell Marketing Co., in June 1918. On 28 November 1921, the Shell-Mex company opened an oil and spirit depot, covering 150sq yd and an oil storage tank at Chipping Sodbury. The annual rental was £16 17s 6d. By February 1925, Shell-Mex rented 165sq yd in the yard at a cost of £14 9s per year. By 1928, this area had been increased to 456sq yd and the rental cost had risen to £39 18s per year. Shell-Mex was still in evidence at Chipping Sodbury into the 1950s, receiving deliveries by rail tanker. The oil storage siding that was laid in the yard in 1926 had been removed by 1966.

Rival oil company British Petroleum BP also rented space in the goods yard, taking 112sq yd from March 1928 for the annual payment of £9 6s.

The goods yard gates at Chipping Sodbury were closed at 2pm on Saturdays. A telephone was installed in the goods yard on 16 October 1922.

The Goods Shed

The goods shed at Chipping Sodbury was the biggest and grandest on the entire line between Wootton Bassett and Pilning. Built of brick and originally roofed with slate in similar manner to the station buildings and signal box, it had an internal loading platform and crane, plus large doors at each end to keep out the elements. It stood on a siding adjacent to the Up goods loop. A small office was built on to the eastern end of the shed. To enable the drivers of locomotives to see the ground signal no. 32 at the station end of the shed, it was fixed to the shed wall; more an 'off-ground signal' than a ground signal. There was a portable platform weighing machine in the shed. Behind the Goods shed were three sidings, the furthest one away from the shed serving the loading bank.

In March 1947, a small area – 40sq yd – of the shed's loading platform was rented to Yate Mills Ltd, of Goose Green, just north of Yate town. This agreement was terminated in December 1948.

The east end of Chipping Sodbury goods shed, showing the office; 1991.
P.D. RENDALL

Staff working in the goods shed were issued with canvas aprons for use when loading and unloading wagons. Gloves were also issued. The goods shed stood into the twenty-first century, but was sadly demolished by Network Rail.

Weighbridges and Other Scales

These were supplied by Birmingham company Henry Pooley and Sons. Pooley's serviced the weighbridges along the South Wales and other lines on an annual basis. Latterly, this company had a travelling workshop-cum-mess coach in the shape of W28790 marked 'Pooley & Sons, Weighing Contractors'. It would be shunted into sidings at the station or goods yard where the staff's services were required and would stay there until the job of servicing, repairing or installing of the equipment had been completed.

It fell to the station master (or other person in charge if the station master was not present) to ensure that red warning lamps and/or flags were placed in such position that the workshop van was adequately protected from shunting movements. If the van was on a siding protected by wheel stops, or the points leading to the siding were clipped and padlocked for a direction other than the siding that the van was on, the lamps and flags would not be required.[12]

There were truck and cart weighbridges in the station yard. The main weighbridge stood where the station approach road fanned out into the station yard. The charges for use of these in 1921 were as follows: truck weighbridge – 1s per truck; cart weighbridge, coal and coke charges – up to 30cwt minimum of 2d per weigh; above 30cwt and not exceeding 50cwt – 4d per weigh; above 50cwt – 6d per weigh.[13]

There was a portable platform in the goods shed that was for weighing items such a sacks and there was a spring balance in the parcels office. Obviously, the spring balance was not for very heavy packages. Private individuals or businesses wishing to send parcels by rail would have them weighed at the parcels office and the necessary payment made according to weight.

Parcels traffic received at the station was delivered free to its destination, provided that the recipient lived within half a mile of the station. A porter, or other staff if the porter was unavailable, would undertake the delivery.

There was not only station and yard staff based at Chipping Sodbury; the line's Signal and Telegraph Department was based here, in a building set in the embankment behind the signal box. There was a board in Sodbury box on which the lineman would write down the location where he was

---

DETAILS OF WEIGHING MACHINES AT CHIPPING SODBURY

- Truck weighbridge: (situated in station yard): 60 tons capacity; size of weighing plate = 19ft 11in × 6ft 5½in.
- Cart weighbridge*: (situated in station yard) 12 tons capacity; size of weighing plate = 12 × 8ft.
- Spring balance†: (situated in parcels office): 5cwt capacity; size = 1ft 8in × 1ft 8in.
- Portable platform:§ (on wheels) (situated in goods shed): 15cwt capacity; size of plate = 2ft 8in × 2ft 0in.

* Replaced by BR 20-ton Pooley weighbridge no. 10509 (Pooley no. B54632), Plate size 20 × 8ft on 1 September 1954.

† Replaced by a dial bench scale of 220lb capacity in February 1958.

§ Condemned May 1953: replaced by Pooley portable platform type 32/972, installed on 2 October 1953. Fitted with backrail. Capacity 20cwt. Platform size: 4ft 9in × 3ft 2in. Reg. no. WR 10427.

---

working, if away from Sodbury. That way, he could be contacted if needed. Mr Giddings was a signal lineman. Charlie Strange and Jack Hatheroe were the locking linemen who dealt with the signal box levers and interlocking. Jack had been a marine during the war and was a survivor of the sinking of the battleship HMS *Repulse*. He had also been a prisoner of war of the Japanese. W.J. Couzens retired from Chipping Sodbury as lineman in November 1945. In the 1960s, Don Parker was the lineman and Perce Starkey was his assistant on the Badminton line, along with Brian Thompson (later a signal technician at Bristol Panel Box) and his assistant Arthur Graham. Des Ollis was their boss. They were later based at Charfield, but eventually went to most places on the 'east side' of Bristol. In October 1957, Len Juggins transferred to Chipping Sodbury as assistant lineman Class 2. Juggins was ex-Gloucestershire Regiment and had been a prisoner of war of the Chinese during the Korean War; this experience affected him for life. In March 1959, Len Juggins left the lineman Class 2 post for a job

as signalman Class 4 at Rangeworthy box, on the LMR Bristol–Gloucester line.

Chipping Sodbury Permanent Way Department

From the opening of the line there was a Permanent Way Office at Chipping Sodbury station, situated in the yard. Here was based the permanent way supervisor and his area ran from Wootton Bassett (83 miles 30 chains) to Stoke Gifford (112 miles 08 chains) on both the Patchway lines and Filton lines and to 112 miles 07 chains on the Avonmouth line. He was also responsible for the East curve from Westerleigh East to Westerleigh North and from Westerleigh West towards Yate, to 1 mile 30½ chains from West box. The entire Malmesbury branch came under the Chipping Sodbury Permanent Way Department from 1933.

Permanent way staff based at Chipping Sodbury in the 1940s included F.A. Febry, Mr Walker and J. Hicks. Those in the 1950s included G. Hicks, T. Hurcom, T. Read, R. Hobbs, T. Wicks, Alfie Archer, Harry Cullum and H. Horlick. As well as their usual duties of patrolling their 'length' and carrying out track maintenance, they were also fogmen for the signal box.

R. Shortman was a permanent way inspector during the 1940s; he died in January 1947 after twenty-five years' service. His widow continued to live in one of the railway houses, Station Villas, built near the station by the GWR when the line opened. Ken Mainstone was a permanent way supervisor at Chipping Sodbury in the 1980s–90s.

Fogmen

During fog or falling snow, the signalman had a fog marker – usually a signal within 400yd (370m) of the box – and if this could not be seen clearly, he would summon the 'fogmen'. These men would come to the signal box to sign on duty in the Train Register before arming themselves with flags, lamps and detonators and trudging off up or down the line to the Distant signal, where they would place a detonator on the line and exhibit a yellow handsignal all the time that the signal was at Caution. Whenever the signal cleared, they would remove the detonator and show a green handsignal.

Fogging was often cold and wet work, as the man would be out in all weathers. They received a small overtime payment for this work. Fogmen used to wear greatcoats with red lapels. These coats were usually kept in the locking room under the signal box and were frequently dusty and moth-eaten, but the men still wore them.

The fogmen had a small hut at or near the Distant signal of the box. This hut was just large enough for one man. It was equipped with a tiny coal-fired stove that the man could use not only to keep warm between trains, but also to warm his food on. A good signalman would ensure that his fogmen always had a supply of coal for the fire. With the advent of colour-light Distant signals, there was no longer the need for fogmen and the huts fell into disuse.

In an ironic twist of fate, when the old signal boxes were closed and demolished there arose a need for some form of shelter for the use of signalmen engaged on handsignalling duties during emergency working or planned engineering work. To this end, small wooden cabins were erected at ground frames and other strategic locations, for use by the signalmen. Just large enough for one or maybe two men, the cabins had a stable door and usually an old chair and a table – put there by signalling staff. Prior to the cabin's occupation for engineering works or single-line working, the cabin would be equipped with a gas fire and gas bottle, a container of water and a teapot and kettle. The gas heater (known as a 'pan heater') could be used to cook on, as well as for heating. One such cabin stood on the Down side of the line at the east end of the Chipping Sodbury layout in the 1980s and was accessed by walking along the lineside path from the yard and crossing the tracks.

The trouble was that the Permanent Way Department seemed to think that the cabins were there for *their* sole use and it was not unusual for a signalman to arrive at the cabin, for example late on a Saturday night, and unlock the door, only to be deluged by a heap of permanent way equipment such as shovels, picks and kango hammers that the trackmen had decided to store in the cabin. Faced with such a problem, the signalman would be forced to stay outside in the cold and/or wet, or to take refuge in his car, but only the latter if he was within earshot of a lineside phone. Meanwhile, the permanent way men were able to make use of a comfy Portakabin or a road vehicle converted to a portable mess van!

Even if the cabin had not been recently occupied by the Permanent Way Department, one had to share the facilities with the odd mouse and an amazing variety of spiders. And the gas bottle could not be kept inside the cabin for safety reasons, so was kept outside; the cabin was thus never draught-proof because the door was left ajar to permit the gas pipe to run through the gap. Such was progress! Other, similar cabins were provided at Pilning station, Patchway Junction, Stoke Gifford East, Westerleigh Junction and Chipping Sodbury.

Snow Duties

Another duty that fell to the Permanent Way Department was that of snow clearance. When falling snow obscured the signalman's marker (as with fog), he would call out the designated 'snowmen'. These were usually the same poor souls who acted as fogmen and, when called, would make their way to the signal box for their duty. One man would be detailed to stay in the signal box and observe the tail lamp of passing trains, whilst others would make their way to the Distant signals to carry out duties as per fogging. The remainder would clear points and signal wires of snow as directed by the signalmen.

Snow duty was not the sole preserve of the South Wales Direct line and was in the *Rule Book.* It was universal across the railway system. Nevertheless, it would happen that some areas were more susceptible to snow than others. The Direct line was particularly prone to snowfall, mostly between Severn Tunnel East and Badminton and, because of the higher ground, heavy snowfall could occur when other areas, such as central Bristol, had little or no snow.

Permanent way staff clearing snow from the junction points at Stoke Gifford. On the background horizon is the 'Brabazon' hangar at Filton airfield. WILF STANLEY

Wrong Type of Snow

Beloved of the media, this is in fact an accurate description. Heavy, wet snow will fall and clog up points and signal pulleys, but, when cleared by brush and shovel or scraper, will stay where it is thrown. Fine, dusty snow that is made up of 'granules' and forms drifts when blown about will get into points and, even when cleared, will just blow back in and freeze. The former type of snow would create problems when blown into the lens hoods of colour-light signals and would obscure the aspect shown; the latter, clogging up points as fast as it was cleared, would cause far more problems and inevitably result in the points being left set for one route only and delays/diversions would be the result.

In later times, there were points heaters, but the gas heaters were only good when lit in advance and with the staff reductions of the 1980s and beyond they were frequently lit after the snow had started. I have heard rumours that these gas heaters were discontinued because of environmental factors, but it is more likely that they were just not efficient enough and were replaced by electric points heaters.

Wet snow has clogged the junction indicator on signal B115 at Westerleigh junction during an unseasonal Easter snowfall in 1987. The signal is obviously showing caution, but the train crew have to phone Bristol Panel Box to find out if the route is the one they want.
P.D. RENDALL

Snow did not stop trains in steam days; hauled by a King, the Up Red Dragon tears through Chipping Sodbury station. WILF STANLEY

Coalpit Heath

At 108½ miles (175km) from Paddington stood Coalpit Heath station. Nowadays, the spelling is 'Coalpit Heath', but when the station was built the platform nameboards, signal box nameplate and other paperwork all referred to 'Coal Pit Heath'. The station was built near the southern end of the straggling collection of houses and shops that comprised the villages of Coalpit Heath and Frampton Cotterell. The main station building stood on the Down side of the line and consisted of a booking office, the station master's office, waiting rooms and urinals. The building was constructed in the same style as the other stations and was on the Down platform. A covered footbridge, no. 289B, linked the platforms. There was a small goods shed with external loading platform situated on the Down side of the line, to the east end of the station. This shed was of similar style to those at Brinkworth, Little Somerford and Badminton. The station entrance was gained by a driveway from the adjacent lane, Ram Hill.

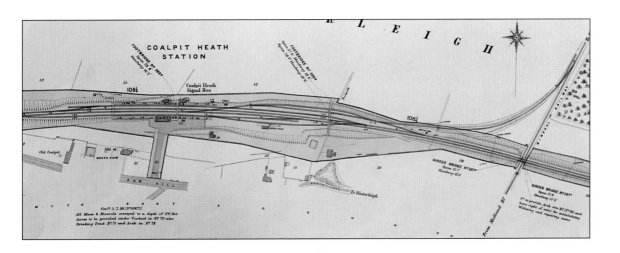

Coalpit Heath station plan; 1903. WILTSHIRE HISTORY CENTRE

Coalpit Heath station in the late 1950s, looking west; the colliery sidings have been lifted. Station master Harry Pike's house can be seen to the far left of the picture. WILF STANLEY

Near the entrance was the station master's house, accessed by a footpath from the approach road. Two cottages for signalmen were erected further along Ram Hill and next to a steel footbridge (no. 288B and known locally as the 'ha'penny bridge'), which carried a footpath over the eastern end of the layout. The station was opened for goods traffic on 1 May 1903 and for passengers on 1 July 1903.

The station and sidings were on a long curve and the points, sited at the east end of the station, were quite a distance from the signal box. Shunting was often held up by the signalman being unable to get locking detection owing to the slack in the long length of point rodding. This meant that the signalman was unable to clear the ground signal. This was often the case when shunting from Down to Up sides and some trainmen used to persuade the signalmen to let them shunt up and down on the Down main line and not use the crossover. A good signalman would not allow this, because on the Down line there was poor sighting and the long curve on the approach to Coalpit Heath from the Westerleigh direction meant that there was not sufficient room to shunt safely, especially if there was a Down train about. A train running by a signal would have been disastrous.

Also sited on the Up side of the lines, just to the west of the station and accessed from a trailing connection in the Down main and crossing through the Up main and Up loop were two further sidings. At the far end of these sidings the line connected back with the Up main via a ground frame of one lever. This lever was interlocked with the signal box by lever no. 12 in the box and was additionally locked with a key, kept in the signal box. From the sidings, a connection ran down a short incline to join with the Midland Railway's colliery branch from

Coalpit Heath in 1983. View from the remains of the Up platform. The small goods shed is still standing and used by an engineering firm. In the background is the 'ha'penny bridge'. T.R. RENDALL

Westerleigh yard (MR) to Frog Lane Colliery at Coal Pit Heath. Although the GWR did move some coal traffic from these sidings over the years, it was not used to any great extent; the majority of coal traffic left via the Midland branch and Westerleigh sidings. The mines were closed by 1948 and the sidings out of use by the same date.[14]

Coalpit Heath was similar to Badminton and Chipping Sodbury in that its platforms were built against the loop lines and the main lines had the straight run-through. Compared to other Direct line stations that had long loops, Coalpit Heath's loops were quite short. In steam days, very long freight trains from Severn Tunnel Junction or from Stoke Gifford yard needed a 'margin' of 30 minutes after leaving Stoke Gifford to enable the train to clear Badminton at the top of the long climb, after which the running was much easier and trains would 'get a move on'.

However, many freight trains were longer than the available space in the loops at Coalpit Heath and if there was no option but to 'loop' them, the train had to draw in so that the guard's van was clear of the loop points, then cut off the engine, which would draw ahead on to the main line. It then backed across to the loop on the other side of the lines and stayed there until the line was clear for it to proceed, when the procedure would be carried out in reverse. When reformed again, the freight train could carry on its slow journey. This procedure would only be carried out if there was sufficient time to do it without delaying trains and if there was insufficient time (or room) for the train to reach a longer loop elsewhere.

The loops being shorter than those at the other four-road stations caused other operating problems, as one signalman in BR days, on his first late shift at Coalpit Heath signal box, discovered. At this time, the early 1950s, Winterbourne signal box was only open on early turn, so Coalpit Heath worked through to Stoke Gifford East after 14.00. The signalman at Stoke Gifford East rang Coalpit up to advise that an Up freight was about to leave Stoke Gifford a short time in front of the Up express, but that 'It [the freight] will fit in your loop.'

When the freight arrived at Coalpit Heath, the signalman duly signalled the freight into his loop, only to find that the train was longer than the loop's permitted forty-five wagons plus loco and brake van, with the result that several wagons and the guard's van were still on the main line when the engine stood at the loop signal. There was only one thing to do; quickly, the signalman pulled off the loop Starting signal and waved the driver to draw the train ahead a little. Then, when the brake van was 'in clear' of the main line, he replaced the signals and the points and asked the driver to back up a little until the brake van stood against the buffers at the end of the short length of track at the Winterbourne end of the loop. He was then able to clear the line of the freight train and was immediately asked 'Is Line Clear?' for the express, which had been standing at Stoke Gifford East.

Now, the express driver, being more than a little peeved at being held up and, approaching Coalpit Heath and seeing the freight crammed into the platform loop, opened his whistle to express his feelings. At that very moment, a Down express was passing and that driver, too, joined in the fun by opening *his* whistle! This cacophony frightened the life out of station master C. 'Harry' Pike (brother of the then station master at Pilning station), who had been sitting in his office reading a paper. Convinced that the prolonged whistling indicated that a collision was about to take place, he dropped his paper and ran from his office as the trains passed safely.

The first station master of Coalpit Heath station was William Eliab Barrington (no relation to the station master of the same surname at Brinkworth). Barrington was a Somerset man, born in 1862 at Coxley, near Wells. His railway career seems to have started at Holt Junction, near Melksham, Wilts, where he was a porter. His next move was to Trowbridge, where he became parcels foreman. From Trowbridge he moved, in 1899, to Broadwey, Weymouth, where he was station master. Lastly, Barrington and his family moved to the station house at Coalpit Heath station when he was appointed as station master there in June 1903. The duties set out in the original station

View from Coalpit Heath signal box looking west. A train of coal empties occupies the Down loop and an Up express passes through on the Up main line. WILF STANLEY

logs by Superintendent of the Line Kislingbury were modified in BR days when the Coalpit Heath station master took on responsibility for covering the station and signal box at Winterbourne and Westerleigh West box.

Coalpit Heath station staff in the period 1903–05 included: porters G. Thomas (from Salisbury in June 1903); Charles Shattock (1903); Harry Tett (March 1905; he went 'missing' later that year); A.V. Brown (from Holt Junction, Wilts, in August 1905); and E. Cornish (from Devizes in 1904). Two signalmen were stationed there: one man who moved there from Fenny Compton in 1903 and W.J. Warner, who came from Worcester in 1903.

Harry Pike was still in charge at Coalpit Heath and also Winterbourne station in 1953 and when the station at Coalpit Heath closed in April 1961. He moved to Shirehampton, on the Bristol–Avonmouth line, as station master.

There never seems to have been any great attempt to provide Coalpit Heath with a decent train service. By 1960, the first Up stopping service of the day was the 06.10 Bristol–Swindon. This called 'all stations' and by then was usually hauled by a Castle Class loco. It was closely followed by the 07.13 Bristol–Swindon semi-fast, which did not call at the station. One morning, a signalman got the two muddled up and put what he thought was the late-running 'Up stopper' into the platform loop to give preference to the semi-fast. However, the first train on this occasion was the semi-fast. The embarrassed signalman had to quickly reset the points and signals in response to urgent whistling from the driver of the 07.13.

Towards the end of the station's life, the 07.35 Swindon–Bristol Temple Meads stopping service was the first Down train of the day; after that there was nothing until evening. In 1953, the signal box was open 06.00 Monday to 06.00 the following Sunday.

In spite of its shortcomings as regards operational matters, most signalmen liked to work at Coalpit Heath. One signalman recalled how the box was a 'nice steady job' on nights. Another, on night shifts, would switch on the station lights in order to be able to see the numbers of the locos passing on Up fitted freights. It was not unusual to see a Britannia Pacific hauling freight trains during the night. The ganger on the Coalpit Heath to Westerleigh length during the 1950s was Bill Reynolds.

Winterbourne

Winterbourne station was almost a 'typical' country station. Two tracks ran through the platforms, which at the east end backed on to Huckford viaduct, a lofty viaduct of eleven arches that spanned the valley of the River Frome, whilst just beyond the west end of the station the lines were spanned by a 31ft (9.5m) span girder bridge, no. 296B, which carried a lane called Hicks Common Road over the railway.

All the main station buildings stood on the Down side of the line; there was a small waiting room on the Up platform. Footbridge no. 295B spanned the tracks from Up to Down platform. A short approach road led from Hicks Common Road to the station. The metal overbridge separated the goods facilities

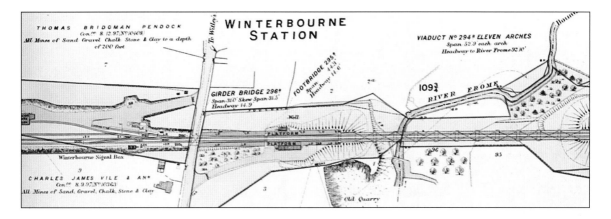

Winterbourne station plan; 1903. WILTSHIRE HISTORY CENTRE

from the station, which was on the London side of the bridge.

Beyond the road bridge, the lines ran into a deep, wide cutting that contained the sidings, goods shed and cattle pens. The brick signal box was built on the Down side of the lines in a niche carved out of the rocky cutting side. Opened with the station in May 1903, the box served a small layout of two crossovers, two Up sidings, a goods shed (the second largest on the line after Chipping Sodbury) and a short siding for cattle pens.

For most of its career, the signal box was a 'day turn only' job, being opened only on mornings. In 1953, it was still a 'one turn box', being open 06.40–14.00, Monday–Saturday. By the late 1960s, however, it was opened over twenty-four hours to provide a 'break section' box between Westerleigh West and Stoke Gifford East boxes; this move became more important when the LMR main line through Mangotsfield was closed in January 1970 and the traffic from that line was diverted to the South Wales main line.

Winterbourne station downside buildings and the footbridge seen from the top of the approach road; 1960. WILF STANLEY

The first station master appointed to Winterbourne station when it opened in May 1903 was William E. Andrews. Andrews' career had been almost entirely local up to that point. He started work for the Great Western in May 1881 as a porter at Patchway station. He next changed jobs when, in 1884, he became signalman at New Passage box, on the Pilning (Low Level) to the Severn Beach section of the Avonmouth branch. Nine years later, Andrews moved to Saltford, on the Bristol–Bath line, where he was booking porter. In 1888, he was promoted to station inspector (in effect, station master under a different name) at Saltford. His next move was out of area, to Evershot, a small station between Castle Cary and Maiden Newton. Winterbourne station was not unlike Evershot, in that it possessed many of the same facilities and was about the same size overall. Just over two years on, William Andrews moved again, to take up the job of station master at Winterbourne. He stayed there for almost eight years before moving on again, to Shirehampton, near Avonmouth. Two years after that, he came back to take charge at Filton Junction.

Initial staff at Winterbourne in 1903–05 comprised porters H. Sambourne, J.C. Smith, T. Clark and F.J. Oliver. Lad porters were A.H. Vile and W.J. Dee. Signalmen E.J. Rogers, P.S. Tyack and E.J. Hasell worked the signal box over three shifts.

The goods shed at Winterbourne was the second largest on the line, being in appearance a slightly smaller version of that at Chipping Sodbury. It had one siding that ran through the shed and another between the shed and the main line, effectively a 'run-round' road. The shed and sidings were approached by a long approach road from Hicks Common Road. A substantial wooden gate stood at the entrance to the yard approach road.

There was little industry in Winterbourne other than farming. The station and yard would have attracted passengers and goods traffic from nearby Frampton Cottrell, but would have been rivalled in this by Coalpit Heath station.

In the 1950s, there was a female porter at Winterbourne – Gladys ('Old Glad') Maggs. She is remembered as having a shrill voice. She worked a middle turn of duty and when the daily goods train arrived, would often carry out shunting moves, assisted by the guard.

It was not all collecting tickets and sweeping platforms if you were a porter; your duties would include keeping all station offices, waiting rooms, platforms and approach roads swept and clear of rubbish and weeded. Any rubbish from the platform was not to be swept on to the tracks, but collected up and burnt or put into a bin. You also had to ensure that the goods shed platforms were swept clear. Not only that, but the porters' duty was also to ensure that the cattle pens were cleaned up and disinfected. As the goods shed and cattle pens were some distance from the station at Winterbourne, it meant that the porter had to walk up the station approach road on to Hicks Common Road, over the bridge and through the goods yard gate and down the road into the goods yard. Manure and straw from the pens had to be swept into a neat heap or placed into bins provided. It was the responsibility of the Civil Engineering Department to dispose of

Looking from Hicks Common Road bridge towards Stoke Gifford, this photo shows the small yard layout and the second largest goods shed on the line; 1960. WILF STANLEY

View from the sidings looking back towards the station, this photo shows the relationship between the station and the yard; one either side of Hicks Common Road bridge. BR Class 9F No.92112 heads towards Stoke Gifford with coal empties; 1960.
WILF STANLEY

the sweepings; any cash obtained for the disposal of the sweepings and any other rubbish had to be given back to the station master for crediting to the Traffic Department.

In the 1950s, it was usual practice on summer Saturdays for Class 2 relief signalmen, if they had no signalling duties that day, to be utilized on station platforms in order to assist the porters. In 1955, relief signalman Ray Whiteford spent several such days at Winterbourne station.

R.H. Curtis moved from Stoke Gifford to Winterbourne as sub-ganger in May 1956. The ganger at Winterbourne in the 1960s was Pete McIvor, who was succeeded by Bob Hair.

At Winterbourne, the Up Home signal was not a ¼ mile (400m) away from the box, therefore the Up sidings connection was within the required 440yd (400m) 'clearing point', which regulations stipulated had to be clear of traffic before a train could be accepted from Stoke Gifford East: shunting was not allowed if a train had been accepted from Stoke Gifford. One signalman related to me how he had

broken this rule one day by accepting an Up train whilst a shunt was being made into the dock. The train had not yet passed Stoke Gifford, but nonetheless this signalman watched proceedings very uneasily and sighed with relief when the wagon was pushed 'in clear'; had it derailed, he would have had to hope that the Up train could stop in time and would not run past his Home signal. Signalmen did not normally take chances like that.

Winterbourne lost some of its facilities even before Dr Beeching got his hands on the railway network. January 1956 had seen the removal of the west end crossover and siding connections, whilst all other sidings were removed under Beeching in January 1964, except the main crossover situated outside the box. Signalling alterations followed in the 1960s with the Up Main Outer Home, Up Main Starting, Down Main Outer Home and Down Main Starting signals being removed not long after the station closed in October 1963. Winterbourne signal box closed in June 1970 under Stage 2 of the Bristol resignalling scheme.

CHAPTER 5

Existing Stations: Patchway, Pilning and Bristol Parkway

The building of the new section of line had the effect of changing the status of the existing Bristol & South Wales Union line from Filton to the Severn Tunnel. Trains from the London and Swindon direction now came mostly via Badminton and, as far as South Wales express passenger and goods services were concerned, this now became the main route, reducing the amount of these trains that had previously come via Bath and Bristol. However, from Stoke Gifford, trains to and from the Badminton line joined the existing route and thus the stations that were already there became more important and were brought up to date to match this.

Patchway Station, Junction and Signal Box

The first station at Patchway had opened in September 1863 on the original single Bristol & South Wales Union line from Bristol to New Passage. It was a single platform situated not far from where Patchway Tunnel signal box was built in later years and near to where the older of the two A38 overbridges stands today. It closed in 1885, being replaced on a site closer to Stoke Gifford by a new station known as 'Patchway and Stoke Gifford', which opened on 10 August 1885. This second station consisted of two platforms being served by double track through the platform, with

the lines becoming single again at each end of the station. A new signal box was opened along with the station.[15] Double track was laid from the Bristol direction into Patchway in 1886 and from Patchway to Pilning in 1887.

With the advent of the new Direct line from Wootton Bassett, a new junction and lines to Stoke Gifford were opened in May 1903 for Goods traffic and July 1903 for Passenger trains. In anticipation of the opening of the new lines, a new, larger signal box was built nearer the junction and opened on 19 October 1902, the 'old' box closing on the same date.

The new station was built in the same style as those on the Direct line, with the main waiting rooms and booking office, along with the station master's office, being on the Up side platform, adjacent to the roadway. There was no dedicated approach road to Patchway station, as it stood close to the lane that ran between Gypsy Patch Lane and Gloucester road (A38) and became known as (not surprisingly) 'Station Road'. The station was provided with a covered footbridge, which, unlike those on the stations on the new Direct line, was glazed. In later years, the signal box became one of the few boxes to be double-glazed; it was fitted with a separate set of sliding windows inside the normal set. This was to reduce the noise from the jet engine test beds that were constructed by Bristol Siddeley

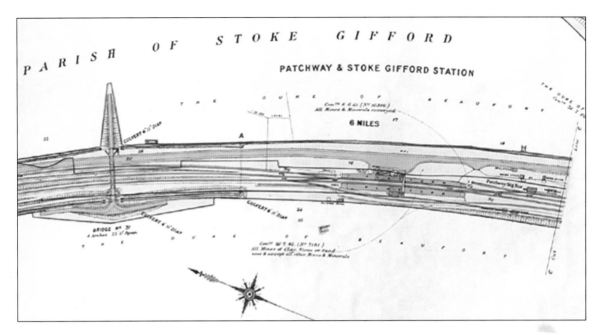

ABOVE: Plan of Patchway and Stoke Gifford station; 1903. WILTSHIRE HISTORY CENTRE

BELOW LEFT: Commemorative stone in Station Road, Patchway, with plaque; June 2013. P.D. RENDALL

BELOW RIGHT: Detail of the plaque; June 2013. P.D. RENDALL

Patchway Railway Station

The railway came to Patchway in 1863 as a single track as far as Pilning and Patchway Station was just here.

There was a weigh-bridge by the station to check wagons were not over-laden. The tall houses in Station Road were built for railway officials, such as the Station Master.

The Severn Tunnel opened in 1885. So many trains brought coal from south Wales that a second track had to be built. The new track was at a different level to make the slope gentler, so the station had to be moved further south to its present site.

Picture courtesy of Mrs W Brewer and text by Lucy Hamid and Alfie Hargreaves

Patchway station. Castle Class 5050 Earl of St Germans passes through with a London-bound service. Look at the neat station yard and the cars. The Down loop is still in situ.
WILF STANLEY

Aero-Engines (later Rolls-Royce) on ground opposite the box.

A refuge siding was also provided on the Up side at the Pilning end of the Up platform. A siding for banking engines was provided next to the signal box on the Up line; a short spur off the station end of this led into a loading dock. The dock could hold about four standard wagons. Goods facilities consisted of a small area behind the dock where a coal merchant had an office and coal stacks.

On the Down side, a long goods loop commenced a short distance on the station side of the junction,

Patchway looking towards Bristol; an unidentified Grange Class comes off the Direct line with a goods for South Wales; 1961. WILF STANLEY

ran behind the Down platform and rejoined the Down main just beyond the platforms. The Filton end of this loop had a long spur to enable very long goods trains that would not fit in the loop to back-shunt, a 'stage' being provided near the Filton end points for the guard to climb on so that he could get a good view of the driver during the shunting move. The method of accessing this spur was for the train to be signalled into the loop and out of the other end, far enough for the guard's van to clear the points that gave entry to the loop. The guard would then climb on to the stage and when the signalman had put the points to 'normal', would handsignal the driver to back the train into the spur clear of the main line.

When the junction was altered to have 'move-able elbows' instead of a fixed diamond crossing, a time lapse was installed to prevent the signalman moving the points in error. Once the road from Stoke Gifford had been set and Stoke Gifford West box had cleared his Down Main Starting signal, the timer prevented the 'elbows' from being moved unless the track circuit had been occupied by a train and cleared again, or the train had been at a stand for two minutes.

The first station master at the new station was William John Moore. A Gloucestershire man, William Moore started his Great Western career in 1876 as a porter at the tiny station of Uffculme, in Devon, having transferred from the Bristol and Exeter Railway. He moved to another small station, Clevedon, in 1877 as booking clerk, taking a similar position at Bridport (West Bay) in 1884. A year later, he moved to do the same job at Broadwey on the Weymouth line where, in June 1890, he became station inspector. Finally, in July 1887, he moved to Patchway and Stoke Gifford station. As well as the duties of a station master already mentioned, in later years the Patchway station master also admin-istered Patchway Tunnel box.

The wartime years of 1940–45 saw Mr Collins as station master and during 1960–62, Mr D.G. Williams was in charge at Patchway station. One of the last station masters was Dick Clark, who was station master during the 1960s, having succeeded Mr Williams. Mr Clark had previously been a sig-nalman at Avonmouth Dock Station box.

Houses for the station master and other officials were built at the western end of Station Road, near the (then) junction with the A38 that crossed the lines at that point. The houses still stand today, but are no longer owned by the railway.

Porters at the new station included W. Russell, A. Wayman, W.E. Read, W. Cockram, and G. Hine. F.B. Stephens was a lad porter. In 1902, porter T. Shergold joined the staff and was shortly joined by porters C. Rushbridge and H.G. Birch. Two more lad porters joined, T.R. Mark and G.Manning. Manning failed to turn up for work in June 1903 and after a week or two's absence was declared as having 'absconded'.

In the 1950s, there was a lad porter still employed at Patchway and an adult porter – Roy Thorning – who later went to Henbury box as signalman. Charlie Watts was a porter at Patchway in the 1950s and is remembered as having served in the

Patchway station, July 2013. Visible through the footbridge is the Rolls-Royce aero-engine works. P.D. RENDALL

RAF during the war. J.A. Davis moved from Coalpit Heath to become a motor driver at Patchway in March 1959.

Herbert Board was the signal lampman from 1903. In addition to the lamps at Patchway station, the 'lampy' also looked after the signal lamps at Patchway Tunnel signal box, when that box opened in 1918.

Apart from the small community that sprang up around the nearby marshalling yard, the village of Stoke Gifford did not expand, but the neighbourhood of Patchway grew in size. As a consequence, 'Patchway and Stoke Gifford' was renamed 'Patchway' from 27 November 1908.[16]

In 1953, the signal box was open continuously, but would close between 06.00–14.00 during periods when the Severn Tunnel was shut for maintenance. In September 1955, W.D. Hockings, assistant lineman at Patchway, moved to Lawrence Hill. The permanent way ganger was Mr Lawler.

Goods facilities were withdrawn from Patchway from 5 July 1965, apart from coal deliveries, which continued for a few years but had gone by 1969. Patchway station had become unmanned by 1970. The station buildings were soon demolished and the footbridge glazing and roof removed. A 'bus shelter' was erected on each platform. The station remains in use today. It has a small car park and is surrounded by various businesses, which include second-hand car dealers. The station sadly now has the overall air of standing in a junkyard.

Pilning Station and Pilning Junction

The original single line from Bristol to New Passage descended from Patchway and passed via a pair of tunnels, the second of which went under Over Lane, from where it shortly passed through the hamlet of Pilning, a small community about 1 mile (1.6km) to the east of the more important village of Cross Hands. When the Severn Tunnel opened, a new line was built to the south and then ran on a higher level for a short distance before descending to the tunnel. The spot where the old line and the new line diverged became a junction; firstly to a siding, then, in February 1900, as the junction for the single line to Severn Beach and Avonmouth. As a result, what with the new station at Pilning, the junction for the line to Severn Beach and the platform later built on the branch at the lower level, Pilning became quite a railway community. In addition to the station, there were sidings and three signal boxes – Pilning Junction, Pilning Station and Pilning Branch, the latter being situated at the bottom of the station approach road where the

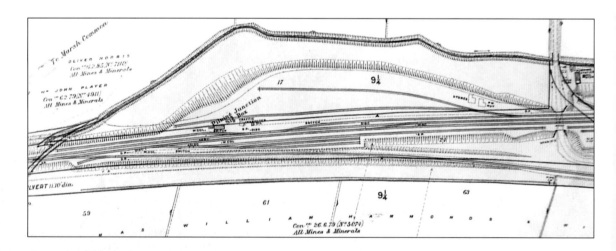

Plan of Pilning Junction, 1903. WILTSHIRE HISTORY CENTRE

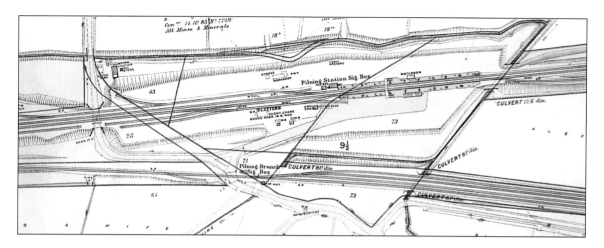

Plan of Pilning Station, 1903. WILTSHIRE HISTORY CENTRE

branch line crossed a road and was more popularly known as 'Low Level'. Further to the west, outside the mouth of the Severn Tunnel was Severn Tunnel East signal box and a mile to the east of the station stood Cattybrook Siding box, the latter serving a brickworks siding.

Pilning station was opened on 1 December 1886. It stood on raised ground in direct line of the winds that blew in across the marshy fields from the River Severn a mile to the west. To the traveller leaving a train at Pilning, the station appeared to be in the middle of nowhere (and still does); the nearest cluster of habitation, apart from the odd house or

farm, was nearly a mile away. The main station buildings were on the Up side platform and reached by a steep approach road from Station Road below. The buildings bore no resemblance to any of the other stations built on the line and were about two-thirds the size of most of them. Those on the Up side contained the station master's office, booking office, parcels office and WC, whilst on the Down platform stood a small waiting room. The footbridge was open and uncovered.

The station was originally named 'Pilning' and received the addition of 'High Level' when the branch 'Low Level' platform opened in 1928. When

Pilning station in the early 1960s; view from the footbridge looking east.
WILF STANLEY

the branch closed in 1968, the main-line station reverted to 'Pilning'.

From its opening, Pilning had a short refuge siding on the Up side of the line, to the west of the station. On the Bristol side of the station, still on the Up side, stood a small goods shed and exterior platform. This shed was built along much the same lines as that at Badminton and other stations. There was a short dock line to the Up platform. However, such was the increase in traffic that a further refuge siding was constructed in 1889, this time at the Bristol end of the station and on the Down side of the line.

In 1904, one of the sidings on the Up side was converted into a goods loop between Pilning station and the junction, then in 1905 a Down goods loop was built on the opposite side of the line. Additional sidings were provided on the Up side. A Down siding for stabling bank engines was provided at the junction.

By 1903, when the Direct line opened, Pilning could boast the largest railway community on the line and in fact probably the largest in the area,

other than that at Bristol. There were fourteen signalmen, six signalmen/porters, six porters, two lad porters and a tunnel inspector. However, between 1903 and 1905 there were a large amount of staff moves in a short space of time, which seems to indicate that many men were only temporary appointments. For example, Signalman A. Chalker arrived at Pilning in March 1903 from Castle Cary on the Westbury (Wilts) to Weymouth line, but stayed only until October 1903 when he moved to Flax Bourton, west of Bristol. In all, seventeen signalmen, eight porters, six signalmen/porters, two inspectors and four other staff came and went during this period. One porter had been a temporary appointment.

The first station master was Frank Charles Cane, who had joined the Great Western in April 1864 as a porter at Warminster station. He had moved to Filton as a booking porter in August 1873, moving to Patchway in the same capacity in March 1877. In August 1877, he became station inspector at New Passage and moved to Pilning Station as station inspector in November 1886. He became station

Pilning Junction signal box.
WILF STANLEY

master in November 1897, but in 1904, at the age of sixty-three, Cane resigned. This may have been due to ill-health, as he was listed as a 'Pensioned Railway Man' in the 1911 census.[17]

To this lonesome but large railway community in July 1905 came station master Henry Jefferies. Jefferies came from Hallatrow station, on the Bristol–Radstock North Somerset line. At the time of his arrival it is known that the staff included: signalmen Biggs, Boon, Ann, Pearce, Govier, Day, Evans and H. Hill; porters included: Turner, Wellman, Matthews, Bolwell, Binning, Hillier and E. Hill; signalmen/porters included: Cossins and Newcombe; lad porters included Master Beer.

Jefferies' duties included daily visits to the four signal boxes that were open and to Pilning Branch box when it was in use (at the time it was only opened 'as required'). In 1928, the Branch signal box, which had been closed as a block post since 1921, became a block post once again with the reintroduction of passenger trains on the Pilning to Avonmouth line and the Pilning station master's duties now included both the Branch ('Low Level') signal box and Low Level platform. He would also administer Pilning Junction, Station and Severn Tunnel East signal boxes.

In 1943, the station master at Pilning was Mr Edwards, who gained promotion to Tidworth, Wilts. He was replaced by Mr H.J. Tidmarsh, who moved to Pilning from Hullavington. During the late 1950s and 60s, the station master was Mr W.A. Pike, who was the brother of Coalpit Heath's station master, Harry Pike. Their father had been on the GWR as well. Mr Pike had previously been station master at Chippenham. F.R. Williams became leading porter at Pilning Station; G. Bishop transferred to leading porter at Pilning in May 1957.

Don (Dinky) Oakhill became a signalman in May 1956 and was still working in Station box when it closed in 1971. All the Pilning boxes were variously worked by members of the Oakhill family; Vic, Joe and Dinky Oakhill all worked at the Pilning boxes and also at Cattybrook. In 1953, all of the main-line Pilning boxes, along with Severn Tunnel East, were open continuously.

In 2013, Pilning station comes under the auspices of First Great Western and is blessed with one morning train to Bristol Temple Meads and one afternoon train to Cardiff – but on Saturdays only. No trains are booked to call at Pilning at any other time, or on any other day of the week. The Strategic Rail Authority website states that during the financial year 2005/06, Pilning was the thirteenth least-used station in the UK. In 2006/07 it was the eighteenth least-used station.

The First Great Western website says that Pilning has ten car parking spaces and no cycle storage. It is, however, 'near a bus stop', so perhaps we should be thankful for small mercies. No doubt we should be happy that it is still there, although it is now sited in a bigger junkyard than Patchway and the approach roads, which in the 1960s boasted rows of commuters' cars parked neatly nose in to the fence, are now so overgrown that one can barely drive a van up there. A 'reclamation' type of yard stands adjacent to the old Up platform building and is guarded by a large, fierce dog. It is certainly not the place to alight on a dark evening, so it is just as well there are no trains!

Cars by Rail

Pilning used to be a busy place. In post-war years when private motoring became popular and before any road bridge was built across the Severn, people wishing to take their car to Wales could either use the ferry across the river, or take the car by train. Those who opted to use the train were advised to contact the station in advance of their journey by 'letter, telegram or telephone' (dial 'Pilning 206') as only twenty-two cars could be conveyed on a train.

To do this, car-carrying flat wagons would be shunted into the end-on loading dock on the Up platform at Pilning station. Cars would be driven on to these and when the loading was complete, the wagons would be shunted out and formed up at the rear of passenger trains. Two shunters were allocated to the station for such shunting moves.

Instructions stated that cars so carried need not have their petrol tanks emptied as long as there were no leaks and the pressure had been released

Assembling a car train at Pilning in the early 1960s. The wooden goods shed and loco water tank are also to be seen. WILF STANLEY

by loosening the petrol filler cap and tightening it again. Additionally, the car engine 'must be run by the person in charge of the car until the carburettor has become exhausted and the engine stops automatically' – a process that could not happen with cars today.[18]

Motorcycles with sidecars could also be carried, but no more than a quart of petrol (2 pints) was allowed in the bike's petrol tank. Waterproof sheets to cover the vehicles were available for a charge of 2s per sheet. The occupants of all vehicles naturally rode in the carriages. Cars thus transported through the tunnel would be off-loaded at Severn Tunnel Junction.

Train services that conveyed motor vehicles from Pilning to Severn Tunnel Junction were the 08.15 (Mondays only), 10.00 and 18.45, arriving in South Wales at 08.33 (MO), 10.18 and 19.03. Return trains left Severn Tunnel Junction at 09.05 and 16.40; arriving at Pilning at 09.22 and 16.57 respectively. Sunday services left Pilning at 10.50 and 19.20, with return services arriving back there at 09.32 and 19.32. The 10.50 outwards and 09.32 return Sunday trains were conditional and ran during September and October, plus on selected dates during December. Services were also liable to alteration on public and bank holidays. The cost for

taking your car by train was 25s for a return journey and 15s one way.

When the new Severn Road Bridge opened in 1966, car trains became less well used and soon ceased to run. The loading bay at Pilning Station then became occupied by the Fire Service emergency train, which would be taken over by the Fire Brigade for transporting them into the Tunnel in the event of mishap. Ironically, this train had been withdrawn from Pilning and stationed at Severn Tunnel Junction by the time it was needed for the first time ever in 1991.

The Pilning Inspectors

Stationed at Pilning Junction, in a cabin situated a short distance to the west of the Junction signal box, were the Pilning inspectors. The duties of these inspectors included giving instructions to banker drivers and signalmen regarding the working of freight trains through the tunnel and regulating the working of the assisting locomotives; for example, three bankers were provided for assisting trains up to Patchway and beyond. One banker turn was known as 'Double Low Level' and entailed the banking loco going down to Low Level to attach to the rear of an ex-Severn Beach or Avonmouth freight. The train would then be pushed up to the

Pilning Branch signal box (Low Level).
R. CUFF/AUTHOR'S COLLECTION

main line and the train loco taken off the rear and run round to attach to the front. The train would then be double-headed through the tunnel. Other tasks were to ensure that the bankers were returned from Patchway as soon as possible to avoid delays to other trains requiring assistance through the tunnel or up to Patchway.

The Pilning inspectors also had responsibility for advising relevant staff if the ventilation fans in the Severn Tunnel became inoperative through some fault. The inspector would normally be advised that the fans had failed by the person in charge at Sudbrook pumping station. The inspector, in his turn, would then advise the signalmen at Pilning Station and Junction, Severn Tunnel East and West, and Severn Tunnel Junction; Bristol District Inspector; the Severn Tunnel Junction East End Inspector and Train Control at Bristol. Drivers of all freight trains passing through the tunnel would be stopped at either end of the tunnel and advised that the fans were out of order. It was essential for train crews to know this, as to be stopped in the tunnel in steam days was not a pleasant experience. Sulphurous smoke would build up and could render trainmen unconscious in a short time.

In the 1960s, Ron Singer was one of the Pilning inspectors; his father, Frank Singer, had been a signalman at Pilning Station box. Mr Sorrell was another Pilning inspector.

In November 1959, Pilning permanent way lengthmen D. Jones, C.S. Thompson and W.G. Marshall all attained a Merit in the PW Maintenance exam, as would be expected of men who maintained the tracks through the Severn Tunnel.

Only brief mention has so far been made of Pilning Branch signal box, or 'Low Level' as it became known after the small, one-platform halt adjacent to the box. The box and its layout really belong to another book as they were part and parcel of the Pilning to Avonmouth via Severn Beach branch line. However, it is necessary to describe them in part to explain what happened when a freight train needed to reverse at Low Level.

The Severn Beach branch started at Pilning Junction, where a facing crossover in the main lines led to a connection in the Up main. From the Up main there was a connection leading to a single line, which descended sharply westwards at a gradient of 1 in 100, crossing a level-crossing. Here, there was a signal box – Pilning Branch Signal Box, to give it its proper name, though it was always known as 'Low Level' to railwaymen. Up until 1928, the single line between the Junction and Branch boxes had been worked by means of a wooden train staff, but on Friday, 22 June 1928, this working was withdrawn and superseded; the single line was henceforth worked by special 'disc' Lock and Block instruments and the line track-circuited. Beyond the box was a small, one-

73

platform halt and it was this halt that was officially known as 'Pilning Low Level'. Here, too, were two loops and at the far end of these loops stood a ground frame, released by means of a key from the signal box.

It was between Pilning Junction and Low Level that elaborate shunting moves known as 'Double Low-Level' took place in order to reverse goods trains to and from the Severn Tunnel. In the case of freight trains for Avonmouth that had arrived via the Severn Tunnel, these would arrive at Pilning Junction and reverse carefully on to the Branch. The level-crossing gates at the bottom of the short incline would be closed against road traffic by the signalman at Low Level box. Once at a stand on the single line, the brake van would be cut off and would run downhill under its own momentum and under the guard's control, over the crossing and on to a loop. The train would next be backed slowly into the platform road. The loco would be cut off and would run round its train and back into the second loop, running round the brake van as it did so. Backing into the first loop, the loco would collect the brake van and then shunt it on to the rear of the train. Next, the engine would run along the first loop again and set back on to the front of the

train via the ground frame, accompanied by the signalman. From there, when the train was ready to leave, the signalman had to walk all the way back to Low Level box to get the single-line token and then all the way back to the locomotive again to hand the token to the driver.

For trains arriving from Severn Beach, the train would come to a stand at Low Level and the train engine would be detached and run round to the rear, where it would back on to the train and attach to the guard's van. The guard's van would be shunted on to a loop and the engine would run round and attach to the other end of the van. The van would then be attached to what was now the rear of the train and the loco would run back to the other end and couple up.

Once the signalman had 'got the road' from Pilning Junction and the latter signalman set the points for the Down refuge siding, the train engine could propel its load up the short incline and into the refuge siding. From there, if the train was a 'double load', it could attach an assisting engine for the journey through to Severn Tunnel Junction.

A klaxon was installed at the west end of the loops at Low Level to enable the signalman to give the driver of a train the signal to commence the

Shunting a freight from Severn Tunnel Junction for Avonmouth at Low Level sidings. The brake van has been placed on the siding and the main train shunted to the through road. The loco will now cut off, run back over the level-crossing and then run round the brake van and train to the far end. It will then attach to the train and pull it forwards, after which it will back on to the brake van and the whole train, having reversed, will now be able to proceed to Avonmouth via Severn Beach. If he could have seen this 'ritual', Dr Beeching would, no doubt, have been convinced that all his plans were right! WILF STANLEY

push up to the Junction: five blasts on the klaxon was the signal to start.

In the case of a passenger train from the Severn Beach direction arriving at Low Level, the train engine had to run round as above and attach to the rear of the train, pushing it up to the Junction as above. If there was a banker available, that had to be attached to the rear at Low Level and pull the train up to the Junction. If assistance through the tunnel was needed, the banker would run round and attach to the front for this purpose.

For Avonmouth-bound freight trains from the tunnel arriving at Pilning Junction, the train would draw up to the Junction Up Main Advanced Starting signal, clear of the junction points. There was a klaxon fixed to the post of this signal and once the points at both the Junction and Low Level boxes were set for the single line, the signalman would give five blasts on the klaxon as the signal for the train to set back on to the single line and down to Low Level. Once in the loop at Low Level, the engine would run round with the brake van, which would be attached to the rear of the train, the engine being coupled to what was now the leading end of the train.

In the event of Severn Beach (or Hallen Marsh Junction if Severn Beach was switched out) not being able to accept the freight, or if priority had to be given to a train from that direction before the freight could be allowed to proceed, the procedure was slightly different, in as much as once the freight had arrived at Low Level, the brake van was initially shunted into the platform line and the train into a loop before the brake van was shunted on to the end of the train in the loop and the loco run round to attach to the front. This left the platform clear for a train to arrive from Severn Beach. Passenger trains for Avonmouth from the tunnel had to be run round at the Junction before going on to the single line.

As Low Level box was at one end of the loops and the ground frame at the other, and as the latter could only be released and operated by the signalman, it meant a lot of walking for the poor old signalman and heaven help him if he arrived at the ground frame and discovered that he had left the keys in

the signal box. Also, each shunt meant a move over the level crossing; although this was released and locked from the signal box, the gates were manually operated, which meant that the signalman was forever opening and closing the gates to road traffic between each move. Cars would build up – even in those days of infrequent motor traffic – so the gates would be shut for the traffic to move off, then the gates would be closed across the road and the whole charade would begin again. Unfortunately, there were usually far more trains requiring shunts at Low Level during the day shifts, thus exposing the Low Level signalman to the ire of the many motorists stuck at the crossing; it did not pay to be a sensitive soul when working at Low Level box, as one's sex and ancestry were frequently cast into considerable doubt by frustrated motorists.

One day, a Bristol Special Class relief signalman, on being allocated a rare shift at Low Level, thought he had got lucky and was looking forward to a nice, quiet turn of duty. Such was the shunting 'nuisance', that after a rough shift of shunts, in and out of the sidings and in and out of the box to operate the gates, this individual, used to very busy boxes such as that at Bristol Temple Meads East, swore he would never accept a shift at Low Level again.

Another annoying factor was that there was no water column at Low Level. Locos requiring water had to be cut off and run up to the 'High Level' station for water; if the loco was on a passenger train, it had to leave its train in Low Level platform and run to High Level first, running round its train on its return from the water column.

Luckily, night shifts at Low Level were quiet affairs. There were usually only two trains to deal with: these were the 01.10 Severn Tunnel Junction to Avonmouth and its return as the 05.05 Avonmouth to Severn Tunnel Junction. After the passage of the 01.10, the Low Level signalman would often walk up the station approach road to the Station box for a cuppa with his main-line colleague.

In 1953, Low Level signal box was open between 06.00 Monday to 06.00 the following Sunday, and on Sundays between 14.00 and 22.00.

Bristol Parkway

Three years after the last of the original stations, Badminton, had closed, a new station was opened on the Direct line on 1 May 1972 – Bristol Parkway.

After the devastation to railway services caused by Dr Beeching's attempts to modernize the railways in the early 1960s, by the end of that decade the new diesel-hauled express trains on speeded-up services were at last clawing back passengers and, with that, some reputation for the bruised and battered railway system. In fact, by 1970 passenger traffic on the Western Region was increasing by 10 per cent per year. It was not only railway passenger numbers that were expanding; there were new, large housing developments at Yate and Thornbury and a huge 'new town' was planned for an area north-west of Patchway. The new M4 and M5 motorways formed a crossroads not far from Almondsbury, on the northern fringes of Bristol. Businesses in the area were booming; ICI at Avonmouth was a huge employer, as was the Rolls-Royce aero-engineering works at Filton. BAC works, where the new supersonic airliner *Concorde* was being built, was working to capacity on that and other projects.

With the streamlining of freight services and the introduction of faster, air-braked company 'block' trains and Freightliner trains, came the beginning of the demise of the old vacuum-braked and loose-coupled slow goods trains. In Bristol, the entire signalling system was also being replaced by modern, electronically controlled signals. A new 'chord' line was being laid between Filton West Junction on the Avonmouth line and Patchway Junction. This new chord would allow trains to run directly to and from Avonmouth and South Wales, alleviating the need for such trains to run to Stoke Gifford to reverse.

By July 1970, plans for a new station to serve the expanding suburbs of north Bristol were well advanced. The local railway management announced the plans for the new station at a meeting of rail staff held in Bristol on 5 July. The new station, consisting of two island platforms linked to each other and a booking office by a footbridge, was to be built on the site of the marshalling yards at Stoke Gifford. It would serve South Gloucestershire, North Bristol and Avonmouth. Car parking for 1,000 cars would be provided on the land at that time occupied by the Up yard. Two InterCity services an hour to Paddington would call at the new station. Later, it was hoped that trains from and to the Midlands, Bristol and the West of England would also call there. Surveys had shown that passenger figures of up to 150 a day could be expected when the new station opened and that this

Welcome for rail station

MAY 1970

The proposal to establish a new inter-city passenger rail station at Stoke Gifford was welcomed today by Gloucestershire highways committee.

Chairman Alderman H. W. Tily (ChippingSodbury) said: "We shall do what we can to support this venture."

The committee also agreed that if a station were established road improvements in the Stoke Gifford area would be necessary.

The improvements to ensure adequate access would be required at Filton Lane and with its junction with the Stoke Gifford road.

Alderman Tily said the British Railways Board intended giving passengers a better service to London and the Midlands and avoiding the necessity of all travellers catching trains at Temple Meads.

From the Bristol Evening Post; May 1970. BRISTOL UNITED PRESS

figure would rise to above 300 when more services called at the station. The new services would be in addition to the Bristol–London service via Bath and would give people living in the Bristol area the choice of around five trains per hour to the capital.

Strategically placed to serve the motorway network, this was to be BR's challenge to the 'age of the car'. The new station was to cost an estimated £200,000 and it was the large car park that was one of the main selling points; by providing such a large capacity for parking, BR was hoping to attract motorists off the new motorways and on to the trains. The new station, as yet without a name, was hoped to be open by October 1971. Local councils approved of the announcement and gave it their support, agreeing that road improvements would be needed in the vicinity of the new station.

Railway staff were not very happy, however. Platform staff at Bristol Temple Meads thought that the new station would see traffic taken away from Temple Meads. Goods yards staff at Stoke Gifford were unhappy at the announcement that the yards would be closed in order to build the new station. Signalling staff were astounded that the yards were about to be equipped with new signalling just before closure.

All in all, though, the new station was a positive innovation for the area. The government plans for residential and business expansion, published a few years earlier as the 'Severnside' plan, had confirmed that roads into Bristol would in future carry more traffic and if the railway was to win passenger traffic back from the roads, the last thing it needed was to expect commuters to travel into the middle of town to catch their trains, especially given that Temple Meads station had limited car parking capacity.

The *Bristol Evening Post* reported the news of the new station on 6 April 1971 with the headline 'Free Car Park Plan with New City Station', including the news that there was the future prospect of trains travelling at 125mph (200km/h) and a 76-minute journey time to London, all in the 'next four years'.[19] When cross-country services started to use the station, the journey time to Birmingham would be seventy-five minutes. In May 1971, it was announced that the station had been given the go-ahead and that work would start soon. It was to be constructed at the west end of the yards, with new road access from North Road to the Up side, where the sidings were to be removed for the car park. The Up and Down main lines were slewed to allow construction of the platforms to commence.

Named 'Bristol Parkway', the new station opened on 1 May 1972 at the cost of just over £50,000. The platforms were given shelters in the now all too familiar 'bus shelter' style and the footbridge was open to the elements. Notwithstanding its somewhat basic provisions, the station proved an almost instant success, with soon over 1,000 passengers per day using the facilities; the car park on the site

ABOVE: *Bristol Parkway by night, late autumn 1972. Note the rudimentary footbridge.* P.D. RENDALL

RIGHT: *By 1978, the footbridge had been given a roof.* P.D. RENDALL

This is 1973 and the car parking facilities at Bristol Parkway were still quite basic but then, so were the cars! An unidentified 'Western' diesel is shunting on the upside and is in remarkably clean condition. P.D. RENDALL

of the Up sidings and the proximity to the motorways being an obvious winning advantage over the limited parking at Temple Meads. Needless to say, after privatization of Britain's railways in 1994, the free car park soon changed to a pay-and-display one.

One of the first station staff at 'The Parkway', as it soon became known, was ex-signalman Gordon Penny, who lived at Old Sodbury and had been a relief signalman until the resignalling made him redundant. After the closure of the old signal boxes, Gordon went to Temple Meads as a platform supervisor and later moved to Bristol Parkway.

Within two years, the station was judged to be a great success and steps were taken to improve the facilities. The footbridge was covered and 'canopies' (resembling windbreaks rather than the traditional canopy) were added. The station stayed this way until the 1990s, when it was rebuilt in a modern style with better booking office, café facilities, escalators to the footbridge and a second storey added to the car-parking area nearest the lines. The Up platform was resignalled to become an island platform.

No.31262 is on an engineer's train in Parkway Up loop. The platform canopies have recently been added, giving some protection to the passengers, who had previously been required to suffer the elements; 1976. P.D. RENDALL

CHAPTER 6

Junctions and Goods Yards

The Westerleigh Junctions

When the Direct line opened, there was a triangular junction made with the Midland Railway's Bristol–Gloucester line at Yate South junction. From two junctions on the Direct line, Westerleigh West and East Junctions, double track ran north and converged at a further junction, Westerleigh North, approximately ½ mile (800m) from the West and East boxes. The 'east curve', that is, the curve that ran from the East box to the North box, was more gentle than the 'west curve'.

The 1903 Westerleigh East box was sited in the 'V' of the junction between the main lines and the east curve. It was a small, wooden box, which, from the 1903 survey, would have been almost identical in appearance to the West and North Junction boxes. Westerleigh West Junction was also situated in the 'V' of the junction, was of wooden construction and differed from the East box in that it stood on a high embankment. Similarly, the North Junction box also stood on an embankment.

From the North Junction, double track continued for about a ¼ mile (400m) before the Up line separated and running to the west, crossed the Midland on a girder bridge and then descended on a sweeping curve round to join the MR at Yate. The Down line continued as a single line on the east side of the MR until it, too, joined the Midland at Yate.

This short branch opened on 1 May 1903, but the GWR and the Midland fell out with each other over operating rights and the branch was closed on 4 February 1907. The dispute was resolved in 1908, the branch reopening on 9 March that year. In spite of, or perhaps because of, the Great War, the branch was taken out of use again on 18 December 1916, but reinstated on 18 February 1918. The status quo continued until 1927, when the branch again came out of use on 19 July. The east curve was taken out of use, along with Westerleigh North and East signal boxes; track and signal boxes were eventually removed, with Westerleigh West box being renamed 'Westerleigh Junction Signal Box'. The lines between there and Yate were used occasionally.

With the construction of the wartime depot at Wapley Common, it was thought strategically necessary to reinstate the East curve again. As is mentioned in the section below on Wapley yard, a new East box was built and a new North box also appeared. This box again stood at the apex of the triangle formed by the lines from West and East boxes towards the LMR. Perhaps surprisingly, in spite of its vulnerable location high on the embankment near a road underbridge, this new North box was built of wood rather than being an ARP (Air Raid Precautions) type, as were the other two boxes connected with the new wartime depot. Perhaps it was thought that the ground in the 'V' of the two

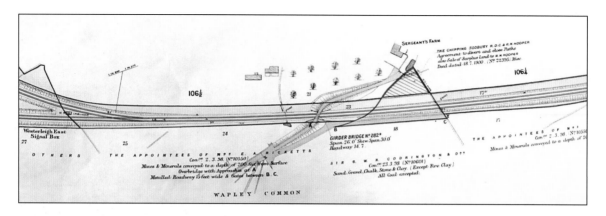

1903 plan of Westerleigh East Junction. The land to the right-hand side of Sergeant's Bridge (centre) was where Wapley Common sidings were laid in 1942. The wartime East box was built just above the figure 18 on the plan. WILTSHIRE HISTORY CENTRE

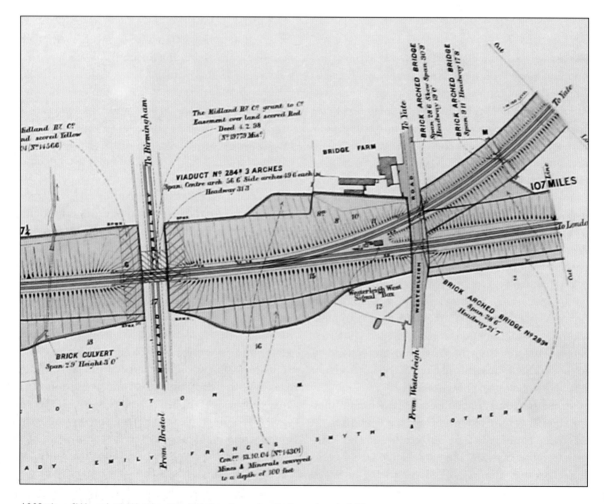

1903 plan of Westerleigh West Junction. Little has changed to the layout here in 110 years. WILTSHIRE HISTORY CENTRE

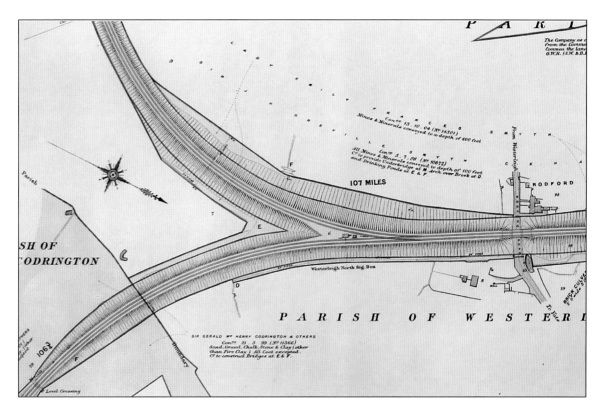

1903 plan of Westerleigh North Junction; East Junction is to the left, West Junction is to the top and Yate South and the Midland are to the right of the plan. WILTSHIRE HISTORY CENTRE

embankments was not stable enough to take the weight of a brick and reinforced concrete signal box; certainly, there have been successive slips of the embankment in that vicinity over the years. The new North box and east curve reopened to traffic on 16 August 1942.

Having served its use during the conflict years, after World War II North box was rarely used. It was

The line climbed steeply from Yate to Westerleigh. An unidentified 9F 2-10-0 struggles up to Westerleigh North with a Washwood Heath–Stoke Gifford coal train in 1962. Pictures of the North signal box are rare; it is just off the right-hand side of the photo. WILF STANLEY

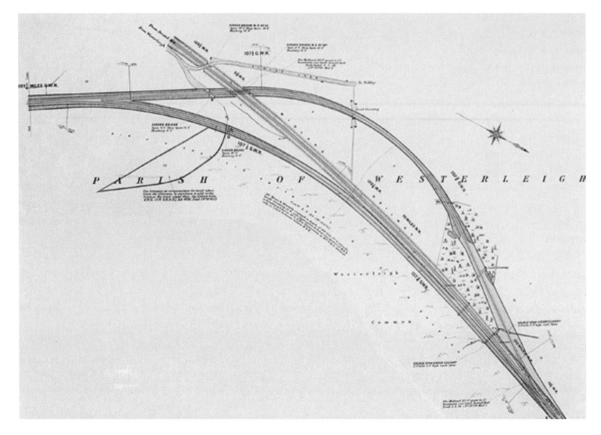

To the north side of Westerleigh North Junction, the line split into two single lines; the Up line continued straight for a while, crossing the Midland Bristol–Gloucester main line via a skew girder bridge, before curving sharply and descending through a small wood to Yate South Junction. The Down line curved to the right and descended to join the main line. In 1970, the Up line flying junction was abandoned and a second track laid alongside the existing Down line. These two then became the main line from Yate South and the MR line was closed, the old Up line becoming a long siding and accessed at Yate South via a new ground frame. WILTSHIRE HISTORY CENTRE

'mothballed' on Wednesday, 12 January 1949 and was officially taken out of use on 4 January 1950. However, it was specially reopened in the 1950s to allow a royal train to stable on the East curve. Relief signalman Wilf Stanley and a Signal and Telegraph Department lineman went to the box to 'tidy up' and make sure that everything still worked. After its regal duty, the North box and east curve fell out of use once more and all the signals and points were disconnected. The next time Wilf Stanley went to the box was years later, in 1963, just for a visit out of curiosity. The box had been vandalized. The signalling block bells and instruments were hanging

off the shelf and windows had been broken, but the track diagram was still there.

Westerleigh West signal box played a crucial part in the working of trains on the Direct line. Open round the clock, it played a significant role in regulating train moves on the main line. For example, it was not unknown for Stoke Gifford to send a freight train up the Badminton line with a very short time margin between the freight and a following, more important, service. If this train was unlikely to be able to reach Chipping Sodbury loop before delaying the following train, Westerleigh West would put the train on to the Up branch to stand clear of the

9F No.92218 comes off the Up branch at Yate South Junction with a train of box vans. The Down line facing junction can be seen.
WILF STANLEY

main line. When the more important service had passed, West box would send the 'blocking back outside Home signal' bell code to Coalpit Heath or whichever box West was in circuit with and reverse the freight back out on to the main line. When the freight was at a stand at the Home signal, the signalman would set the junction for the Up main line again and signal the train on its way. This was, of course, before World War II and the advent of Wapley yard with its loops.

After the closure of Wapley Common box in 1965, Westerleigh West seldom stood trains on the Up branch in this manner; by then, the density of

freight traffic on the Direct line beyond Westerleigh West had diminished to the point where trains could either be recessed at Westerleigh East to allow a more important train to pass, or run to Chipping Sodbury loop.

However, right up until the end of the manual signal boxes, it was common for Down goods trains from the Midland line to be held at West Junction's Outer Home signal on the Down branch line if Stoke Gifford yard was full and could not accept them. After the 1970–71 resignalling, the Up branch became signalled in both Up and Down directions, so both lines could be used in the Down direction if

Westerleigh West Junction circa 1962. In the background, above the farmhouse roof, can be seen the formation of the east curve. The branch to Yate curves away to the left of the photo. In the foreground is the viaduct over the Midland main line.
WILF STANLEY

necessary. This will be discussed in Chapter 13 on signalling.

Up until January 1970, West Junction only played a small part in moves to and from the LMR line at Yate. When the old Midland line closed and all Bristol–Gloucester traffic then ran via the West Junction and Yate, the box became very much busier.

Westerleigh West signal box was in use round the clock, seven days a week until it was closed in May 1971, when control of signalling was transferred to Bristol signal box.

Westerleigh West had a permanent way gang based in a cabin there; Bill Reynolds was the ganger and Alfie Dee one of his men in the 1950s; Pete McIvor was there in the 1960s.

Filton Junction

Opened originally in 1863 as a single platform, Filton station stood on a site where the coal concentration depot sidings were built in the 1930s and 1950s. The Bristol and South Wales Union line, originally single, was doubled in 1886 and another platform provided for the new Down line. With the advent of the Direct line, a junction was made in 1897 to give access to the works site for construction of the line to Stoke Gifford; the new tracks were

laid on an embankment between Filton Junction and Stoke Gifford West Junction. A new station was built in the 'V' of this junction and opened in July 1903. There were four platforms serving all lines, so passengers could catch trains bound for South Wales and the Direct line. The station itself was at the top of the embankment and the buildings stood level with the platforms, but several storeys high at ground level. The station was opened as 'Filton'. When the Avonmouth line was built in 1910, another junction was made at Filton to connect with this line, enabling traffic to run to and from Avonmouth and Filton. The station was renamed 'Filton Junction'.

With this new chord making a junction at Filton West Junction with the Avonmouth line from Stoke Gifford West, trains and locos were able to turn without recourse to a turntable or running to Bristol. This was achieved, for example, by a loco wishing to turn running smokebox leading from Stoke Gifford to Filton, where it would reverse down the chord on to the Avonmouth line at Filton West. From Filton West, the loco would be able to run smokebox first again back to Stoke Gifford.

The Filton station master in November 1899 was Edward Charles Cavill. A Somerset man, born in the village of Compton Martin, Cavill joined the GWR as a 'railway policeman' in May

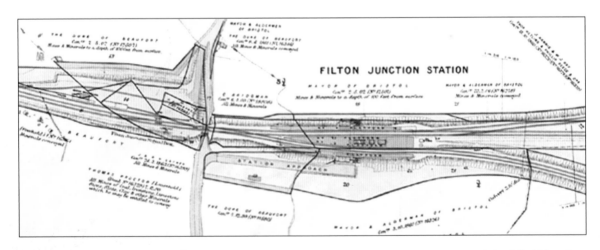

1910 plan of Filton Junction. The lines to the left were quadrupled in April 1933. The lines to the lower right run to Stoke Gifford West, the lines in the middle right run to Patchway and those on the top right to Filton West Junction. WILTSHIRE HISTORY CENTRE

Castle Class No.5013 Abergavenny Castle *has run from Stoke Gifford to Filton Junction, backed down to Filton West Junction and is now running back up to Stoke Gifford again. The lines to Avonmouth vanish under the bridge; 1959.* WILF STANLEY

1884. In 1885, he became a signalman at the original Patchway signal box and lived with his wife in a house on Station Road at Patchway. In September 1893, he was promoted to station inspector at Filton and became station master there in 1894, moving to the new station when it opened. He and his wife lived in the station master's cottage at Filton until Cavill died 'in harness' in May 1913, aged forty-nine years.

Filton Junction underwent many changes over the years. The lines from Bristol were quadrupled in 1933, with a goods running loop being provided between Filton Incline box and Filton Junction. After local train services on the Direct line ceased in 1962, Filton continued to use its platforms on the Stoke Gifford chord, but this lasted only until 1968, when they were taken out of use. The South Wales platforms remained in use, although the station became unstaffed and the buildings demolished. The station was once more named 'Filton'. The opening of Filton, Abbey Wood station to the south of the junction in May 1996 saw the final demise of the 1903 station. Nothing now remains of the station at rail level, although the remains of the lower-storey buildings can still be seen on the west side, at ground level.

The first Filton signal box stood to the south of the original single platform; this box closed in 1886 and was replaced by the second box to the east of the new Down platform. This, in turn, was replaced

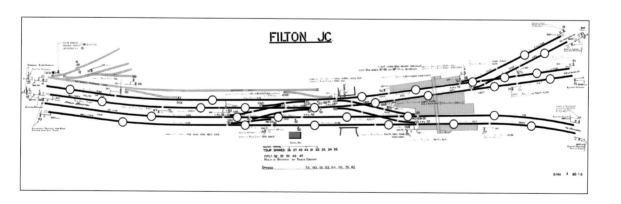

A 1960 signalling diagram of Filton Junction. AUTHOR'S COLLECTION

Filton Junction in 1962 looking towards the station from the Bristol end. Note the coal-concentration depot sidings on the left and the mound of coal. WILF STANLEY

by Filton Junction box in 1903. Subsequent altera-tion and enlargements took place in 1917 and 1932. The box eventually closed under Stage 7(B) of the Bristol resignalling scheme in February 1971.

There was a small yard on the Up side, with a small goods shed and loading platform; this was replaced by a larger goods shed in the 1930s and later in that decade extra sidings were also added. Later still, in the 1950s, two more sidings were added for use by the National Coal Board, which opened a new drift mine at nearby Harry Stoke in

September 1954. The goods sidings were generally used on the early shift and mainly for coal traffic in later years.

The mine was not a success and the sidings were little used, but a new coal-concentration depot was built in the yard in 1965, after the end of public goods facilities in July of that year. This depot had a wagon tippler that would turn a single wagon over, so tipping its load into a hopper. Later the same year, Bristol Mechanised Coal Co. took over the remaining sidings. After Bristol Panel signal box took control of the layout in 1971, access to the coal depot sidings was via a new ground frame, 'Filton North Ground Frame', which was unlocked by an Annett's key, released by the panel box and gave access to the yard from the Up goods loop. Coal traffic continued to use the sidings for many years and in the 1980s the yard was served by a working from Exmouth Junction; usually a Class 37 loco and around six coal hoppers. The sidings closed in December 1995.

View from Filton Junction station towards Bristol in 1968. R. CUFF/ AUTHOR'S COLLECTION

Original station staff at Filton Junction included W. Pound, R. Shield and H.J. Antell (lad porters); J. Bartlett, W.M. Keate and C.H. Mason (porters); and J. Dowse, J.H. Pearce, A. Way and H. Crossman (signalmen). Pearce's appointment was a temporary move from Pilning. Signalman E. Jakeways had moved to Filton from Flax Bourton in 1903, but left later the same year to move to Ashley Hill box, Bristol. His replacement was W. Parsons, who moved from Ashley Hill box to Filton. In 1953, and until it closed in 1971, Filton Junction signal box was open continuously.

Mr T. Powell was station master here in the 1950s. He came from the Gloucester area and lived with his family in the station house (still there, but now a nursery). By the time he became Filton Junction's station master, the post was also responsible for the work at North Filton Platform (on the Avonmouth line) and Horfield platforms, which were situated nearer to Bristol, on the four-track section between Filton Junction and Ashley Hill.

Wapley Depot

As World War II began in earnest after the 'phoney war' period of 1939, so the Government realized that in the event of enemy action crippling the country's major ports, food and material supplies could be seriously affected. The Ministry of Transport undertook to construct several large sorting depots at safe distances from the major ports. Bristol's Avonmouth Docks was one of those ports.

The depots needed to be sited away from the ports so that enemy bombing of the port could not destroy the depot. Also, the depot needed to be within a fairly short rail distance of the port. The main objective of the MoW in siting the depot was to increase the amount of goods that could pass through the port by clearing the goods as quickly as possible from the port and sorting them for distribution at a safe, distant location. This would serve another objective in that it would remove the goods from the danger of being destroyed by enemy air raids. Once sorted at the distribution depot, the goods could then be transported to their destinations by less congested routes, both by rail and road.

The depot would consist of four huge sheds; each measured 500×100ft (150×30m) and was designed to receive five trains per day of mixed loads totalling 250 5-ton wagons, which would represent the discharge of eight ships simultaneously.

A similar figure of outward trains of sorted goods was expected to leave the depot daily.

The new depot would cost £300,000 and was to be operated by the Ministry of War Transport on behalf of the Port of Bristol Authority (PBA). The PBA would be responsible for supplying both the labour force and the policing of the premises.[20]

Accordingly, land was found near the GWR main line between Chipping Sodbury and the original Westerleigh East junction. So in 1940, the Ministry of Transport requisitioned an area of pasture land on which to build the huge goods depot. The planned depot would be connected to the South Wales Direct line by rail. Adjacent to the GWR main line would be series of reception and departure sidings, leading to the 'arrival' and 'departure' and the depot itself, which would be sited over a ¼ mile (400m) away from the main line, near Yate, in South Gloucestershire.

From the reception sidings alongside the main line, the tracks narrowed to two, which passed through gates into the depot complex, where there were further reception sidings capable of holding five trains. Proceeding into the shed area, to the west of the site were the arrival sidings (marked A on the plan), which were capable of holding 750 wagons. On the east side of the sheds lay the outwards sidings (marked B on the plan), which had room for 500 wagons. Near here stood a railway weighbridge. Between the arrival and outwards sidings was a turntable for turning locomotives.

On either side of the long sheds were covered platforms for the purpose of offloading wagons. The rails that ran alongside the sheds were set in concrete, enabling road vehicles to be loaded on one side, whilst goods were offloaded into the shed on the other.

In a move that brings to mind modern warehouses of the twenty-first century, the sheds were equipped with mobile electric trucks that had elevating platforms, 1-ton mobile cranes and hand trucks. Outside in the stacking areas were two 2-ton cranes and two 10-ton cranes.

Office accommodation blocks, a staff canteen, stores, workshops, battery-charging room and an incinerator were provided. There was an up-to-date fire fighting system.[21]

Alterations to the Signalling and Trackwork

The depot required considerable railway alterations in the area. The existing Westerleigh East Junction and signal box that controlled the mainline end of the curve to Westerleigh North (GWR) and thence to the London Midland and Scottish Railway (LMSR) line at Yate had stood out of use

since 1927, along with the curve itself and the North box. Now the curve was to be brought back into use and a new signal box built at Westerleigh North. New Up and Down loops were to be built, both on the Up side of the main lines. To start with, in August 1941 a contractor's siding was laid in, connected to the main line and operated by a ground frame. Work proceeded quickly and just under a year later, in July 1942, the depot with its sidings was complete. The East Junction crossover, which had been removed in 1929, was now laid in again and, along with the reinstated junction, was connected to a new East box.

Three new signal boxes were required to operate the new complex; the new Westerleigh North box already mentioned, which was a wooden box of standard GWR construction, equipped with a frame of sixteen levers and seven spaces; a new Westerleigh East box and a new signal box at the

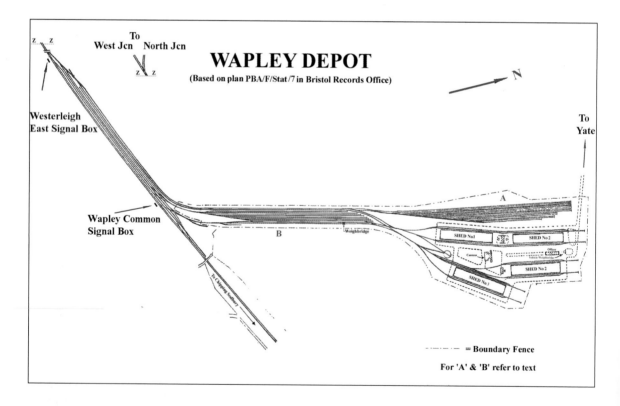

Plan of Wapley depot and sidings. Based on a plan in the Bristol Records Office.

Wapley Common signal box and reception sidings, looking west. To the right of the picture, the sidings run into the depot itself. 1960.
WILF STANLEY

Chipping Sodbury end of the loops; this latter box was named 'Wapley Common' after a nearby patch of common land in the parish of Wapley.

Westerleigh East and Wapley Common boxes were both of the GWR ARP type, later designated 'Type 13' by the Signalling Record Society. These boxes were quite unlike the signal boxes normally seen around the system prior to the war. They were built of brick and reinforced concrete with thick reinforced concrete roofs. Blast walls were built around the door at ground level, which gave access to the box; there were no outside stairs. There were no windows in the locking rooms and in the case of

Westerleigh East box, the lever frame was situated at the rear of the operating floor, a practice more associated with the LMSR. This was possibly for sighting purposes, as there was an overbridge very close to the west side of the box. However, having been in Westerleigh East box when it was in use, I am of the opinion that the sighting of Up trains would have been quite adequate with the levers in the front.

Westerleigh East had a 44-lever frame containing 11 spaces and Wapley Common was equipped with a 59-lever frame in which there were 10 spaces. Wapley Common's levers were at the front of the box, as was normal.

Westerleigh East signal box, looking east. The Down loop has by now been recovered, leaving just the connection to the Up loop and sidings; 1960.
WILF STANLEY

Trains were loaded at the docks very quickly and despatched to Wapley depot. On arrival, they would be signalled into either the Up loop or one of the two reception roads. From there, the train would proceed into the main reception sidings (next to the outwards sidings). Here, the train engine would be uncoupled and could go to turn on the turntable. The depot pilot loco would be attached and the wagons drawn alongside the sheds for unloading. As each batch of wagons was unloaded, they would be uncoupled and pulled up into the head shunt, from where they would be propelled back into the outwards for remarshalling. Trains that were unable to be unloaded on arrival would be shunted into the arrival sidings to wait their turn.

The USAAF takes over Wapley Depot

It was ironic that as the depot came 'on stream' in early 1942, so the threat of enemy air raids had diminished and thus the need for the goods to be cleared away from dockside areas as quickly as possible was no longer there.

By this time the Americans had entered the war and large numbers of American troops were being sent to the UK. With the troops came a vast amount of stores and supplies. This massive supply chain had to be accommodated somewhere and many warehouses were requisitioned for this purpose.

As it was no longer fulfilling the purpose for which it had been built, Wapley depot became one of the warehouses where American supplies were stored. The depot became a Port Intransit Depot for the US Army Air Force 8th Air Force and was known by its security title of 'Base Air Depot Area (BADA) American Air Force number 515'. Side by side with the (now lesser) use by the PBA, the depot became full of aircraft spares and equipment for the 8th Air Force. It also handled post for the soldiers of the American forces.[22]

The working was very similar to that of the original intended purpose as an inland sorting depot; American supplies were shipped to the west coast ports (in this case, Avonmouth), where they were offloaded into rail wagons and transported to the storage depots. With the advent of D-Day in 1944 and the subsequent movement of forces into Europe, the supply chain moved in its wake and by 1945 Wapley depot was little used by either the Americans or by the PBA. For a while, the GWR pondered over whether to build a large wagon repair depot there, but plans failed to come to fruition and the site was eventually taken over by the Royal Navy for storage of naval stores. Later still, it was used by the Ministry of Transport (Sea Stores Division) for the same purpose. Mr Gallop was in charge of the yard during 1944.

A panoramic view of Wapley depot after closure. No.1 shed to the left, No.2 shed to the right. The 'A' sidings were to the left of No.1 shed. Rusty rails can just be discerned in the grass in the centre foreground. AUTHOR'S COLLECTION

Wapley Depot Post-War

After the war, the GWR decided that the two signal boxes, Wapley Common and Westerleigh East, did not have enough work to justify them being opened round the clock. In 1948, both Wapley Common and Westerleigh East boxes were open 06.00 Monday to 06.00 the following Sunday morning. In 1953, Wapley Common was open Monday to Saturday 07.10–14.30 and Westerleigh East was temporarily closed. By 1956, Wapley Common signal box was open 07.20–14.20, with Westerleigh East open as required between 05.30 and 16.00, Monday to Friday, and 06.00–14.00 Saturday. Sunday opening was again 'as required'. From 1966–71, East box was open one shift only, six days a week and Sundays as required.

Wapley Common box could be frustrating to work at times because when Westerleigh East was shut trains could not use the Down goods loop, so signalmen relied on Chipping Sodbury to margin trains to Coalpit Heath, or more usually Stoke Gifford, as Coalpit's loops were short.

During the 1950s, Wapley yard was served by the 07.00 Stoke Gifford–Swindon local trip freight. This called 'all stations' as required and carried the travelling shunter. Cyril Batten was based at Chipping Sodbury, but lived at Coalpit Heath. He would walk or cycle to Coalpit Heath station and take up residence in the signal box until his train was due. On its arrival, he would climb aboard and travel with the guard to Wapley depot. There, the train would often have to be backed into the Up loop at Wapley, owing to East box not being open. Once 'in clear' it would be 'shut in' to carry out its work in the Sea Stores Depot. There would usually be around half-a-dozen wagons for the Sea Stores.

Once its work was complete, the freight would move on to Chipping Sodbury, where further work was done. In due course, it would proceed on up the line and on arrival at Badminton would be put into the goods loop there. It would meet with the Down Swindon–Stoke Gifford local freight and the crews would swap footplates and continue with the work; the Swindon crew working the 07.00 Up goods on to Swindon whilst the Bristol crew worked back to Stoke Gifford yard.

Wapley Common signal box had one regular signalman from 1949 to 1965; this was Alan Flook, who had worked at the box at Marston Magna during the war and on the closure of Wapley Common box in 1965 moved to Westerleigh East box as the sole regular signalman. The box was now opened on a day shift only.

The development of Yate as a new town in the 1960s saw a new dual-carriageway road, Heron

A photo as rare as hen's teeth! Viewed from Wapley Common signal box, BR Britannia Class No.70022 Tornado *speeds the Up* Red Dragon *past Wapley yard on 6 May 1960 – the day that Princess Margaret married Anthony Armstrong-Jones.* WILF STANLEY

Way, cut through the reception 'A' sidings and the depot sheds were now isolated from the rail system. Still used by the MoT for Sea Stores, the site was recognizable by the many ships' anchors and chains that lay alongside the No.4 shed.

The Down loop between Wapley Common and Westerleigh East having been removed in December 1959, trains had still been able to use the Up loop, Up departure and reception sidings alongside the GW main line to gain access to the depot. With the removal of the connection to the Nos 1 and 2 reception sidings, this left just the truncated Up loop, Up reception and a spur leading into the 'A' sidings. These sidings were used for the storage of railway Civil Engineering Department trains before weekend engineering work and often saw ballast trains stored there during the week, to be taken out at weekends for use all around the district. Sometimes wagons were stored there for cleaning out if their next trip would contain a different load.

Between 1965 and their closure in 1971, the sidings were used for the shunting of slower trains if a faster, more important service was 'catching them up'. For example, a slow freight might be allowed to depart from Stoke Gifford yard when a passenger or parcels train for the Badminton line was in the Severn Tunnel. The signalman at Stoke Gifford East box would send the 'shunt train for following train to pass' signal, 1–5–5, to Winterbourne box, who, having no means to shunt the train, would pass it on to Westerleigh West. The trains could not be shunted here either, so Westerleigh West box would pass the signal on to Westerleigh East. East box would shunt the train into the Up sidings and clear the line for the faster train to pass. Once it had gone, the train would be backed out on to the main line again and when the points had been put to normal, could continue on its way.

This manoeuvre was actually a carefully worked-out plan on behalf of Stoke Gifford yard. Needing the space, they knew that if Westerleigh East was open, the train could be recessed there; it would not have time to gain the Up loop at Chipping Sodbury.

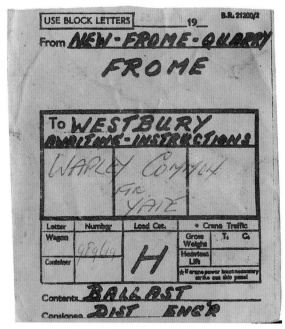

Wagon label from ballast wagon stored at Wapley Common reception sidings in 1969. AUTHOR'S COLLECTION

06.00 SPECIAL WESTBURY TO BRISTOL EAST DEPOT AND WAPLEY COMMON 7Z04, SATURDAY, 21 FEBRUARY 1970

To convey 26 Dogfish of ballast and plough van to detach 10 at East Depot (to go forward on 08.00 special to Wapley Common) then convey remaining 16 to stable at Wapley Common, returning Light Diesel to Westbury.

As well as Civil Engineering trains, during the late 1960s an ex-GWR tender was to be found in the sidings (still known as Wapley yard). The tender may have been part of a weedkilling train at one time or employed as a sludge tank, but, whatever its use, once no longer needed, it found its way into Wapley yard. The site of Wapley depot is now almost completely obliterated by a housing development that has occurred in stages since the mid-1980s.

Ex-GWR tender stored at Wapley Common sidings in 1970.
P.D. RENDALL

A 1970 SNAPSHOT

The following vehicles were to be found parked against the stop blocks on the spur near Westerleigh East box as late as 1970:

- M79486, 13 tons, Wolverton LMS lot no. 1521, 1948
- W30606, 10 tons, GWR
- W104563, GWR, Swindon 1924
- W80675, GWR
- Six-wheel vehicle W3030, GWR, 14 tons.

Stoke Gifford Yard

At the western end of the new Direct line, a triangular junction to the existing Bristol and South Wales Union line was created. One line led to Filton Junction and Bristol, the other to Patchway and ultimately the Severn Tunnel. At the junction, a marshalling yard was built and named after the nearby village: Stoke Gifford. The yard was built in a cutting at the east end and on an embankment at the west end. It was rather an exposed position and as such was vulnerable to west winds bringing rain. Fog would often form across the Down side yard. Wooden refuge platforms for shunters and other staff to use during train movements were built standing out from the embankment on the Down side.

Initially, the yard had Up and Down goods loops, five Up and five Down sidings and a spur from the Up sidings into a brickworks; this latter spur was equipped with a run-round adjacent to the Up yard. In the yards, both Up and Down sidings had long shunting spurs. All of this was opened in May 1903 for goods and July 1903 for passenger trains.

Two signal boxes were needed to control the layout – these were Stoke Gifford East and Stoke Gifford West, the latter being at the junction of the lines to Patchway and Filton.

Wapley Common No.2 shed, seen from the A432, Kennedy Way, Yate.
AUTHOR'S COLLECTION

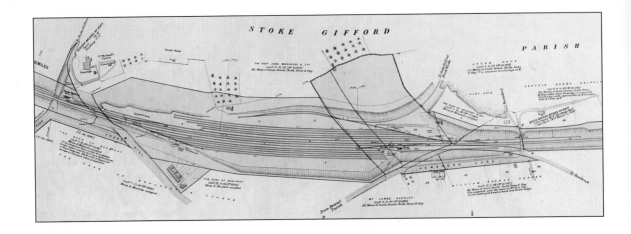

Plan of Stoke Gifford sidings, 1903. WILTSHIRE HISTORY CENTRE

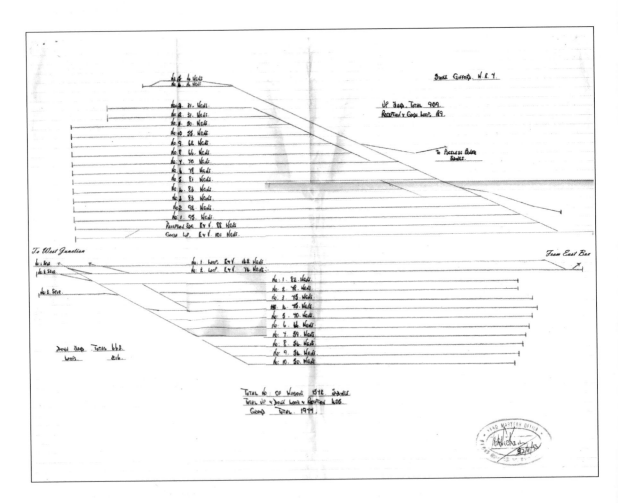

Plan of Stoke Gifford sidings in 1953, drawn by the yardmaster. The stamp in the lower right-hand corner states 'Yardmaster's Office, Stoke Gifford, WR. 22–11–53'. AUTHOR'S COLLECTION

This aerial view will help to explain the layout of the junctions: Bristol Parkway station is right in the centre of the photo; the main line runs in from the right and at Parkway there is a three-way split. The lines to Bristol turn left towards Filton Junction. The South Wales line curves upwards, passes through Patchway and then disappears off to the top of the picture. From Parkway, the Avonmouth line heads off left, between the Filton and South Wales lines to Filton West, where it is joined by a branch from Filton Junction. The line then runs alongside Filton Airfield and off to Avonmouth. The light-coloured triangular area between the Avonmouth and Patchway lines is Stoke Gifford Tip.
P.D. RENDALL.

By 1918, the facilities were being overwhelmed with extra traffic and so additional sidings were provided on both sides of the yard. The Up side was extended to fourteen sidings, a reception loop and an additional shunting spur and the Down side was extended to ten sidings, an additional goods loop and an additional shunting spur. The original Down goods loop (now renamed 'Down Goods Loop No.1') had a connection with the Down Filton line at its farthest end, enabling trains to leave the Down yard whilst another train was signalled down the main line towards South Wales.

Even these additions proved insufficient and another spur was added to the Down side layout in 1926. On the Down side, the sidings were split into two sections for operational purposes; trains from No.1 section could shunt into No.2 spur independently of trains shunting into No.3 spur. A similar arrangement applied on the Up side.

Both Down loops and the Up loop were worked under the Permissive Block system. The Up reception line was worked as a siding.

Although Stoke Gifford West was the larger of the two boxes, both East and West boxes proved to be very busy jobs, with freights arriving and departing round the clock on the loops and reception lines and transfers from Up side to Down side. The yard despatcher would advise the East or West box

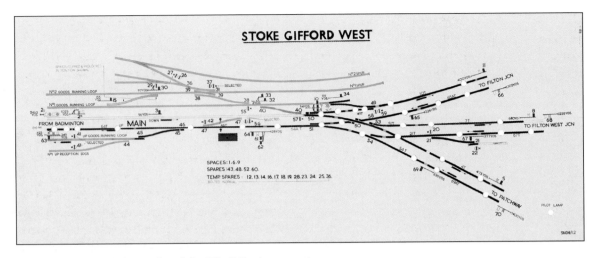

The final signal box track diagram from Stoke Gifford West box. AUTHOR'S COLLECTION

signalman which freight trains were booked to call at the yard. Despatchers were always on the phone giving orders for freight trains ('let 'em run' or 'in the loop') and the signalman could be on his feet all shift. Other phone work included freight train enquiries and – in East box – advising West box of the whereabouts of Down trains.

The East end crossover from Up to Down main lines was situated beyond the road overbridge (No.303B – latterly known as 'Pearce's Bridge' after the construction company that had offices on the north side of the railway) and some distance from the signal box. To facilitate shunts or transfers from Up to Down yard, or vice versa, that required

shunting out on to the main lines, there was a 'backing hooter', or klaxon, installed near the Up Starting signal. When a train shunting from the yard had come to a stand on the Up main line near the signal, the signalman would reset the points and signals for the Up or Down side as required. Once this had been done, the signalman would operate the klaxon by means of pushing a brass bell-push in the East box. The noise of the klaxon would indicate to drivers and shunters that it was in order to set back into the Up or Down yard as required.

At the west end of the Down yard stood a tall water tank for loco purposes and there were water cranes at both ends of the loops. Brick cabins on the

Diesel No.42 on a train of coal hoppers passes Stoke Gifford Up side pilot Cl 08 No.D3185 busy shunting on 31 May 1967. Note the 'backer' coupled next to the pilot. R. CUFF/ AUTHOR'S COLLECTION

Down side at the west end contained accommodation for the shunters and carriage and wagon examiners. On the Up side, between East box and the overbridge, stood a wooden shed used for parking staff pedal and motor cycles. This was accessed via a path that ran from the north side of the bridge and sloped gently down to track level.

In the 1920s, the yard depot master was C.W. Chidsey. In 1945–46, Mr Hannam was in charge. In 1963, it was Arthur Ellis, who had been a controller before moving to Stoke yard. Ellis' staff of around fifty men included clerks Ron Chaney and John Rice, telegraphist Bill Cox, Up side yard inspector Reg Shergold (who had previously been a shunter), chargeman carriage and wagon examiner Ern Humphries, head shunters Sid Alford, Reg Humphrey and J. Peacock and shunters John Hughes and Don Drew.[23]

Such was the number of staff employed at Stoke Gifford that the railway ran a workmen's train from Bristol to the yards. This was the 05.25 Dr Day's Sidings to Stoke Gifford. The train usually consisted of a pannier tank and one coach. It returned to 'Doctor's' at 06.15. The 'Workmen's', as it was known, also proved a useful train for staff not employed at the yards; for example, Bristol signalman Joe Stockham used it from Bristol to Filton Junction, where he would get off and walk home, and signalman Terry Dart would also travel up on it from Bristol to Filton Junction, where he would get off and walk down the branch to Filton West Junction box for his shift.

Being in a strategic position regarding traffic, Stoke Gifford yard was busy round the clock. The Up sidings had a capacity to hold over 900 wagons, plus an additional 180 wagons on the Up reception line and the Up loop. The Down yard could hold 663 wagons plus a further 200 wagons on the two Down loops. At its peak, there were two Up side and two Down side pilots (shunting locos) employed there. There were two Down side pilots working up to the end of the yard's main life and one Up side pilot. The GWR pannier tank was a favourite for yard pilot duties across the system, but was superseded in the 1950s by the soon to be ubiquitous English

Electric diesel shunter (later Class 08). The pilot was almost permanently coupled to a flat wagon with footboards and lockers on it. This was known as a 'shunter's truck' to the uninitiated, but was more commonly known to staff as a 'backer'.

Traffic

Stoke Gifford was dealing with over 400 trains a week during the 1950s–60s. This amounted to around 6,000 wagons. During the severe winter of 1962/63, the yard handled an additional 1,000 wagons a week, this latter figure being mostly extra coal. Coal was one of the main commodities handled through the yard, with ten coal trains per day arriving. Trains conveying not only coal but agricultural materials, military traffic in the form of explosives, fertilizers from and to Avonmouth, loads of spent ballast courtesy of the Civil Engineers and in fact almost anything one can think of would arrive from all parts of the country.

Trainloads would arrive on the loops or reception lines and, once the train engine had been cut off and the pilot coupled on, would be broken up and remarshalled into new complete trainloads for other destinations. These would then be taken forwards by a fresh engine, or 'tripped' to local depots such as Avonmouth or Bristol.

LONG FREIGHT TRAINS

Certain trains are authorized to take a load of 60 or more wagons between Stoke Gifford and Swindon (via Badminton) and *vice versa*. When it is necessary to shunt these trains, Up or Down, for other trains to pass this must as a rule only be done at the Stations where there are Platform Loop Lines or Refuge Sidings constructed to hold such trains and, except to avoid serious delay to more important trains, they must be allowed to proceed to the next Station where there are Through Lines or suitable Refuge Sidings.

Excerpt from *BR Sectional Appendix to the Working Timetables and Books of Rules and Regulations*, Bristol Traffic District, October 1960.

View across Stoke Gifford yard in the early 1960s, looking west. WILF STANLEY

Fast freight trains formed up in the yards would serve places such as Cornwall, Newton Abbot, Exeter, Taunton, South Wales, Gloucester and the Midlands and the London area at least once a day. Stoke Gifford had a very good record for punctuality and even if a train arrived late on the reception road, the yard staff would work so efficiently that lost time would be saved. This was useful in cases such as train 6V95, the 02.00 Carlisle to Stoke Gifford, which was one of the longest running trains on the Western Region, arriving at Stoke Gifford at 13.44 – just under twelve hours after leaving Carlisle.

View from Stoke Gifford West signal box looking east across the yard. WILF STANLEY

A Class 47 runs through Stoke Gifford in 1989 with three nuclear flasks bound for Sellafield. T.R. RENDALL

By 1968, the yard was host to traffic from the nuclear age in the shape of atomic flasks for fuel rods. These would travel down from Sellafield on specially arranged services. An example of one of these was on Friday, 31 May 1968, when five empty flasks were sent down on 4V35, the 02.00 (Friday) Carlisle to Bristol West depot. Three flasks were to travel from West depot to Bridgwater for Hinkley Point Power Station and two flasks were for Berkeley Power Station in Gloucestershire. On arrival at Stoke Gifford, the two Berkeley flasks would be detached and the train would proceed on its way. The two flasks at Stoke Gifford were next to be attached to the 02.45 (Saturday) Stoke Gifford to Washwood Heath service (5M72) and would be taken back up the Gloucester line and detached at Gloucester New Yard, whence they would be worked back down the line again on a special working 07.00 (Saturday) Gloucester to Sharpness Docks for offloading. The flasks would be conveyed to Berkeley Power Station by road.

A well-known train in steam days was 'Long Tom', the 01.30 Old Oak Common to Stoke Gifford, so nicknamed because of its regular load of 100 wagons. Another train that terminated at Stoke Gifford was the 18.40 Swindon–Stoke Gifford Class 8 freight, headcode 8BOO. This must have been one of the slowest freight trains on the line, as even in diesel days it usually ran very slowly down the line and saw the inside of most goods loops on its journey west.

The reason for this slowness was that it frequently conveyed diesel shunting locos in its formation. These were 'outshopped' from Swindon works and were for destinations in Bristol, South Wales and the West of England. With traction motors 'demeshed', the locos could only travel at 25mph (40km/h). On arrival at Stoke Gifford, the shunting locos would be moved forwards to their destinations by local 'trip' workings. Engines conveyed thus to Bristol Bath Road diesel depot and other loco sheds would have their traction motors re-engaged at their destination shed and would, in time, make their own way to the destination yard at the flat-out maximum speed of 20mph (32km/h)! 8BOO also carried ex-GW Siphon G vans labelled 'ENPARTS'; these carried spares and stores from Swindon works and were also bound for locomotive depots.

In the late 1960s, Stoke Gifford yard was often host to lines of scrap steam locos. These were not permitted to run through the Severn Tunnel, so they ran usually via Gloucester, being stabled or margined at Stoke Gifford Up side until there was sufficient gap in the timetable to let them run forwards. In the beginning, these moves were usually made at night to ensure they did not get in the way of normal services, although there were those who claimed that this was done to avoid the scrapped steam locos being seen by the public at large. Later, it became impossible to confine these trains to nights only, as there were so many scrap

Trains of scrap steam locos bound for South Wales scrapyards became a common sight in Bristol during the late 1960s. Here ex-SR locos 34017 Ilfracombe *and 34032* Camelford *in the company of BR Standard Class 5 4-6-0 No.73089 are seen passing through Bristol East depot behind a 'Western' diesel. They will make their way to Stoke Gifford, then to South Wales via Gloucester.* THE LATE COLIN WEEKS/AUTHOR'S COLLECTION

locos to get rid of, and for a while they became a normal sight round the clock.

Normally, scrap engines ran in trains of not more than five scrap engines, with brake van and sometimes a couple of empty wagons as 'spacers' or 'runners'. Engines sent for scrap were sometimes in excellent condition, condemned simply because steam was being eradicated, rather than because they were beyond useful repair. On other occasions, engines were sent for scrap in deplorable condition and frequently did not make it to their destination in one journey, developing overheated axle boxes or other faults en route.

On Friday, 4 February 1966 condemned 2-6-2 tank loco no. 82044 was held at Stoke Gifford sidings for a while, having been originally meant to be moved to Gloucester a week previously, on service 7M09, 03.54 Stoke Gifford to Gloucester. After its temporary stay at Stoke Gifford, the condemned loco was sent forwards to Buttigeig's scrapyard, Newport, South Wales, by train 6B65, 23.15 Stoke Gifford to Gloucester (declassified to Class 8). Towed by a diesel, it travelled at 25mph (40km/h) to Gloucester via Westerleigh West Junction and Yate. At Gloucester, 82044 was placed in a siding until Monday, 7 February, when it was attached to 8T75, the 17.10 Gloucester to Severn Tunnel Junction to continue its way to Newport.

Life in the Yard – Signal Boxes

Such was the workload of the yard that many signalmen steered clear of yard boxes. Signalman Terry Dart, who had started his railway career at Filton West junction in 1948, did not like them. He once warned a colleague: 'Keep out of yard boxes. You never have any control over the job; everyone else tells you what to do!' Stoke Gifford East was one of those boxes where, as one signalman told me: 'You were always shunting; rushing up and down the lever frame and answering phones and bells. The pilot was always shunting and the shunters always shouting or phoning moves to you ... it was a box where you never sat down!'

Nonetheless, there were signalmen who *did* adapt to yard life and still found time to do other things. One of the later East box signalmen was Harold Goodway, who played the trumpet and often switched the box out early on Saturday late turn in order to play in a band. Another was Mike Goodfield, better known nowadays as a railway photographer whose work graces the pages of several leading railway magazines. Both became

An Up London express hauled by an immaculate Castle Class passes Stoke Gifford West signal box in the early 1960s. WILF STANLEY

guards after the signal boxes closed and Goodfield later became a train crew supervisor.

With junctions to Filton, Filton West and Patchway, plus the tip sidings (on the Avonmouth branch) to deal with, apart from the two Down side pilots and the loops and reception roads, Stoke Gifford West box was a very busy job, open continuously and being double-manned on all shifts in later years. A 'booking boy' (usually a relief signalman) was employed at the box in the 1940s and 1950s to allow the signalmen to concentrate on the signals and points and leave the booking and telephone work to the 'boy'. Stoke Gifford West was a Class 1 box in the 1950s, when signalmen there included Walt Webber and Frank Sparks. One of the last signalmen to work Stoke Gifford West before it closed

Stoke Gifford East signal box, 1970. BRYAN DYSON/AUTHOR'S COLLECTION

in February 1971 was Mark Taylor, who had been signalman there during the 1960s. In 1953, both Stoke Gifford boxes were open continuously, but, by the late 1960s, East box was closed on Saturday nights.

One of the characters of the line was signalman Stan Horn. Stan had left the Army in the late 1940s and started on the railway at Henbury box, on the Filton West–Avonmouth line. From there, he had gone to Avonmouth Goods Yard box (Town Goods) and then to Pilning station – where he became widely known for his expertise with margin working. After Pilning station, he went to Stoke Gifford West and then to Dr Day's until that box closed in 1970.

Stan liked to know what was happening all about him and also to try and make sure that things happened as he liked, in order for him to be able to work the job successfully. This annoyed some people, but most agreed that Stan knew the job, his train crews and the service inside-out. Whilst working at Stoke West, Stan employed his knowledge of the workings of other boxes and train movements to great advantage and it used to be said of him that he 'worked all the boxes around him' when on duty. When the box was later demolished, several old Train Registers dating from the opening of the line were discovered under the floor. What became of them?

As bad weather – snow in particular – could be disruptive to rail traffic, steam lances were kept in the 'locking room' underneath Stoke Gifford West and East boxes and also Pilning station box. These lances were accompanied by a 20ft (6m) length of hose. The idea was that the hose could be connected to the steam-heating pipe on steam or diesel locomotives and the lance used to clear points of accumulations of snow. Bags of salt were also kept with the lances; salt had to be spread on areas cleared of snow by the steam lance in order to prevent the thawed snow icing up again. Signal linemen and the Permanent Way Department were not always amused by having salt spread on point slides and locking bars, as this would cause corrosion, but it was the most efficacious way of keeping trains moving.

May 1945 GWR notice concerning the use of steam lances to clear snow. AUTHOR'S COLLECTION

The Tip Siding

As mentioned above, the tip siding branched off the Up Avonmouth line. The tip was where all sorts of railway rubbish was dumped as a sort of early landfill scheme. Mostly it was spoil and spent ballast that was dumped there, although rumour said that in the early 1960s Swindon works sent down wagon loads of scrap from steam locos to go in the tip. Some of these wagons were said to include loco name and number plates.

Trainloads going on to the tip siding were almost always propelled from the loops. Instructions stated that not more than fifty wagons could be propelled without a brake van from East to West in the Down direction along the Up loop. The move could not take place until the signalman had set the points from the loop to the tip siding and cleared the signals for the move. The shunter had to pin down sufficient wagon handbrakes to allow the driver to be able to hold the train. This was because the line descended sharply from the loop to the tip. Additionally, a man had to ride on the leading vehicle (or on a vehicle as close to the leading vehicle as he could get) in order to be able to give handsignals to the shunter riding on the 'backer' next to the loco. Because there was little noise from a rake of wagons being propelled, a third member of staff was to stand at the junction by West box to keep a lookout and warn any staff working in the vicinity of the movement. Movements to and from the tip sidings were not permitted after dark or during fog or falling snow.

Similar instructions applied to the propelling of empty coaches from Filton West Junction up to Stoke Gifford West. Carriage sidings had been added to the layout at Filton West in 1942 and empty carriages often needed to be propelled to Stoke Gifford,

where they would then be in the correct order to go to Bristol. Instructions allowed a train of not more than '112 wheels' to be propelled to Stoke Gifford West in clear weather and in daylight. Under these conditions, such trains could also be propelled as far as Stoke Gifford East box. After sunset, a man had to be appointed to place three detonators at Stoke Gifford West, on the Up line from Avonmouth at the Up Avonmouth line Home signal before Stoke Gifford West could accept the train from Filton West and permit the move to take place. During fog or falling snow, propelling moves from Filton West to Stoke Gifford were banned.

Morale was always good at Stoke Gifford yard and the May 1956 edition of *Railway Magazine* carried a short piece about G. Ellaway and B. Campbell, two goods guards at Stoke Gifford yard who won a bronze plaque in the men's duet singing at a festival of drama and music held at Reading. Campbell also won a silver plaque for senior tenor solo.

There were two permanent way gangs based at Stoke Gifford: the west end gang and the east end gang. Bill Reynolds was the west end ganger during the 1960s. An amusing story is recalled concerning the time in the summer of 1966 when the permanent way supervisor at Stoke East detailed his gang to start the annual burning of the scrub on cutting it at the east end of the yard. But there was a breeze blowing and once the fires had been started, they

A view from Patchway, looking south. The Class 47 and train are passing between Filton Junction and Bristol Parkway; the Stoke Gifford tip sidings can be seen in the middle of the picture, with the lines to the left going to Bristol Parkway and those to the right to Filton Junction and Avonmouth. The area to the left will be the site of the new SET depot.
P.D. RENDALL

quickly spread out of control and into the adjacent field. The gang spent the next hour or so frantically beating out the flames.

New Station to be Built

In August 1970, with the approach of the Bristol area resignalling and with the announcement that a new station was to be built at Stoke Gifford and the resultant closure of the yards, there was a doubt in the minds of the staff representatives as to whether the loss of freight traffic would be balanced by the possible increase in passenger revenue as claimed by the railway management. It seemed to the staff that freight traffic was being neglected at the expense of trying to develop passenger traffic. Delays regularly occurred in the Stoke Gifford–Patchway areas owing to the volume of both freight and passenger traffic. How could the new station benefit when this was the case?

At a meeting in Bristol during August 1970, the management advised staff that the Patchway and Stoke Gifford areas had not yet experienced the benefits of Multiple Aspect Signalling. Most delays were due to freight traffic crossing from Up to Down yards, or vice versa, and reversal moves at Stoke Gifford. With the Up yard closed and trains from Avonmouth running direct to South Wales via the new chord line at Filton West, these practices would be avoided. The staff pointed out that the current running times from Bristol to Birmingham were slower than they had been in steam days. The management's reply was that planned work would soon raise the average speed over this line to 90mph (145km/h).

On another point and considering the need for rail staff to get to work at the proposed new station, the staff said that they were greatly concerned that the lack of road access to the proposed car park, coupled with the current congestion caused by traffic to and from the factories of Rolls-Royce aero-engineering and British Aircraft Corporation at Filton and Patchway, would result in the roads around the area becoming clogged. But they were unaware that talks had already been held between British Rail and Gloucestershire County Council to discuss these needs.

But, as was well known to local railwaymen, difficulty was already being experienced in getting freight trains away from sidings in central Bristol, in particular the St Philip's Marsh area. With extra freight traffic and trip working conveying crippled wagons to stable at Marsh Junction instead of Stoke Gifford, surely delays would be encountered? Failing that, why not start some freight workings from Bristol West depot in future? Staff were unable to comprehend how BR could just shut such a large yard as Stoke Gifford without losing all the traffic and revenue that the yards brought to the company.

A suggestion was duly put forward by someone from the staff that perhaps Winterbourne would be a better place for the proposed new station. There was plenty of space in the cutting where the goods yard had stood. Sadly but understandably, the railway staff were still thinking in terms of a 'steam age' station, not a major road/rail interchange that BR was planning to build at Stoke Gifford. It had to be pointed out to the railwaymen that the question of land ownership came into the equation if one considered Winterbourne. What this amounted to was that the land at Stoke Gifford already belonged to the railway, whereas to build a station at Winterbourne would require the purchase of a considerable amount of land over and above the railway-owned land already available.

In addition, road access, if thought bad at Stoke Gifford, was hopeless at Winterbourne; the existing (and only possible) entrance to the goods yard site was from Hicks Common Road, which was little more than an upgraded country lane. The old Winterbourne station site was far too small to enable the development of a new 'park and ride' station and was at the top of a hill with access from a narrow road. At Stoke Gifford a reasonable road existed, from which access to the new station could easily be created via a new road through the west end of the Up sidings. There could be very little practical argument against Stoke Gifford being the site of the new station.

Winterbourne yard; it was quite obvious that a new Parkway-style station and large car park would not fit here. WILF STANLEY

The yard staff at Stoke Gifford made plain their feelings at the proposals for the new station. They stated that they felt they had been 'led up the garden path'. Recent work had been carried out to improve and update the staff facilities at the yard and the staff were angry that this work had been allowed to go ahead by the management, while all the time plans were being made to close down the yards. This was truly an example of further poor industrial relations on the management's side. The closure of the Up yard, along with the closure of the signal boxes, would, it was estimated, ultimately lead to some thirty redundancies in the area. Ultimately, the Up loop and reception roads at Stoke Gifford would remain, along with one siding on the Up side to hold crippled wagons.

Moves towards Closure

By September 1970, further details of the plans for Stoke Gifford were revealed by the local railway management. At a meeting between the management and local union representatives, BR admitted that imminent plans to divert four freight trains away from Stoke Gifford yard had been thwarted by the Southern Region. The Southern had refused to accept the diversion of these freights via Westbury, Dilton Marsh and Salisbury, at least for the next six months. The trains concerned were: 7V07 (11.55 Eastleigh to East Usk); 7V68 22.58 (Eastleigh to Severn Tunnel Junction); 8O70 (03.35 Severn Tunnel Junction to Eastleigh); and 8O77 (16.00 Severn Tunnel Junction to Eastleigh). These services would have normally run via Swindon and Reading to reach the Southern; each was booked to call at Stoke Gifford as required. BR had planned to divert the services to run to Westbury via Bristol without calling at Stoke Gifford at all. Now that the Southern region had refused to accept the diversion, for the forseeable future these services would continue to run via Stoke Gifford and Swindon.

It seemed that a slight ray of hope was visible to the yard staff, although what followed made it plainer than ever that the yard would eventually close and the site be used for the proposed new station. The BR management announced that a proportion of the traffic at present catered for at Stoke Gifford would be transferred to Bristol West depot yard. This, the staff foresaw, would pose problems, as there were only two existing services from West depot that could clear extra West of England traffic; these were the 19.25 Avonmouth–Ponsondane and the 20.38 Burton–Tavistock Junction. Severn Tunnel Junction yard representatives were afraid that with future congestion likely at Bristol West depot, it would not be long before somebody eventually decided that trains which conveyed Gloucester traffic to West depot would instead be routed to Severn Tunnel yard, which was already working almost to capacity. BR replied that as a matter of principle this would not happen. (To see what could happen when railway managers and politicians made decisions about railway closures one does not necessarily have to study the Beeching Report; once the second Severn crossing road bridge was planned and the approach road on the Welsh side planned to pass very close to the Severn Tunnel yard, that yard was closed almost overnight along with its loco stabling point.)

Existing railway wagon repair facilities and carriage and wagon staffing levels would need to be looked at, as much of the Stoke Gifford traffic was to be henceforth dealt with and marshalled at Gloucester New yard and at Bristol West depot; it was possible that the need would arise for extra

staff at these locations to cope with the increased traffic flow. There was also the need for proposed alterations at Gloucester New yard to be carried out.

The Stoke Gifford staff representatives posed a question to BR managers, regarding a rumour currently circulating that there was to be no new station at all, but it was in fact just a ruse to shut the Up yard. BR said that there was no foundation in the rumour; the sidings closure *was* necessary in order to build the new station.

The Bristol Panel signal box staff committee, composed of two signalmen, Sam Slee and Brian Lockier, were of the opinion that BR should not be announcing plans for the Stoke Gifford yard closure until the new train workings had been finalized. Not only that, but what about the investigation into the siting of the new station at Winterbourne? At a previous meeting, BR had given an assurance that this would be looked into and now they were being informed that this was '*still* being looked into'. The management seemed to be implying that all the work put into the relocating of trains to other yards would be of no use at all if Winterbourne was found to be the best site. It appeared to the staff that the primary aim

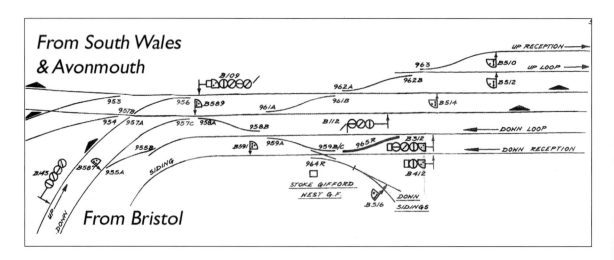

Stoke Gifford west end after resignalling; note the troublesome west ground frame. This from a 1971 resignalling handout; there was full provision for the yard when they knew it was going to be closed, but no apparent provision for Bristol Parkway, which was under construction.
AUTHOR'S COLLECTION

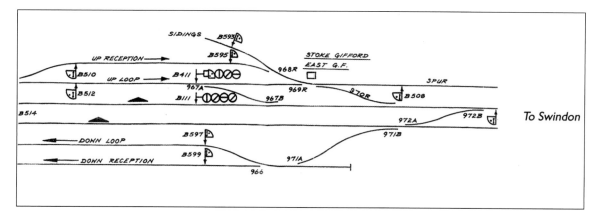

The same at the east end. AUTHOR'S COLLECTION

of the management was to reduce local freight trip working whether or not the new station was built. The management replied that whilst enquiries were still being made as to the status of land ownership at Winterbourne, the traffic plan was considered the basis on which to build the future service.

In reality, it was highly unlikely that the BR management was even *considering* Winterbourne as a site for the new station. As noted above, there were too many limitations against the use of the Winterbourne site. All things considered, the idea to site the station at Stoke Gifford had been fairly well thought out. Strategically placed for both the Bristol and South Wales main lines and for the M4 and M5 motorways, as well as for planned future expansion in the North Bristol and Severnside areas, there can be little doubt that Stoke Gifford was the logical site for the station. The question remains as to why remodelling and resignalling could not have been carried out to allow for more flexible use of the station, the new signalling instead being installed as if the freight yards were to remain open and in full use.

But, in retrospect, the aspects of the Beeching plan that dealt with freight traffic showed that the future held no place for the short-wheelbased and frequently slow and ancient wagons which made up the majority of BR's freight rolling stock

at that time. The future lay with company block trains and Freightliners using vehicles that were roller-bearing fitted, had air brakes and could travel at high speeds between loading and unloading points. These mostly ran as fixed formations and did not need to call at goods yards for remarshalling. The old freight yards were a thing of the past. Thus Stoke Gifford was destined to pass into history.

Post-Closure

Both Stoke Gifford signal boxes were closed over the weekend of 20–22 February 1971. A new ground frame controlled the entrance and exit of the Down yard, whilst the Up yard was soon to be closed. The new signalling brought into use hardly affected the working of the goods yard at Stoke Gifford. The new ground frame on the Down side controlled a new 'compound' point in the Down sidings. Considering that most compound points were at that time being replaced by sets of crossovers, it was something of a surprise that a ground frame was coupled to one. The set-up gave trouble almost from the start and was eventually replaced by a simpler layout.

In the event, Stoke Gifford remained concerned with freight traffic throughout the 1970s and well into the 1990s, even though during that period the 'powers that be' seemed to have planned for the

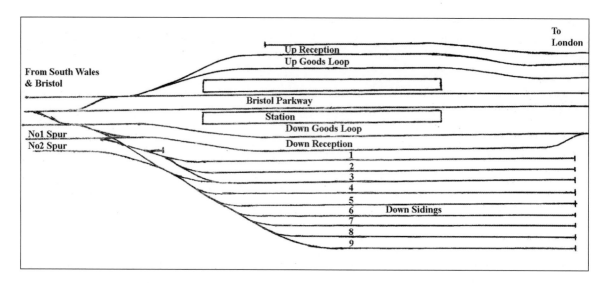

How Bristol Parkway station fitted into the layout. AUTHOR'S COLLECTION

Even into the 1980s, Stoke Gifford Down sidings was busy. (L–R): two sidings of empty stone tipplers for Tytherington quarry; fuel tankers for Avonmouth and empty Procor stone hoppers for Tytherington; a row of empty stone hoppers; a row of empty coal hoppers for Avonmouth Royal Edward yard; a row of loaded coal from Royal Edward yard and a loaded stone train from Tytherington. P.D. RENDALL

future to be one where freight traffic would rapidly leave the railways and transfer to the roads. Those years saw Bristol's East depot closed and West depot did not last long after the resignalling of that area late in 1971. However, due to the Port of Bristol Authority and BR falling out over the releasing of Avonmouth's Royal Edward yard in 1978, freight traffic to and from Avonmouth returned to Stoke Gifford, using the Down sidings. To this was added the stone traffic from the quarry at Tytherington and the (then) Avon County Council rubbish train, the 'Binliner', which used the Up reception.

Stoke Gifford remained open as a freight yard until 1991 – twenty years after its full closure was proposed. After 1991, some freight still used the Down yard, but after that the sidings became mainly used by Civil Engineering traffic – a function it still carries out at the time of writing.

After privatization of Britain's railways in 1994, Stoke Gifford sidings became a part of EWS freight. Carriage and wagon staff were still based at Stoke Gifford until the late 1990s to deal with wagons off engineering trains that required repairs. From 1994, Railtrack Great Western had a presence in the Down side yard with Mobile Operations Managers having an office in a Portakabin.

Pugsley's Siding

As mentioned above, there was a spur from Stoke Gifford Up sidings into a brickworks. This spur was on the furthest side of the yard from the Up main line and was equipped with a run-round loop adjacent to the Up yard to enable trains to and from the brickworks to be shunted. The furthest of the two run-round sidings was dedicated for run-round purposes. The brickworks had been opened in 1902 and supplied bricks for the building of the railway and for Chipping Sodbury Tunnel. It lasted until 1915, after which it fell into disuse and the buildings had been demolished by the 1930s.

There was a short incline of 1 in 32 down into the brickworks yard, which in later years was the premises of a scrap merchant and known as 'Pugsley's Siding'. In Pugsley's, there were other sidings; the points in the yard were set for the main or 'straight' siding and locked that way, the keys being kept in the yard inspector's office until needed. GWR and later BR locos were allowed to work the sidings; all moves had to be during daylight and accompanied by the yard inspector or foreman.

The site of Pugsley's scrapyard and sidings is now covered by the approach road to Bristol Parkway station car park from Bradley Stoke.

CHAPTER 7

Tunnels

The Direct line descended at a gradient of mostly 1 in 300 from Hullavington to Stoke Gifford. To do this, it had to pass through the Cotswold Hills. Whilst between Wootton Bassett and Hullavington the line was able to cross the landscape by means of embankments and shallow cuttings, crossing the hills without drastically changing the ruling gradient meant that the engineers who built the line had to tunnel through the hills.

Alderton Tunnel

The first tunnel necessary was near the village of Alderton, in the county of Wiltshire. Alderton Tunnel was 506yd (463m) long and unventilated.

The GWR plans of the line drawn up in 1903 have an interesting note to the effect that the GWR reserved the right to 'construct and maintain a tunnel for four lines'. This is very interesting

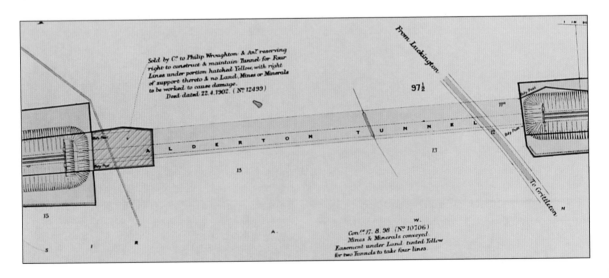

Plan of Alderton Tunnel, 1903. Note the April 1902 agreement that the GWR had the right to '... construct and maintain a tunnel for four lines ...' WILTSHIRE HISTORY CENTRE

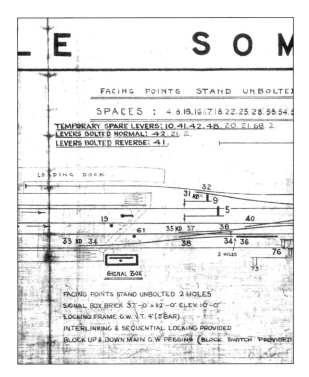

1940s GWR plan of Little Somerford showing that the signal box was apparently built of brick. Wishful thinking or forward planning?
AUTHOR'S COLLECTION

indeed, as it brings into mind the possibility that the Great Western intended to quadruple the line through the tunnel. Obviously, just quadrupling through the tunnel alone would have little impact on train running and could have caused a bottle-neck, so there must have been grander plans behind the scheme. Looking at the surveyor's plans of the line it would appear that the most sensible place to commence a four-track section would have been at, or on the approaches to, Little Somerford. From there it could have run through Hullavington and the twin bores of Alderton Tunnel, to Badminton, becoming two tracks again after leaving Badminton station. The four-track section would almost cer-tainly have ended at Badminton, as the financial cost of building two twin-track tunnels under the Cotswolds to Chipping Sodbury would have been prohibitive. Certainly, the GWR did not purchase, or have the option to purchase, any more land around Chipping Sodbury Tunnel.

This possibility of two twin-bore tunnels at Alderton brings to mind the 'puzzle' of the large wooden signal boxes at Little Somerford and Hullavington. Very likely, had the four-track section been built, the existing wooden signal boxes would have been rebuilt in brick, probably on different sites. Little Somerford station would have stood on a four-track section, as would a new Hullavington station.

With the advent of the High Speed Trains (HSTs) in 1976, line speed through Alderton Tunnel was restricted to 110mph (177km/h), compared to 125mph (200km/h) for most of the rest of the line. This was due to the fear that a build-up of air pressure caused by two HSTs passing in the unven-tilated bore could cause windows in the trains to be broken by the pressure.

Chipping Sodbury Tunnel

At 4,444yd (4,064m) long, this was the longest tunnel on the line, other than the Severn Tunnel, which was really part of the original Bristol and South Wales Union Railway (B&SWUR) line.

The tunnel was equipped with a 'tell-tale' wire. This was a wire that ran the entire length of the tunnel, on the Up side wall, at a height of 5ft (1.5m) from the ground. A mild electric current passed through the wire. The wire was connected to a special bell in both Badminton and Chipping Sodbury signal boxes. Should a train fail in the tunnel, or stop through accident or other circum-stances, the guard (or fireman, if a light engine) had to immediately break the wire and coil the loose ends up to prevent them dangling in any water and thus making the circuit again. This action would ring the alarm bells in the signal boxes and trains could be prevented from entering the tunnel on the opposite line until the reason for the wire being broken could be ascertained. Necessary steps could then be taken to provide assistance to the train in the tunnel.

The alarm wire was not the only method of con-tacting the signalmen at either end of the tunnel. Telephones were provided on the Down side of

the lines at ½-mile (800m) (intervals throughout the tunnel, as well as in huts outside either tunnel mouth. These connected to the signal boxes via an exclusive telephone circuit. They were located as below:

- No.1: in a telephone hut outside the London end of the tunnel at 101m 6 chains
- No.2: inside the tunnel at 101m 46 chains
- No.3: inside the tunnel at 102m 6 chains
- No.4: inside the tunnel at 102m 46 chains
- No.5: inside the tunnel at 103m 6 chains
- No.6: in a telephone hut outside the Bristol end of the tunnel at 103m 48 chains.

The phones inside the tunnel were in wooden cupboards situated in refuges in the tunnel wall. All such cupboards were lit by a lamp (oil in early days, later electric). The phones were tested by the permanent way patrolman twice a week. When the signal boxes were closed in 1971, the tunnel phone circuit was transferred to Bristol Panel signal box.

The west end of Chipping Sodbury Tunnel, 1985. T.R. RENDALL

Viewed from the A38 road bridge at Patchway, a Hall Class loco on a parcels train emerges from Patchway Up Tunnel in 1959. The Down tunnel, on the higher level, is just out of sight round the curve. WILF STANLEY

HST set 253030 emerges from Patchway Down Tunnel at the Pilning end. *P.D. RENDALL*

Patchway Tunnels

There were actually three tunnels between Patchway and Cattybrook; two on the Down line and one on the Up line. The two Down line tunnels were on a higher level, as they had been built as part of the works of the B&SWUR, which was on a steeper gradient than the later new Up line. The first Down tunnel was a single bore of 1,246yd (1,140m) that was known as 'Patchway Old Tunnel'. Upon emerging from this tunnel, there was a short cutting of 198yd (180m) long, before entering the shorter tunnel known as 'Patchway Short Tunnel'; this was 62yd (57m) long. Leaving this tunnel, the Up line could be seen at a lower level.

The Up line entered the newer tunnel, which had been built when the line was doubled in 1887. This tunnel, known, not surprisingly, as 'Patchway New Tunnel', ran for 1,760yd (1,610m). None of the tunnels was ventilated.

Ableton Lane Tunnel

Ableton Lane Tunnel took the double-track line under the road of the same name. The 97yd (89m)-long tunnel was between Pilning station and the mouth of the Severn Tunnel. Owing to its short length, there was no need for ventilation.

The west end of Ableton Lane Tunnel, view towards Pilning. *WILF STANLEY*

The Severn Tunnel

At 7,688yd (7,030m) long, this is the longest railway tunnel in the United Kingdom and is a recognized feat of Victorian engineering. The tunnel, as is well known, carries the main lines under the River Severn and is steeply graded from each entrance down to the bottom of the incline. The gradient from Severn Tunnel West down into the tunnel is at 1 in 90, whilst the gradient from the East end down into the tunnel is 1 in 100. At the bottom is a very short stretch of level track.

Like Chipping Sodbury Tunnel, there is a 'tell-tale' wire through the tunnel, which must be broken by a member of the train crew in the event of accident, emergency or breakdown. Severing the wire used to cause a bell to ring in Severn Tunnel East and West signal boxes; when these were superseded, the alarm was transferred to Newport Panel signal box.

In steam days, before any freight train entered the tunnel it would be stopped in the loop at Severn Tunnel West (for Up trains), or Pilning Loop (for Down trains). Here, the guard would release any wagon brakes he had applied to control the train on the descent towards the tunnel. Whether the train had a pilot through the tunnel or not, the guard would screw on his van's handbrake before the train entered the tunnel in order to keep the couplings taut. There would always be residual steam and smoke lingering in the tunnel in spite of the ventilating fans and train crews working loose-coupled trains needed to know exactly where the downward gradient ended so that the guard could slowly release his van brake as the driver(s) opened their regulators. If one or the other was 'out of sync', any 'snatch' on the train could result in a broken coupling and a runaway.

In order to assist train crews to know where the downward gradients ended, a single white light was permanently displayed to drivers at approximately ¼mile (400m) before the bottom of the tunnel. It was at this point that drivers would start to open the regulator. At the bottom of the grade, two

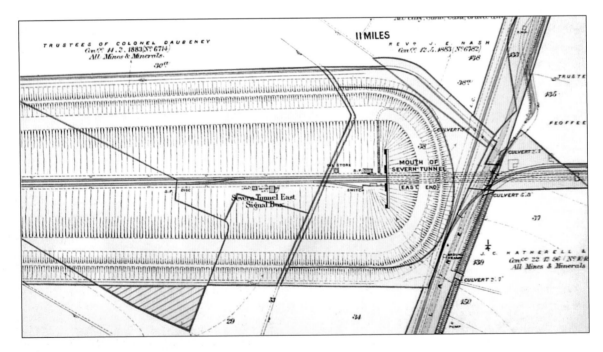

1903 plan of the East end of the Severn Tunnel, showing the original site of the East signal box. The single line over the tunnel mouth is the Pilning Low Level–Severn Beach branch; the short siding off the branch is to the Severn Beach pumping station. WILTSHIRE HISTORY CENTRE

white lights were displayed and this was the point at which the driver would open his regulator wider and the guard would release his handbrake fully, as both knew that the climb out of the tunnel was starting. Nowadays, the white lights have been replaced by blue lights, one on each side of the tunnel just before the bottom of the gradient in each direction. One light refers to normal direction moves and the other is for reversible moves.

Although comparatively 'easy' graded overall, the line was nevertheless quite a hard job in steam days. The smoke and steam were bad enough for the driver and fireman, especially if there was a banking loco attached, but it was even worse for the poor old guard at the rear of the train.

Once through Severn Tunnel Junction and into the tunnel, drivers and firemen of Up trains, both freight and passenger, were aware that they had some 18 miles (30km) of hard slog up to the top of the climb at Badminton. Once past those two white lights that indicated that they had reached the bottom of the tunnel, drivers would open the regulator and the battle was on. With express engines hauling a full load of over 400 tons (400,000kg), speed was often only 20–30mph (32–48km/h) through Pilning. Patchway would be topped at around 20mph. Reaching Badminton, the hard work was over, but it had often been a very tiring time for the fireman.

Compare that to diesel days, especially after the curve from Patchway to Stoke Gifford West was eased in the mid-1960s. It was then common for Up express trains to emerge from the tunnel and pass Pilning at around 60mph (97km/h), Patchway at around 50mph (80km/h) and 70mph (113km/h) achieved at Badminton. The High Speed Trains, of course, put even those figures to shame: maximum permitted speed between Pilning and Patchway is 90mph (145km/h); 110mph (177km/h) through Chipping Sodbury and Alderton; with 125mph permitted between Hullavington and Wootton Bassett.

The hardest job of all lay with the permanent way staff who worked in the tunnel. Day was night all the year round for them. You could always distinguish a Tunnel Gang trackman by the white

An Up High Speed Train emerges from the East end of the Severn Tunnel, 1982. P.D. RENDALL

donkey jackets he would wear for visibility. Tunnel men were known as 'tunnel rats'. Weekend tunnel closures took place at intervals throughout the year and this was when the tunnel examination train would come out from the Civil Engineering depot at Ashton Gate, Bristol; lights would be strung along the side walls of the tunnel and track maintenance, ballasting and a host of other jobs would also take place.

On occasions, the tunnel ventilation fans, which were situated towards the Welsh end of the tunnel and blew air into the tunnel to dispel the smoke, were switched off and this added to the feeling of gloom. Many diesel loco crews found that the lack of ventilation affected them more with diesels than it did with steam engines; it was not a good place to be, but the job had to go on.

The tunnel emergency phones were tested daily by the permanent way staff patrolling the tunnel. In those days, you could set your watch by a train and it was quite common for a tunnel permanent way man or patrolman to phone either West or East signal box if a train did not pass them at the usual time, to ask 'Everything all right, mate?' This was, of course, a normal part of 'teamwork' – something that all railwaymen did from the early days of

PRIVATE AND NOT FOR PUBLICATION.   Signal Notice No. S.2139.

GREAT WESTERN RAILWAY.
(For the use of the Company's employees only.)

SIGNAL ALTERATIONS - SEVERN TUNNEL EAST & WEST INTERMEDIATE BLOCK SECTIONS

On **Sunday, May 11th, 1947**, between the hours of 6.0 a.m. and 5.0 p.m., or until completion, the Signal Engineer will be engaged in **taking out of use** the Intermediate Block Section signalling in the Severn Tunnel.

The following signals will be taken out of use :—

Severn Tunnel East End.
Down Main Intermediate Block Home Signal (Light Signal).
Down Main Intermediate Block Home Repeating Signal (Light Signal).
(The above Signals are fixed to the Tunnel wall.)
Down Main Intermediate Block Distant Signal.
(Lower Arm on Down Main Starting Signal.)

Severn Tunnel West End.
Up Main Intermediate Block Home Signal (Light Signal).
Up Main Intermediate Block Home Repeating Signal (Light Signal).
(The above Signals are fixed to the Tunnel wall.)
Up Main Intermediate Block Distant Signal.
(Lower Arm on Up Main Starting Signal.)

At the same time the **A.T.C. Ramps** situated in the Tunnel to the rear of the Up and Down Intermediate Block Home Signals, also the Ramps to the rear of the Repeating Signals and the Ramps outside the Tunnel at the Up and Down Intermediate Block Distant Signals, together with all Track Circuits in the Tunnel, **will be taken out of use.**

The Block Section will now be Severn Tunnel East End—Severn Tunnel West End.

Occupation of the Locking Frames at East and West End Signal Boxes will be required for the purpose of altering and testing the Locking.

During the time the work is being carried out, Severn Tunnel East Down Main Distant and Severn Tunnel West Up Main Distant Signals will be disconnected, and placed at Caution.

District Inspector Newman, Newport, and District Inspector Old, Bristol, to make all necessary arrangements for safe working in accordance with Rule 77, and provide the necessary handsignalmen.

ALTERATIONS TO THE APPENDIX TO No. 4 SECTION OF THE SERVICE TIME TABLES.

INSTRUCTIONS FOR WORKING THROUGH THE SEVERN TUNNEL AND ON THE INCLINES AND SIDINGS BETWEEN PATCHWAY AND SEVERN TUNNEL JUNCTION.

VIDE NOTICE No. S.1916, dated APRIL, 1943, and subsequent amendments thereto.

The following alterations to be made :—

Page	Clause	
3	4	**Delete** paragraph 6.
3 & 4	5	**Delete** whole of clause 5 completely—Severn Tunnel Intermediate Block Signals.

Page	Clause	
7	10	**Delete** first paragraph (re A.T.C. apparatus).
8	10	**Delete** last two paragraphs (re American Engines).
10	15(a)	**Delete from** first sentence of second paragraph :— " by reason of the Intermediate Block Home Signal being at Danger, or " Third sentence of second paragraph :— " passed the Intermediate Block Home Signal for the opposite line " **to be substituted by** *has not* " already entered the Tunnel at the other end." **Delete** fourth sentence (last) of second paragraph.
13	15(c)	**Delete** fifth, sixth and seventh paragraphs (vide additions contained in Notices S.2032 and S.2063), with exception of last three sentences of seventh paragraph (Notice S.2032):—

These to now read :—

In the event of a train parting in the Tunnel and the rear portion of the divided train is to be drawn to the Box in advance and the opposite line is unoccupied, an engine, the Driver of which must be in possession of Wrong Line Order " D " must be admitted into the Section in accordance with Regulation 14.A, and the Fireman of such engine must obtain from the Guard of the disabled train Wrong Line Order " A." When this has been done the engine must return to the Signal Box in rear and an engine (or two engines coupled) may then be admitted to the Tunnel on the authority of Wrong Line Order " A " for the purpose of assisting forward the rear portion of the divided train. The Guard of the disabled train, after acting in accordance with the provisions of Rule 183(c) must proceed towards the Signal Box in advance and pilot the assistant engine(s) to the rear portion of the train.

Page	Clause	
13	15(c)	**Delete** the following from the fifteenth paragraph :— " or a train is allowed to proceed to the Intermediate Block Home Signal,"
14	16	**Delete** reference in Notice S.2048 to the Up and Down Intermediate Block Home Signals, and repeaters, in the sketch shewing the siting of the Trolley Wheels. **Also delete** the distances shewn on the sketch, between the Up and Down Intermediate Signals and the Trolley Wheels.
19	23	**Delete** paragraph (1). **Delete** from paragraph (4) :— " except that ' Line Clear ' must be obtained through the Tunnel in accordance with paragraph (1) above."

ACKNOWLEDGE RECEIPT TO HEAD OF DEPARTMENT.

W. R. STEVENS,
Superintendent of the Newport Division.

R. G. POLE,
Superintendent of the Bristol Division
Temple Meads Station,
Bristol, May, 1947.

Received Notice No. S.2139, re Intermediate Block Sections—Severn Tunnel.

Mr. R. G. POLE, ...Department.
Divisional Superintendent's Office, ...Station.
Bristol.   ....Sign.

GWR 1947 notice giving details of the removal of intermediate block signalling in the Severn Tunnel. AUTHOR'S COLLECTION

Reverse side of GWR 1947 notice. AUTHOR'S COLLECTION

Class 50 No.50009 draws the tunnel inspection train out of Bristol Ashton Gate Civil Engineering depot in 1989.
P.D. RENDALL

The original Severn Tunnel East signal box. AUTHOR'S COLLECTION

railways, but that some officials seem to think they invented in the 1990s.

As there was little room in the tunnel in the event of mishap or accident and access was via the tunnel mouths or the narrow shaft down from the pumping station, emergency trolley wheels were located in the tunnel between the tracks at a 14-mile (22.5km) post on the Welsh side and at 12 miles 40 chains on the English side. These wheels (on axles) were set in boxes buried in the ballast and were placed lengthwise to the running line. The tops of the wheels protruded 9in (230mm) above rail level. Spare rails were also kept in the tunnel at various locations.

As mentioned elsewhere, the working through the tunnel was by Special Lock and Block, allowing one train in either direction to be in the tunnel at any one time. During World War II, intermediate block signals were installed in the tunnel to speed up the movement of traffic; these were removed after the war.

During the same war, the East and West signal boxes were replaced by ARP construction boxes, having brick walls and reinforced concrete roofs. In spite of the tunnel being a strategic target for the Germans, there is no evidence that the Luftwaffe

ever tried to bomb it. Had they done so and the tunnel been flooded, it would have taken years to pump out and rebuild.

In the event of any emergency arising in the Severn Tunnel in diesel days, it was decreed that any empty passenger train, capable of being driven from either end (in other words, a Diesel Multiple Unit [DMU] or High Speed Train) could be requisitioned for use by the Fire Service to transport personnel and equipment into the tunnel.

Portable Headlamps

Special portable headlamps are provided for use when examining the line through tunnels. One such headlamp was kept in the Permanent Way Office at Stoke Gifford for use in examining Alderton, Chipping Sodbury, Patchway and the Severn Tunnels in the event of track circuit failures, obstructions or other mishaps. The headlamp was fixed to the front lamp bracket of a locomotive and plugged into a socket in the loco cab. It could not be used on Sprinters or other DMUs.

The locomotive examining the line had always to be accompanied by a competent person. This could be a signalman if the line was being examined for other than a track defect; if the latter, he had to be accompanied by a permanent way inspector. Accidents were rare indeed, but there were isolated incidents such as broken rails and track circuit failures. Should a driver report a 'bump' in the track whilst passing through the tunnel, it had to be examined using a special headlamp. Most times this was done, the lines were found to be clear, the train most likely having just run over a piece of ballast. However, during the construction of the Second Severn Crossing in the early 1990s, pile-driving took place in the river bed very close to the course of the tunnel. On more than one occasion, the shock waves from the pile-driving caused a brick to be dislodged from the tunnel roof. This would hit a passing train, or one would run over the brick. On each occasion, the lines had to be examined, causing considerable delays.

CHAPTER 8

Signal Boxes and Block Posts

There were three signal boxes on the entire South Wales Direct line whose purpose was not to control a junction, station or goods yard. These were: Patchway Tunnel box; Cattybrook Siding box; and Severn Tunnel East box.

Patchway Tunnel Box

Between Patchway station and Cattybrook Siding, the Up and Down main lines ran on different levels; the old Bristol and South Wales Union line was the Down line and the newer Up line, being built on easier gradients, was the lower level. Both lines passed through separate tunnels. Such was the concentration of traffic on the line in the early years of the twentieth century that it was deemed necessary to open a small signal box between Patchway and the mouth of the tunnels. This box opened on 29 August 1918. It was named 'Patchway Tunnel signal box'.[24]

A long 'sand drag' was put in the Up line just before the Up Home signal. The purpose of this was to prevent any 'breakaways' from running back down the incline into the tunnel and beyond. The two lines ran in a deep cutting at this point; a signal box situated at the side of either line would not have been able to command a view of both tracks, so the new box was built perched on the bank between the Down and Up lines. Being level with the Down

PRIVATE AND NOT FOR PUBLICATION.   SIGNAL NOTICE No. S.1298.

GREAT WESTERN RAILWAY

(For the use of the Company's servants only).

SPECIAL INSTRUCTIONS FOR WORKING TRAINS THROUGH
CHIPPING SODBURY TUNNEL.

*(Page 114—Appendix to No. 4 Section of the Service Timetables.)
Additional Clause.*

When a corridor train comes to a stand in Chipping Sodbury tunnel and it is necessary for the engine to be detached and run forward for assistance, the Fireman must remain with the train and the Engine Driver must take his engine out alone; and on arrival at the station in advance must obtain assistance from the station staff.

SPECIAL INSTRUCTIONS FOR WORKING TRAINS THROUGH
THE SEVERN TUNNEL.

(Page 114—Appendix to No. 4 Section of the Service Timetables).

If a passenger train which has to be divided in the Severn Tunnel is worked by two Guards (or by one Guard and a man assisting), the second Guard or the man assisting must remain with the passengers in the rear portion, and the Fireman must ride upon the last vehicle of the front portion. If the train is worked by one Guard only, the Fireman must remain with the rear portion and the Engine Driver must take the first portion out alone; and on arrival at the station in advance must obtain assistance from the station staff.

When a corridor train comes to a stand in the tunnel and it is necessary for the engine to be detached and run forward for assistance, the Fireman must remain with the train and the Engine Driver must take his engine out alone; and on arrival at the station in advance must obtain assistance from the station staff.

ACKNOWLEDGE RECEIPT TO HEAD OF DEPARTMENT.

H. R. GRIFFITHS,
Superintendent of the Bristol Division.

Bristol, August, 1927.
S.S.P.W.B./S1298.

GWR 1927 notice with instructions for the working of trains through the Chipping Sodbury and Severn Tunnels. AUTHOR'S COLLECTION

Patchway Tunnel signal box in 1962. Grange Class No.6828 Trellech Grange on a Cardiff–Portsmouth service has got the road towards Filton at Patchway station.
WILF STANLEY

line, it appeared from that viewpoint as a ground-level signal box, but from the Up line it stood high above the line. The box being thus sited, if the signalman needed to speak to drivers of Up trains for any reason, he had to walk down a steep path to track level. On one occasion, signalman Dave Dart had to do just that. The train came to a stand and Dave set off, hurriedly, down the bank. Too hurriedly as it turned out, because he lost his footing and skidded along until his progress was arrested by the 6ft driving wheels of the locomotive. Poor Dave was winded, but apart from bruised ribs, no damage was done.

All Down freight trains signalled as 1–4 or 3–2 bell code (i.e., not fully fitted with the vacuum brake) were instructed to stop at Patchway Tunnel box to pin down wagon brakes before proceeding. This involved the guard walking the length of the train, applying handbrakes on wagons until the driver was happy that he had sufficient braking power to hold the train on the steep descent to Pilning. When this was achieved and the train was on the move again, the guard would throw out a written 'tally' list of the train's load to the signalman, who would phone Pilning Junction with the details. The tally was then put on a spike on the desk for collection later by officials.

Patchway Tunnel was a busy box with one train after another. By the 1950s, many signal boxes were being equipped with locked Starting signals to prevent accidental clearing of the signal when a preceding train was still 'in section' between one signal box and another. Oddly enough, although there was a tunnel ahead of the box on the Down line, the Patchway Tunnel Starting signals were not locked by the block. Had this been the case, the Starting signal could not be pulled to the 'clear' position unless the line was clear and the signal box ahead (in this case Cattybrook) had given 'Line Clear' on his signalling instrument, thus releasing the Patchway Tunnel starter.

During the 1950s, there were so many vacancies in the signalling grades that twelve-hour shifts were the norm. A relief signalman could work a week of twelve-hour nights at Patchway Tunnel box, double back for a 14.00–22.00 Sunday turn at Patchway Station box, then follow that with a week of twelve-hour days back at Patchway Tunnel box. This was tiring and also meant that reliefmen were kept at boxes with vacancies, so every so often new signalmen were recruited. These were normally started off at smaller boxes.

One such 'learner' was started at Patchway Tunnel box. Unfortunately, this lad could not get it into his head that you needed 'Line Clear' before you could permit another train to enter the section ahead, even if the Starting signal was *not* locked by the block. One day, when the signalman's back was turned, the learner signalled a Down train and replaced the signals behind it as it passed. Okay so far; but on giving the 'Train Out of Section' signal to Patchway station he was immediately asked 'Is Line Clear?' for a light engine – a banker returning to Pilning. He accepted this engine as he was quite legitimately allowed to do – and was then given the 'Train Entering Section' signal. However, the preceding train had not cleared Cattybrook and the learner should not have pulled his signals off. Nonetheless, he promptly cleared all the signals.

The signalman, whose back had been turned, heard this going on and rushed to the levers, but the loco had already passed the Down Distant signal and was steaming past the box. They could not put the signals back in time to stop the engine before it passed the Starting signal. Luckily, the banker, for once, was in no hurry and drifted down past the signal, watched by the horrified signalman and the unconcerned learner. By the time the engine was passing Patchway Tunnel's starter, the first train had cleared the section and Cattybrook sent 'Train Out of Section' for it. Patchway Tunnel quickly 'asked the road' for the banker and all was well. A little 'cooking of the books' was required, but no damage done. The learner left the railway shortly afterwards.

Night shifts were very busy, consisting mostly of freight trains. The signalman would be lucky to get ten–fifteen minutes' break on the odd occasion when a freight called at Pilning and nothing else was able to run on the Down line until it had cleared the section.

Most Up freight trains were usually long and heavy and banked up from Pilning. The bankers normally left the train at Patchway station and had to be crossed over there to return to Pilning. There were about twenty bankers to return to Pilning during an eight-hour shift.

When the diesel 'Blue Pullmans' arrived, they produced a new phenomenon; the Up Pullman would be signalled sometime after a preceding train had cleared the section. This train normally had a banker and the smoke from the banker would, as usual, linger in Patchway Up tunnel. As the Pullman entered the tunnel, so its speed and air displacement would push the smoke out of the

tunnel at the Patchway end, so the smoke billowing out of the tunnel was always visible before the 'Blue Pullman' appeared: 'it was as if a giant hand was pushing it out', said one of the signalmen.

Cattybrook Siding Box

Some distance from the west end of the Patchway Tunnels stood another small signal box. This was known as Cattybrook Siding and, as the name suggests, a siding tailed off from the Down line to cross the Up line and run into a brickworks. The small, twelve-lever box was the oldest signal box on the line. It opened in July 1886 and replaced a box known as 'Over Sidings signal box', which had stood on the B&SWUR single line 5 chains further west since about 1880, to control the connection into the brickworks.

The brickworks (Cattybrook Brick Co.) was served by a daily trip from Stoke Gifford yard. This was known as the 'Brickie' and left Stoke Gifford around 11.45, after the passage of the 08.55 Paddington–Cardiff express. Usually headed by a pannier tank, it would run to Cattybrook with a few wagons. There, it backed across the Up main line and into the brickworks, where it shunted as required. When its work was complete, the 'Brickie' whistled up to come out and would then run down the line to Pilning Junction, where it would be put in the Down goods loop. From the loop, the engine would run round its train, remarshal the guard's van at the end and return to Stoke Gifford.

Another, unusual, duty of the signalman at Cattybrook box was to give permission for blasting to take place at the quarry adjacent to the brickworks. Blasting was timetabled to take place daily at 11.20 in daylight and in clear weather. To allow this to take place if required, the signalman had to ensure that a Permanent Way Department ganger was posted at a spot on the lineside 'as near as possible to where the blasting is to take place'.[25] This man was to have with him a red flag and some detonators to protect the line should the blasting cause an obstruction. Once the ganger had been asked by the brickworks' foreman for permission to set

9F 2-10-0 No.92220 Evening Star *has only been in service for a few months. It is seen here starting away from Patchway Tunnel box after stopping to pin down wagon brakes on a train of coal empties for Severn Tunnel Junction. WILF STANLEY*

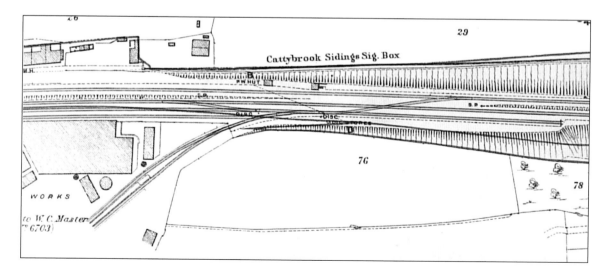

Plan of Cattybrook Sidings, 1903. WILTSHIRE HISTORY CENTRE

A lovely summer's day in 1963 and the 'Brickie' shunts at Cattybrook Brick Co. A scene of idyllic delight.
WILF STANLEY

off the charges, he had to phone the signal box and if there were no trains signalled or imminent, the signalman could give permission, but only after advising his colleague in Patchway Tunnel box and then sending the 'blocking back' 3–3 bell signal to Patchway Tunnel for the Down line and having that signalman send the same signal for the Up Line.

Once the blasting was over and the brickworks' foreman had assured the ganger that 'all charges had been successfully fired or withdrawn', then the ganger could, if all was safe to do so, advise the signalman that normal working could resume. The ganger had then to visit Cattybrook signal box and initial the entries that the signalman had made in the Train Register concerning the blasting. The 'blocking back' signal could then be withdrawn.

Cattybrook signal box was open Monday–Saturday round the clock, closing at 22.00 on Saturday night. The box opened on Sunday with a short Sunday turn, 16.45 or 17.30 to 19.00 to break the long section between Patchway Tunnel and Pilning Junction.

For many years during the 1940s and 1950s, Cattybrook signal box was worked by various members of the Oakhill family – Vic, Joe and Don (Dinky) Oakhill.

Severn Tunnel East Box

The first Severn Tunnel East signal box stood just outside the east end of the Severn Tunnel. It opened on 14 May 1888. It controlled little more than a few signals, a crossover and a throw-off point. The small signal box stood for fifty-four years until replaced in 1942 by a wartime ARP box. This latter box stood in a cutting a little way up the line from the mouth of the Severn Tunnel and was located at the western end of Ableton Lane Tunnel, approximately a ¼-mile (400m) nearer Pilning than the old box. It was constructed in typical ARP style, being built of brick with a flat, reinforced concrete roof. Owing to sighting difficulties, it was not as high as the ARP boxes at Wapley and elsewhere. It had control of signals, facing and trailing crossovers and connections to and from new Up and Down goods loops laid in on account of the increase in traffic due to World War I.

Tunnel East was a strategic location in the Western Region railway network on the English side of the River Severn and as such 'all eyes looked towards it'. Everyone from signalmen to station masters and controllers would be interested in the times of trains as they emerged from the tunnel. Any delay would reflect on workings elsewhere

A Hall Class 4-6-0 on a Portsmouth–Cardiff working is about to pass Cattybrook signal box. Note the 'moth-eaten' concrete signal post and its replacement post on the far side of the box. WILF STANLEY

and so, when a train was delayed for some reason, it was not unusual for even Paddington to be 'on the blower' to find out how 'such and such a train' was running.

It was not an easy place to work; the lines were in a cutting that became deeper as it approached the tunnel mouth. Freight trains would labour up the incline from the middle of the tunnel and emerge in a cloud of steam and smoke that hung around the tunnel mouth, making it difficult for the signalman to see the tail lamps of the brake vans when they followed out of the murk. On one occasion, a signalman had an Up freight 'on the block' and when it stormed out of the tunnel he was at the window, eager to spot the tail lights on the brake van. Satisfied that the train was complete, having seen the lamps, he gave 'Train Out of Section' to Severn Tunnel West box and was immediately asked the road for another train. He accepted this and set the Tyers Tunnel Lock and Block instrument to 'Line Clear' and was then given 'Train On Line'. He acknowledged this signal and was then suddenly seized with doubt. Had he actually seen the tail lamps of the preceding train? If not, there might be wagons still in the tunnel. He ran down the box steps and peered up the line to where the rear of the train was slowly vanishing into the gloom cast by palls of smoke from the train engine and the assisting loco. No chance; the lamps were obscured. The poor man had to wait for many nail-biting minutes

before the train passed Pilning and 'Train Out of Section' was given and he knew that the train had been complete.

Other signalmen who worked Severn Tunnel East also testified that frequently they could not see the tail lamp for smoke and/or fog, and would phone Pilning station box to ask the signalman there to confirm 'train complete' before they 'cleared back' to Tunnel West.

It was not just smoke and steam; being near the River Severn, the cutting at Severn Tunnel East got a lot of fog. This would roll in off the river, mix with the residual smoke and steam and congregate in the cutting. On such occasions, fogmen were often required. The fogman was usually a member of the permanent way gang and his duty on such occasions was to stay in the signal box until a train was due. Then he would descend to track level and observe the tail lamp of the train, thus confirming that the train was complete and shouting this information to the signalman.

Saturdays at Severn Tunnel East were the worst. Train after train ran through the tunnel and any delay or blockage reacted on services all over the region. As traffic built up through the morning, so a succession of Down trains began to receive 'distant checks' as they caught each other up. Later still, the checks changed to delays as trains were stopped at the Starting signal waiting a clear passage.

Carrying an indeterminate headcode, a Class 47 has emerged from Ableton Lane Tunnel with an Up freight. Photograph taken summer 1968 after the Severn Tunnel end of the Down goods loop had been taken out of use, as can be seen by the missing signal on the bracket, middle distance, left-hand side of the lines. R. CUFF/AUTHOR'S COLLECTION

There was a rule at Tunnel East which said that should a Down train become divided approaching the tunnel, it must not be permitted to enter the tunnel. This was obviously because of the danger of the rear half catching up with the front half and derailing in the tunnel. But what was a signalman to do if this happened? Most signalmen agreed that they would break the rules and give the driver a green handsignal or light authorizing him to pass the Starting signal at Danger and proceed on into the tunnel; the chance of the rear portion catching the front portion safely, they reckoned, was more likely than it colliding and derailing – which is precisely what would happen if they stopped the front portion at the Starting signal. Luckily, it never happened.

The Up Starting signal with its accompanying arm for the Up goods loop and Distant signal for Pilning station was very close to the mouth of Ableton Lane Tunnel and with the clouds of smoke and steam that accompanied a train's exit from the 'hole' (as the Severn Tunnel was known), it was difficult on occasions for a driver to see the signal. One day, signalman Dave Dart had a passenger train steaming hard through the tunnel, but he did not have the road ahead. When the train emerged from the tunnel it was steaming hard up the grade surrounded by clouds of steam and smoke and the driver failed to see the Up Starting signal at Danger. However, as he passed the signal, so the driver realized that it stood at Danger and he did not have the road. He slammed on the brakes. The signalman, watching out of the box window, saw the restaurant car staff performing quite spectacular dances as they fought to keep their balance with hands full of trays of food.

A margin of twenty minutes was required for a freight to run from the Down loop at Severn Tunnel East to be clear of the loop at Severn Tunnel West. Freights were supposed to be 'looped' either side of the tunnel as necessary to allow a safe margin for passenger trains. Signalman Stan Horn was quite aware of this when he worked at Pilning station box, but he also knew many of the drivers. Each trusted the other and Stan knew that the drivers would not let him down if he gave them the chance to 'have a run'. So, with a passenger train imminent, Stan would let the freights run down the main line and wave to the drivers to 'get a move on'. The freights would thunder down past Severn Tunnel East and into the 'hole', passing Severn Tunnel West with ample time for the passenger train to follow without delays.

This worked well until the advent of the Cross-Country DMUs. These ran quicker than steam-hauled local passenger trains and one day the inevitable happened; Stan let a freight have a run and the following passenger was a Cross-Country set. It was at a stand at Severn Tunnel East's Down Starting signal before the freight cleared the tunnel. After this, the authority for margining the trains was taken away from Pilning station box and given to the Pilning inspectors, who were 'cautious', to say the least, and all freights thereafter ran down the loop. This practice now caused delays to freight trains and freights occupied loops and sidings for miles around, waiting a path through the tunnel. It was not long before Stan Horn and his mates on the other shifts were asked to take up the margining again. Not surprisingly, the answer was unprintable!

Those Cross-Country sets almost cost a guard his life one day. A Down goods was stopped on the Down goods loop at Severn Tunnel East and the guard climbed down from his van to come to the signal box to carry out the rules. Dave Dart watched as this man walked nonchalantly down the Up main towards the box, oblivious to the fact that there was a passenger train formed by a Cross-Country set, in the tunnel, coming towards him. Dave Dart was a churchman and did not swear, but on this occasion he felt that something other than a polite warning was required. 'I had to yell "Get out of the bloody way!" at the top of my voice!' he recalled. It worked. The guard leapt off the track as the DMU shot out of the tunnel. The guard afterwards thanked Dave, saying that the shout had undoubtedly saved his life.

Voices in the Night …

In its lonely and isolated position next to a short tunnel and near to the dark mouth of the Severn Tunnel, the wartime brick and concrete box at Severn Tunnel East was a strange place. In the night-time the darkness could play havoc with the imagination and it followed that the right sort of atmosphere was created in which stories could breed. The atmosphere could be something akin to Charles Dickens' *The Signal-Man*. At Tunnel East, men could hear voices; voices, it was said, that could be heard muttering to themselves in the dead of night.

Several signalmen I have spoken to could testify to hearing these voices. Soft, whispering, voices,

they were said to be. Chattering away in hushed tones in the dead of night; it was never possible to pick up quite what it was they were saying, but they 'were there all right'. However, there does not seem to be any record of anyone refusing to work there because of the 'voices'; men accepted the phenomenon, it seems.

There was a parallel – Dainton Tunnel box, on the main line between Newton Abbot and Plymouth, sat in a similar position to Severn Tunnel East box. It was just outside the mouth of Dainton Tunnel itself, although not in a cutting. The box in question was erected in 1965, replacing an earlier structure. Sidings used to run behind the box and had once served an old quarry. It was said that on a still night, voices could be heard whispering and muttering to themselves …

In both cases the answer was to be found in water. Streams ran close to both signal boxes and the 'tinkling' sound made by gently running water was taken by some as sounding like voices; imagination did the rest.

On the plus side, Severn Tunnel East box had electric heating, which, as one signalman recalled, was 'very nice. You didn't have to keep a fire in or get the coal up at the end of your shift'. A negative was that there was nowhere to park a car or motorbike other than on the main road that ran between Pilning and Severn Beach, where the vehicle was not visible from the box. After finishing at 06.00 after a night shift, signalman Bert Tyler walked up to the road, only to find that someone had pinched his Lambretta scooter during the night.

Such were the trials and tribulations of working at Tunnel East.

The June 1942 Severn Tunnel East signal box, which was closed in July 1969; photograph taken in 1968. WILF STANLEY

CHAPTER 9

Passenger and Freight Workings

Just reading through old timetables and signal box Train Registers shows what traffic used to run on the line. Aside from the normal day-to-day express passenger and local services, there was the flood of excursions during holiday times, football specials, rugby specials and even an excursion from South Wales to London on the occasion of evangelist Billy Graham's appearance at Wembley Stadium in 1955.

Named Trains

As befitted an express route, the Direct line saw many prestigious 'named' trains both in steam and diesel days. Most of the named expresses were post-World War II, the exception being 'The Bristolian',

Headboards from some of the Direct line's expresses; photographed in the National Railway Museum. WILF STANLEY

which was inaugurated on 9 September 1935. These included expresses such as 'The Red Dragon', 'The Bristolian', 'Capitals United', 'The Devonian', 'Pembroke Coast Express' and 'The Cornishman' plus the 'South Wales Pullman' – both steam and diesel versions. In HST days during the 1980s and 1990s, there were a few new named trains in the shape of 'The Brunel Executive' (07.25 Taunton–Paddington, calling at Bristol Parkway 07.54); 'The Armada' (06.25 Plymouth–Newcastle); 'The Devon Scot' (07.25 Plymouth–Aberdeen) and 'The Cornish Scot' (07.52 Penzance–Edinburgh.) By this time the two 'old stalwarts' left from steam days, 'The Devonian' and 'The Cornishman' had altered destinations. 'The Devonian', which for years had run between Paignton and Bradford, now ran between Paignton and Newcastle in the Up direction and between Leeds and Paignton in the Down direction. 'The Cornishman' ran from Penzance to Edinburgh (instead of Aberdeen) in the Up direction and started at Dundee in the Down.

In the 1960s, the first named Up train of the day was the 'Capitals United Express'. This was the 06.30 Swansea–Paddington, which in 1960 was timed to pass Stoke Gifford at 08.54.[26] Headcoded 1A13, this train was booked for Castle, County or Britannia haulage if 400–420 tons (400,000–427,000kg) and if 350 tons (356,000kg) it could be hauled by a Hall. King Class locos were also used

The Down 'Capitals United Express' thunders through Chipping Sodbury behind a Britannia Class 4-6-2. WILF STANLEY

on this train, but mainly before the advent of the Britannia Class.

Signalman Wilf Stanley recalled being on duty at Westerleigh West box one day when the Up 'Capitals United Express' was signalled. Although it had a clear road, the train, hauled by a Castle Class loco, approached the box very slowly with clouds of steam issuing from the front end. The loco had suffered a failure of the front nearside cylinder cover. The driver coaxed the loco and train to Chipping Sodbury, where he stopped on the Up main and explained to the signalman there what had happened. In the Down loop at Sodbury there was a freight train headed by a GW 28XX 2–8–0 freight loco. There was no option but to use this and when the Castle had limped off into the Up loop, the '28' was uncoupled from its train and run back up the Down main line to the east end of the station, from where it backed down on to the 'Capitals'. A quick change of crew and the train

then proceeded on its way, tender first, somewhat late and without the express headboard. Whether someone forgot to put the headboard on to the freight engine or someone's pride would not allow them to put such a distinguished headboard on to a freight loco is not known. The '28' was taken off the train at Swindon and replaced by a spare express engine. Later that morning, the Castle, assisted by a pannier tank loco, limped tender first back to shed, stopping at Westerleigh West and other boxes for examination before going on its way, the headboard still proclaiming that it was the 'Capitals United Express'.

Another of the line's well-known expresses and the second Up 'named' train of the day was 'The Red Dragon', which first ran on 5 June 1950 and started using a headboard in 1956. This was the 07.30 Carmarthen to Paddington and would emerge from the Severn Tunnel climbing hard to pass Patchway at 10.54. After the slight easing of the

The Up 'Red Dragon' storms up to Patchway behind 9F 2-10-0 No.92220 Evening Star. *WILF STANLEY*

left out, 92220 *Evening Star* was noted on 'The Red Dragon' on more than one occasion.

The 06.30 ex-Paddington–Swansea was a Britannia working. The Britannias were frequently seen on less glamorous jobs on night shifts, such as express freight and parcels trains; one was sometimes seen on the 03.50 Whitland–Kensington Milk, although this was normally a Castle duty (it usually passed Winterbourne around 19.00) and the return working was 10.35 Kensington–Whitland Milk empties.

The third Up express that passed Stoke Gifford at 12.27 was 'The Devonian'; 1N45, 09.15 Paignton–Bradford and 12.28 from Bristol Temple Meads, which was timetabled to run via Filton Bank to Westerleigh West Junction, where it left WR metals for the LMR. This train was often double-headed; the pilot engine usually worked back to Gloucester. The motive power was usually a Class 5 loco: a Black Five or a Jubilee.

On occasions, there would be another afternoon Up express, 'The Cornishman', which would run through Stoke Gifford around 16.02 and after 'The Devonian'. Although 'The Cornishman' was not normally booked to run via Stoke Gifford and Westerleigh West, but was booked to run via the LMR line through Mangotsfield, both it and 'The Devonian' were able to run via Filton, Stoke Gifford and Westerleigh West Junction, from where they regained Midland metals via the branch to Yate

gradient through Stoke Gifford it was climbing all the way to Badminton, which was passed at 11.06.

The usual motive power for this train was a Castle, although when the BR standard Britannias were allocated to Cardiff Canton shed, the South Wales men put up some good timings with them. Those 'Brits', often seen on 'The Red Dragon', bore good old GWR names such as *Morning Star*, *Polar Star* and *Western Star*, but just to show that the Britannias did not have the monopoly of astral names and that Swindon workmanship was not

Before the Britannia Class took over, the normal motive power for 'The Red Dragon' was an ex-GWR King. Here the 'Dragon' hurtles past Winterbourne with an unidentified King in charge. Note the 'lowmac' parked in the cattle dock siding. *WILF STANLEY*

South Junction. 'The Cornishman', which began in June 1952, was mostly headed by a Castle Class and I can recall, as a small child, seeing a very smartly turned-out 5072 *Hurricane* heading the Down 'Cornishman'; alas, not on the Badminton line, but running through Mangotsfield.

Express number four and undoubtedly the pride of the line, was the Up 'Bristolian'. Although this train ran down to Bristol via Bath, it returned to the capital via Badminton. Running in later years as headcode 1A92 and starting from Bristol at 16.30, this train was a 'racer'. Timed for a 'special load' of seven coaches, this train had originally been planned for ex-GWR King Class haulage, but was soon found to be suitable for a Castle, which was able to keep time easily. The train normally had a King at its head on Fridays when it was more heavily loaded. The timetable allowed nine minutes to reach Filton Junction from Temple Meads, but it was not unusual to do it in eight minutes. From there, the train was allowed one hour and thirty-six minutes to Paddington, often reaching speeds of 100mph (160km/h) between Hullavington and Little Somerford. For such speeds, the line needed to be kept clear of slower trains; at Chipping Sodbury box, when the 'Is Line Clear?' bell signal

Post-nationalization, WR trains could use the LMR routes; 'The Cornishman' is shown here passing Kingswood Junction on the Bristol–Gloucester main line in 1958. This was a frequent route for this train. WILF STANLEY

was received for the Up 'Bristolian' it was just off Stapleton Road.

However, it was not just the Kings and Castles that made a name for themselves on 'The Bristolian'. Although it rarely happened, other locos sometimes had the opportunity to show what they could do on the service. A good example of such an

A fine shot of the Up 'Bristolian' climbing Filton Bank and passing Ashley Hill in 1958. WILF STANLEY

By 1961, 'The Bristolian' was in the hands of Warship Class diesel-hydraulics. It is seen here passing through Chipping Sodbury.
WILF STANLEY

RECOLLECTIONS BY ERIC HOLWELL – DRIVER, BRISTOL BATH ROAD SHED

Eric recalls working 'The Bristolian', which started from Paddington in the morning and ran to Bristol via Bath, returning via Badminton in the afternoon:

> We had a King Class to start with, then they told us that we were to have a Castle next time. We thought this would be a backward step as we thought the Castle wasn't powerful enough. But with a Castle we took eight minutes from Temple Meads to Filton Junction and were doing almost 100mph at Hullavington. From then on it was always a Castle on this train – they were wonderful locos.

Eric preferred GW locos to the BR standards, but his overall favourite, though, was the HST.

occasion occurred on 15 September 1954 and was duly noted by train running expert and author Cecil J. Allen in an article about the Hall Class in the May 1964 issue of *Railway World*; 'The Bristolian' left Bristol on time behind Castle 5073 *Blenheim Castle*. However, all was not well and the train struggled to keep to time. It was stopped at Little Somerford, where the brakes were found to be leaking. After examination by the train crew it was decided that *Blenheim Castle* was unfit to take the train forwards, so the loco off a freight train standing in the loop

was requisitioned. This loco was 7904 *Fountains Hall*, which proceeded to leave Little Somerford fourteen minutes late with 'The Bristolian' and arrive in Paddington seventy-two minutes later, having improved on the normal timings by over six minutes![27]

From 1960, 'The Bristolian' was normally headed by a D600 or D800 Class Warship diesel.

Up express number five was the 'Pembroke Coast Express', the 13.05 Pembroke Dock to Paddington. Regularly heavily loaded and therefore headed by a King Class, this was a long-distance service, passing Patchway four hours and forty-two minutes after leaving Pembroke Dock and arriving in London six hours and forty minutes after starting. This service was also booked for Castle, County or Britannia haulage according to loading.

Less than an hour after the 'Pembroke Coast Express' had sent the dust on the platforms flying, the Up 'South Wales Pullman' followed. Timed past Chipping Sodbury at 19.08, this train consisted of the prestigious Pullman cars; mere mortals did not travel on *this* train! Leaving Swansea at 16.31, this train was another that was allocated a King, Castle, County or Britannia according to *The Working Timetables*, but the usual loco was a Castle. However, it was noted on more than one occasion being headed by a 9F 2–10–0.

In May 1961, the Western Region announced that from September of that year, it was taking what was described as a 'big step forwards' with the introduction of new passenger timetables covering most of the main lines in the region. The reasons given were that long-distance passenger traffic had grown steadily since the war and this had been provided for with additional trains. The opportunity was now being taken to 'rationalize' the timetable and to provide new services that would give regular interval departures from main-line stations. It was claimed that by spacing departures at regular intervals, the Western Region would be able to give the public a greater choice of trains. In addition, business folk would find morning trains to London and evening trains back home. Many services would include a buffet or restaurant car. The General Manager of the Western Region, Mr J. Hammond, admitted that the new services would keep down costs, which he said was 'especially important with the costly new diesel locomotives now coming into service'.[28] Most of the current services were still steam-hauled, but further changes would come when more diesels were brought into service.

For the South Wales Direct line this meant an almost hourly service, with trains leaving Paddington at fifty-five minutes past the hour and leaving Cardiff on the hour. All new trains would call at Neath, Bridgend and Port Talbot, except the 'Pembroke Coast Express' and the 18.55 Paddington–Fishguard Harbour express, which connected with the ferry to Ireland; both of these trains would run non-stop between Cardiff and Swansea.

The Down 'Capitals United Express' would leave London at 08.55 for Cardiff and West Wales, with the Up 'Capitals' leaving Milford Haven at 11.10 and Cardiff at 15.00. The 'Blue Pullman' diesel set would now form the 'South Wales Pullman', leaving

A poor shot, but nonetheless worth including – the Down 'South Wales Pullman' behind an immaculate Cardiff Canton shed Castle is about to pass Westerleigh West signal box. Photo thought to be 1960. WILF STANLEY

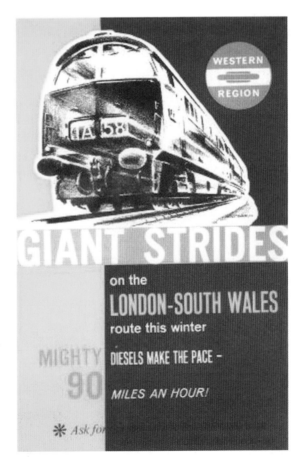

WESTERN REGION

GIANT STRIDES

on the

LONDON–SOUTH WALES

route this winter

MIGHTY DIESELS MAKE THE PACE –

90 MILES AN HOUR!

✱ Ask for

A Western Region advertising notice, 1961. AUTHOR'S COLLECTION

Swansea at 06.40, Cardiff at 07.50 and Newport at 08.08, arriving in Paddington at 10.15. Its return working would leave Paddington at 16.55 and run non-stop to Newport, arriving there at 19.02. It would reach Swansea at 20.40. It would not call at Neath in either direction.[29]

This brought about the fastest-ever timings between London and Swansea with the diesel Pullman reducing the journey to three hours and thirty-five minutes for the Down service and three hours and forty-five minutes for the Up service. The 'Blue Pullman' diesel sets replaced the usual rake of Pullman coaches in their livery of cream and umber, but the 'Wells Fargo' Pullmans (as they were known to railwaymen) were kept as standby in case of diesel failures, or for use when one of the three Pullman diesels was away for maintenance.

Of all the stations on the line, only Badminton saw any of the new hourly trains call at its platforms. The 13.55, 15.55 and 17.55 Down ex-Paddington called at Badminton at 16.03, 17.46 and 19.56 respectively, whilst on the Up line, the 06.26 ex-Swansea called there at 09.07 and the 12.05 ex-Milford Haven called at 17.04.

With all these expresses needing to have clear runs, one may wonder how local trains and freights, plus light engine moves and bankers returning to Pilning, fitted in with the timetable, but they did. Nowadays, the line is mostly used by HSTs and block freight services – there are no local stopping passenger services to 'get in the way' of the expresses, but in the days of steam, signalmen and station staff relied on the train crews and vice versa. Without the cooperation of all staff the intense train service could not have run.

Undoubtedly, when the local stopping passenger services finished in 1962 there was greater leeway for faster trains, but by 1966 the named expresses had all gone other than the diesel 'South Wales Pullman'. From the start of the new Western Region summer timetable on 18 April 1966, the line saw a speed-up in some of the services that ran via Badminton. The 08.20 Swansea–Paddington and the 19.00 Paddington–Swansea were both booked to be hauled by a pair of Class 37 diesels working in multiple.

It was not just new engines that were appearing on the line. In April 1967, BR introduced a new carriage – this was the first of three 'lounge cars'. These were coaches without the usual seating pattern of compartments, instead having 'lounge compartments'. Two of these compartments were installed, each with four swivel armchairs fixed to the floor. Each lounge compartment had ten seats altogether. The rest of the coach comprised three 'normal' First Class compartments, each having the usual six seats. The first of these coaches went into service on a daily Swansea–Paddington service. The train

It is 1963 and the 'South Wales Pullman' is now a 'Blue Pullman' set. An Up service speeds through Pilning station; a faster, if not exactly a more comfortable, ride. WILF STANLEY

would then work a Paddington–Bristol run and return to Paddington again to work its last trip of the day back to Swansea.

Further dieselization saw the Paddington–South Wales services taken over by Class 52 Western diesels and Brush type 4 Class 47s. The sole Class 53, D0280 (later 1200) *Falcon*, also occasionally appeared on a London service. The Westerns were still in charge of the Paddington–South Wales expresses right into the mid-1970s and the introduction of the air-braked Mark 2 coaching stock in the early 1970s saw an upgrade in comfort so far as the travelling public were concerned. Westerns were still in charge at this stage, many having been fitted with dual air and vacuum braking systems. There was (arguably) no finer sound than that of the music of a 'Thousand' – as they were known to railwaymen – with a rake of air-braked Mark 2s behind, speeding down the Badminton line with its twin Maybach engines in full voice.

As the 1970s progressed, the introduction of Mark 2(d), (e) and (f) coaching stock, which was air-braked and equipped for electric train heating (ETH), meant that the Western diesels were unable to haul this stock; the coaches, being dual-braked and dual-heated, were equipped for electric train heating, but the Class 52s were not. After 1973, the Westerns were gradually moved off passenger trains on this and other lines to make way for Class 47- or 50-hauled Mark 2 ETH stock. The Class 50s were allocated to the Western Region after being displaced from the West Coast main line by electrification – and these locos had been fitted with ETH as built. Class 52s were still to be seen on freight trains, though. However, they were 'non-standard', being diesel-hydraulic, and the future was the majority diesel-electric fleet.

A sad sight came on 26 February 1977 when two Westerns, Nos 1023 *Western Fusilier* and 1013 *Western Ranger* headed a special 'last run' from

The HST had taken over most of the Paddington–South Wales services by 1981, but some were still in the hands of the Class 47 and Mark 2 stock. One is seen at Bristol Parkway. P.D. RENDALL

26 February 1977. Western Fusilier *and* Western Ranger *speed through Chipping Sodbury with the Paddington to Swansea leg of the 'Western Tribute' railtour, the last runs of the Class 52 diesel-hydraulics.*
P.D. RENDALL

Paddington to Swansea via Badminton and back to Paddington via Bristol and Plymouth. I stood on the remains of the Up platform and watched them speed through Chipping Sodbury that morning. Well-known railway photographer George Heiron, who, in photos and paintings had recorded much of the comings and goings along the Direct line over the years, was among others also there. George took up his position on the Down side cutting slope nearer to the tunnel to record the end of an era.[30] How sad to witness the end of a diesel era when steam-hauled trains had vanished from the same line only a few years before. When the Westerns were withdrawn, the services were taken over by Class 47 and English Electric Class 50 locos before the HST services became the norm and transformed the London runs.

After the closure of the LMR Mangotsfield route in January 1970, all trains that previously ran via that route now ran via the Badminton line and Westerleigh West, making the 'bottom half' of the Direct line quite busy and giving Westerleigh West box a more 'strategic' role regarding regulation of freight traffic. The resignalling of the line with four-aspect colour-light signals in 1971 allowed for faster, more frequent services, with trains able to follow each other at closer spacing running under Caution signals. Ironically, having equipped the line to take more trains, the tail end of the Beeching Report's implementation began to take effect and the freight traffic gradually became concentrated into block trains; Stoke Gifford yard effectively

closed and the four-aspect signals (fine for closely spaced commuter traffic) were an anomaly until the HST arrived and the Westerleigh–Wootton Bassett section of the line was resignalled again in 1975.

Local passenger workings on the line were always slow. The 06.10 Bristol Temple Meads–Swindon called at all stations and the 07.13 Bristol Temple Meads to Swindon was a semi-fast service via Badminton and calling at all stations except Coalpit Heath. It was usually hauled by a Castle.

The 17.25 Swindon–Bristol Temple Meads ran down via Badminton and returned via Bath. After nationalization things altered little, although costs changed and services speeded up when diesel units were introduced to the line. Wootton Bassett station, being a junction, had the benefit of two lines from which to gain revenue. In the summer of 1960, a Special Cheap Day Return ticket from Wootton Bassett to Bath Spa was advertised as costing 5s 6d and the same to Bristol Temple Meads was 7s (27½ pence and 35 pence respectively). Both journeys were via Bath, rather than Badminton, and were advertised in a British Railways promotional leaflet as being by 'Diesel Trains'. In 1962, the same journey would have cost 6s 6d and 8s 6d (32½ pence and 42½ pence respectively).

In 1960, there were six Down trains between midnight and midday, the first being at 00.49, followed by 06.29, 07.42, 08.53, 10.05 and 11.17. There were a further seven between midday and midnight: 13.18, 16.18, 17.08, 18.01, 18.33, 19.25 and

The 13.27 Bristol Lawrence Hill–Swindon was often hauled by an engine on a 'running-in turn'. Here it is a Castle Class loco arriving at Chipping Sodbury with the lightly loaded service. Note the wagons in the loading dock and the old van in the neat station yard. WILF STANLEY

21.59. By 1962, this had changed to four between midnight and midday: 06.29, 08.42, 07.53 and 11.04; and three between midday and midnight: 17.32, 18.23 and 19.45. None of these ran via Badminton, as the Direct line local services had been withdrawn as uneconomical before Dr Beeching could get his hands on them.

Brinkworth, Little Somerford, Hullavington, Chipping Sodbury, Coalpit Heath and Winterbourne – all 1903 stations – were closed before the Beeching plan, *The Reshaping of British Railways*, was announced. The plan closed Wootton Bassett station as well. Ironically, Filton, Patchway and Pilning Stations stayed open and are open to this day, although Pilning Low Level (an

anachronism by then for many years) was closed under Beeching. Badminton, of course, lasted a few more years thanks mainly to the Duke of Beaufort; it should have been saved for good. Filton Junction firstly ceased to be a junction so far as passengers were concerned, then was replaced in the 1990s by a new station a little further towards Bristol, that of Filton Abbey Wood.

After Beeching, some slower trains from Bristol ran to Gloucester and beyond via Westerleigh, but there were no local stations for them to call at on the LMR line until BR reopened some in the 1980s.

There were, of course, many parcels trains and in the 1950s the 00.45 ex-Paddington was the Down Papers. The conveyance of newspapers by rail was

Shorn of almost all its canopies, Chipping Sodbury station Up side building stood for many years after closure, used as offices for a road haulage company. Photo taken in 1977. P.D. RENDALL

a long-standing business until the advent of computers, whereby newspaper copy could be sent to local printers and copies printed off in provincial towns and cities for distribution by road; there was then no need for papers to be solely printed in London and distributed by rail.

In the 1990s, a parcels distribution depot was built on the Up side of the line at the east end of Stoke Gifford. Sadly, this did not last long as all parcels traffic was allowed to go on to road transport within a few years.

After the closure of the LMR main line through Mangotsfield in January 1970, the line saw an additional service in the shape of the Bristol–Newcastle service, which conveyed Royal Mail coaches on the rear. This train came on to the line at Stoke Gifford West and turned off at Westerleigh West Junction to regain the line to Gloucester.

Once, in the 1960s, LMSR loco 46220 *Coronation* worked through to Bristol from Crewe with only a couple of through coaches – this is thought to have been during the 1962 snows – and when Patchway signalman Jim Coles saw it approaching he was quite surprised, saying afterwards: 'I wondered what on earth that huge engine was!' It seemed that Coronation Pacifics were not authorized to run via the tunnel, so on its arrival at Bristol, 46220 was sent to SPM whilst the powers that be decided where it would go next. It is thought it returned via the tunnel to Pontypool Rd.

Wartime Working

The main effect of the Great War of 1914–18 was the difficulty in staffing stations and yards as men went to war. This was eased to a certain extent when the Government forbade men working on the railway from joining up, as their work was essential to the war effort. After that war, there was a shortage of labour as a result of so many men not returning, or being unable to work owing to war injuries. World War II saw similar restrictions on railway staff joining up and the threat of air raids brought about the necessity to draw up emergency plans. In the event of enemy action damaging or blocking a

line so as to prevent the passage of trains, diversionary routes had to be worked out to prevent undue delays to trains.

The Great Western drew up plans and published these to station, yard and signalling staff. The plans were contained in a booklet dated June 1940 and entitled 'NOTICE shewing the Arrangements for the Diversion of THROUGH trains to Alternative Routes in cases of EMERGENCY'.[31] In the booklet were instructions to cover all eventualities. The station master at the station nearest the obstruction was responsible for advising (by telegraph) the officials and stations concerned in the diversion. Messages had to be relayed using a code laid out in the booklet. As each area was allocated a code consisting of letters and a number, this had to be included in the message. The South Wales Direct route was coded as 'B.D.7'; the Stoke Gifford to Patchway was coded as 'B.D.8'; and the Patchway to Pilning section was coded as 'B.D.9'. If the line between Wootton Bassett and Stoke Gifford was to be obstructed, trains would be diverted via official routes: South Wales trains would run via Box and Bristol (Stapleton Road), Stroud, Gloucester and Lydney; London and Bristol expresses via Box; Birmingham and Bristol expresses via Mangotsfield LMS; and Swindon and Bristol local trains via the Westerleigh loop, Yate and Mangotsfield.

Should the obstruction be between Yate South and the Westerleigh junctions, or between Westerleigh West and Stoke Gifford, then arrangements were on hand to divert trains over the LMSR lines to Bristol, but only after being authorized by the Divisional Superintendent at Bristol. This officer, in turn, had to contact the Divisional Superintendent of Operations, LMSR, Derby via 'Telephonic Communication' through the LMSR Control Office at Gloucester; if this was damaged or otherwise not available, then 'Post Office telephones' could be used.

In the event of the blockage being on the Stoke Gifford–Patchway lines, the diversionary routes were via Filton West Junction and Filton Junction. Obstructions on the 'B.D.9' Patchway–Pilning section would necessitate diversions as follows: Bristol and Crewe trains via Stoke Gifford, Yate, Standish Junction, Stratford-upon-Avon, Birmingham and Market Drayton; and Bristol and Hereford trains via Stoke Gifford, Yate, Standish Junction, thence Gloucester (GWR) and Ross-on-Wye. South Wales traffic had to run via either Stroud, Gloucester and Lydney or Stoke Gifford, Yate, Berkeley loop, the Severn rail bridge and Lydney, or via Ashley Hill (Bristol), Henbury, Hallen Marsh Junction (Avonmouth) (reverse) and over the single line through Severn Beach to Pilning Low Level and up to Pilning Junction, where the train would once more reverse if it was to pass through the Severn Tunnel. Diversions over the LMSR or Severn and Wye lines had to go through the same procedures for authorization, with trains that would normally use the Severn Tunnel being diverted via Gloucester.

There were, of course, rolling-stock restrictions on the various lines over which GWR main-line traffic would have to pass in such cases. For example, GW 33XX 4–4–0 engines numbered between 3300–3455 could run on the LMSR lines between Yate and Mangotsfield and between the LMSR Kingswood Junction and the Clifton Extension line. 2–6–0 locos of the 26XX, 43XX, 53XX, 63XX and 73XX Classes, plus 4–6–0 29XX (and 49XX and 59XX versions), 40XX and Castle Classes could also use the LMSR routes, as could 2–6–2 tank engines in the 45XX, 55XX, 41XX, 51XX and 61XX Classes.

However, main-line coaching stock measuring 64ft 6in (19.7m) long by 9ft 3in (2.8m) wide was forbidden to use the LMSR route. The instructions do not appear to state what the station master had to do if a blockage occurred that would require diversion

In the event of a wartime blockage of the line between Wootton Bassett and Stoke Gifford, GWR trains could run from Swindon to South Wales via Bath and Filton Bank, regaining the South Wales route at Filton Junction. Here, in peacetime 1964, Castle Class No.5044 Earl of Dunraven climbs past Stapleton Road. WILF STANLEY

of a Badminton line train over LMSR metals and the train contained wide-bodied rolling stock.

Naturally, it was not just the Great Western that would need to divert trains if lines were blocked; the LMSR had reciprocal arrangements to divert its traffic. If the LMSR line was blocked between Gloucester and Yate, trains had to be diverted via Lydney to Severn Tunnel Junction (reverse), then via the Severn Tunnel, Patchway and Filton Junction to Bristol. There were no arrangements for diverted LMSR trains to use the branch from Yate to Westerleigh and thence via Stoke Gifford to Filton and Bristol.

LMS locos of the 4–6–0 5XP (Jubilee) Class, 5P5F (Black Five), 5P4F 2–6–0 (Taper and parallel boiler), 4–4–0 4P Compound, 4–4–0 3P and 2P, 2–8–0 8F, 0–8–0 7F and 3F and 4F 0–6–0 were permitted on the diversionary route.

In 'cases of mishap', the railway companies had arrangements for 'mutual assistance between rail and omnibus companies'. On the Direct line, arrangements were agreed that in the event of a blockage of the line the Bristol Tramways and Carriage Company Ltd. would operate bus services between Wootton Bassett and Filton Junction. Alternatively, buses could be obtained from 'any reputable operator'. In peacetime 1970s and up to the present day, local diversion or blockages usually result in Turners buses being used.

Freight

Apart from the usual coal traffic, the line saw trains of sugar beet, petrol, bananas, oils and petrol, carbon black, fertilizer and ammonia – all from Avonmouth; coal from Washwood Heath yard, Birmingham, to Stoke Gifford and beyond, and empties back; coal from South Wales; milk from West Wales and Somerset to London; Freightliners; and car trains from Dagenham. Later, there were nuclear flasks and roadstone from local quarries. All of these trains ran on an almost daily basis – and all now gone from the railways.

Many freight trains started from Avonmouth Docks and would run to Stoke Gifford and the Direct line via Henbury. If the train was for South or West Wales, it would reverse at Stoke Gifford; if for Bristol and beyond, it would run via Filton Junction (Midland trains normally left Avonmouth via Clifton and ran via the Mangotsfield line). Banana traffic was heavy after World War II and when a ship arrived it was unloaded quickly and the bananas put into railway box vans. These were classed as 'perishable' goods and all banana trains would

Likewise, in the case of enemy action blocking the LMSR lines south of Gloucester, LMS trains could run to Bristol via Lydney and the Severn Tunnel to Patchway, Filton and thence via Filton Bank to Bristol. This is a peacetime working with an ex-LMSR Jubilee Class 4-6-0 heading a freight past Patchway Tunnel box.
WILF STANLEY

A Beyer-Peacock Hymek diesel-hydraulic D7094 blasts through Badminton station with a train of banana vans from Avonmouth, 31 May 1967. *R. CUFF/AUTHOR'S COLLECTION*

run to their destinations as 'specials' when ready. A 'boxer' message (a box-to-box telephone message) would be passed up the line in advance to warn all concerned of the times of the train, which must not be stopped if that could be avoided. For example, the following message was sent on the afternoon of Saturday, 7 May 1966: '17.00 Avonmouth–Carlisle Bananas, Time. Load 35', which meant that the train would leave on time as published in the daily train notice and would convey thirty-five vans. The train duly passed Westerleigh West Junction at 18.00 following a Swansea–Paddington express. In the 1960s, banana trains ran from Avonmouth to Crewe via the Severn Tunnel and to London and beyond via Badminton; motive power was often a D7XXX Hymek.

As mentioned, much other traffic started from Avonmouth and it was a long climb from the docks up to Stoke Gifford and to Badminton. Eric Holwell started on the GWR in 1940 as a loco cleaner. Progressing from there he became a fireman and later in 1956 became a driver on steam and, later, diesel. Eric recalled: 'It was a long drag if you started from Avonmouth with a 28XX Class 2–8–0 on a train of oil tankers. It was slog, slog, slog all the way up to Badminton.' And frequently the train would see the inside of many goods loops on the way as its slow progress resulted in it having to be recessed for more important trains to pass.

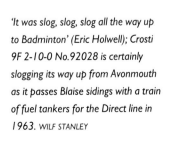

'It was slog, slog, slog all the way up to Badminton' (Eric Holwell); Crosti 9F 2-10-0 No.92028 is certainly slogging its way up from Avonmouth as it passes Blaise sidings with a train of fuel tankers for the Direct line in 1963. *WILF STANLEY*

Winter 1963 and 9F 92244 leaves Avonmouth Royal Edward yard with the Avonmouth–Bromford Bridge fuel tankers. This train ran up the Direct line as far as Westerleigh West, where it took the branch towards Yate. WILF STANLEY

Another train from the Avonmouth line was the Avonmouth to Bromford Bridge Esso fuel tankers. This was hauled by Stanier 2–8–0 locos or BR 9F 2–10–0s in steam days and normally comprised 4-wheel tankers. By the late 1960s, the tankers were bogie 100-ton tankers and a Brush Class 47 was the usual motive power. This train left the Direct line at Westerleigh West to run to Bromford Bridge via Gloucester. Other freight that passed through the line between Westerleigh West and Stoke Gifford West included the Gloucester and Westbury cement.

But it was not just passenger and freight traffic on the line. There were also parcels trains, troop trains, pigeon specials and farm specials. Today, there is the odd train of imported coal from Avonmouth's terminal and occasional Freightliner trains. Passenger workings are HSTs, plus the now-ubiquitous Sprinters. Where ten-coach trains hauled by Class 45/46 or 47 diesels used to rumble over Westerleigh West Junction, heading north, now a four-coach multiple unit trickles by.

The Up and Down local freights that stopped at all stations started from Stoke Gifford and Swindon respectively. After working as required at stations en route, they usually met at Badminton and swapped crews. The 04.05 Acton–Severn Tunnel Junction freight, signalled 1–2–2, was a mixed freight. It was usually headed by a 28XX loco and would make its slow, trundling way from London to South Wales, seeing the inside of most goods loops on its journey (as did most freights during the daytime).

Regular freights included coal trains from South Wales on the Up line and coal empties on the Down. These ran both to and from Bristol and to and from the Badminton line. Most coal was usually for loco purposes. One regular freight was known as 'AD & ED' as it ran from Alexandra Dock, Newport, South Wales, to Bristol East depot. Another regular freight in the 1950s was the 11.10 Milford Haven to London Milk, comprised of six tankers and frequently hauled by a Castle Class, as the loaded milk tanks were heavy.

There were also specials conveying almost anything from farm equipment to (in later years) locomotives for display at depot Open Days. One regular freight train was the Tavistock and Crewe, which always ran up the main to Filton and then via Stoke Gifford, Westerleigh and Yate and on to the LMR line to Gloucester. The regular guard on this working was one Brian Harbour.

It was mentioned in the section on Stoke Gifford yard above that the line saw many scrap steam locomotives during the years 1966–70, all being towed off to scrapyards, usually in South Wales. However,

Castle Class No.7011 Banbury Castle approaches Coalpit Heath with a short Down Milk empties train for Milford Haven.

WILF STANLEY

the procedure was reversed on 10 October 1970, when one engine that had previously been towed through the area on its way for scrapping made the journey again, but in the reverse direction. Ex-Somerset and Dorset (S&D) Railway Class 8 freight engine No.53808, which had languished in Barry scrapyard since withdrawal, had been bought by the Somerset and Dorset Railway Circle and was being towed via Charfield, Westerleigh West and Stoke Gifford to Bristol, from where it would be moved by rail to the old S&D station at Radstock, where the society planned to restore it to working order.

MOVEMENT OF ELECTRIC LOCOMOTIVE E3044 AFTER APPEARING AT BATH ROAD OPEN DAY

Saturday, 18 October 1969, 6M68 19.45 Bristol West Depot to Crewe Conveys Electric locomotive 3044 in the following schedule:

- Bath Rd Diesel Depot   Dep 20.00
- Bristol East   20.06
- Filton Jcn   20.26
- Patchway   20.28
- Pilning Jcn   GL
- Pilning   Arr. 20z40 Dep. 20z50
- Severn Tnl East   21.00
- Severn Tnl West   21.12
- Severn Tnl Jcn   Arr. 21*16 Dep. 21*38
- Hereford   Arr. 23c42 Dep. 23c47

3044, normally in store at Bury, had been to Bristol Bath Road Depot for exhibition at an Open Day (it was there for the 1968 Open Day as well).

GL = Goods Line
z = stops for examination
* = Stops or shunts for other trains to pass
c = Stops only to change crew

Personal Observations

Although I have an interest in steam traction, my personal memories and observations of the Direct line stem from the late 1960s onwards, when I had much experience of the workings of the line, from manual signalling days through my time in the loco maintenance department and later as a panel signalman and supervisor.

My earliest memory is of discovering Stoke Gifford yard and clambering up the bank on the Down side to stand on the shunters' refuge platform to watch the shunters at work. How they managed to remember which 'cuts' to make in a rake of wagons and then shunt them out on to different roads to make different trains always amazed me. Likewise, I loved to sit on the 'hump' at the top of the cutting above Stoke Gifford East box, from where one had a marvellous panorama across the yards and could watch not only the seemingly continuous shunting going on, but also the procession of Up and Down trains speeding through to and from South Wales and Filton. Not quite so regular were the trains to and from the Avonmouth lines.

I remember Chipping Sodbury, too; the station was closed and the footbridge had been removed when I first went there to visit the signal box, but the station buildings were still there. There was an old LMSR carriage in the loading dock. I was told the story of how signalman Chilston (Chilly) Frampton had cycled into the yard one day on his way to the signal box when a shout distracted his attention from where he was looking – he rode his bike straight over the side of the loading dock. Luckily, he was not hurt.

There was a variety of motive power to be seen on the line in those days. It was not just the 'Thousands' and Class 47s on passenger workings, but also Class 45 and 46 diesels on passenger and freight trains diagrammed from Bristol to the Midlands via Westerleigh West Junction; these, of course, increased after January 1970 when the LMR line was closed and all traffic to and from Bristol and the Midlands ran via Filton and Westerleigh West to Yate.

Then there were the D8XX Warships, D63XX locos, D7XXX Hymeks, Class 37s and 'visitors' from other regions that slipped through the net of loco changing at Gloucester. The following are some of my observations during those years:

- 6 March 1970 – D5619, Brush Type 2, ran down from the LMR to Stoke Gifford on a freight. In January 1972, ten of these locos were transferred to Bristol Bath Road shed and were henceforth frequently seen in and around the area, particularly working to and from Avonmouth and Stoke Gifford. For the record these were: 5692, 5695, 5823, 5824, 5826, 5827, 5828, 5837, 5842 and 5843. Often seen working in pairs, they were prone to catching fire.
- 19 April 1970 – Class 25 locos D7516 and 7595 worked a tank train down from Gloucester to Avonmouth.
- Saturday, 13 June 1970 – D6537 and D6543 were both observed from Cattybrook box as they worked Cardiff to Portsmouth trains.
- June 1970 – D8000 and 8118 worked a fertilizer train off the LMR down to Avonmouth.
- August 1970 – D8159 and 8188 double-headed a freight off the LMR and down to Avonmouth. On that same day, other locos seen passing Winterbourne were: Class 47s 1548, 1700, 1701 and 1743; Western 1062; and Class 45 D15.
- On an unrecorded date in 1970 – D6327 failed in section between Stoke Gifford and Westerleigh West whilst coming up from Stoke to Swindon. The load was only two wagons.
- Again on an unrecorded Sunday in 1970 – D6310 and D6320 was spotted at Westerleigh double-heading a coal train down to Stoke Gifford yard.
- D7039 was seen at Westerleigh one Sunday with an Eastern Region viaduct inspection train.

Pulverized fuel ash from Aberthaw power station in South Wales was transported through the Severn Tunnel, through Pilning, Patchway and Filton Junction down to Bristol, and onwards to the offloading site at Puxton, near Weston-super-Mare. These trains consisted of thirty-five

Hymek D7081 at Stoke Gifford East with an Engineers' train. WILF STANLEY

'merry-go-round' hoppers full of the dusty ash, which was known as 'fly ash' (not without good reason – you could see the trains coming from quite a distance by the cloud of ash surrounding them, which allowed time for the signalman to shut his box's windows). The 'Puxton Fly Ash', as it was known to railway staff, was almost always hauled by a pair of Class 37 locos. Some of these pairings were: 6978 and 6921; 6927 and 6954; 6907 and 6968; 6608 and 6604; 6910 and 6941.

As mentioned previously, the sole Class 53 Brush type 4 prototype *Falcon* was frequently seen both in its two-tone green livery as D0280 and in BR blue livery as 1200. I saw it in green passing Westerleigh West box on the Down road on 30 July 1969.

As mentioned above, scrap steam engines were a common sight from 1967 onwards as they were hauled off to scrapyards. Not so common was the occasional train of scrap coaching stock. Whilst the steam locos were forbidden to pass through the Severn Tunnel and thus were always heading east from Stoke Gifford and north from Westerleigh, so the scrap coaches were heading west as they were permitted to pass through the

Pairs of Class 25s, rare in Bristol during 1970, became quite common by 1973 as members of the class were transferred to Bristol, Bath Road shed, to replace scrapped Hymek diesel-hydraulics. 25168 and 25080 shunt at Stoke Gifford Down side in summer 1973. P.D. RENDALL

What a good advertisement for modern British Rail! On the opening day of Bristol Parkway station in 1972, the Up 'South Wales Pullman' ran by minus one carriage and the rear power car. The station's early sparse protection from the elements is obvious. P.D. RENDALL

tunnel. I saw such a train pass Winterbourne on 15 May 1970; in the middle of the formation was a condemned SR electric unit. I was convinced it was a scrap 4-LAV unit and recorded it as such, but stand to be corrected.

And of course, there were the 'Blue Pullmans'. Lovely to see as they sped up or down the line, these looked wonderful in their original Pullman livery of Nanking blue and white, but after being repainted in the modified Pullman colours of blue and grey they became dirty and shabby very quickly. My abiding memory of the grey Pullmans was of seeing the Up evening service from South Wales to London rattle through Bristol Parkway station on the day the station opened: the Pullman was conspicuous by the lack of a rear power car.

CHAPTER 10

Test Trains and Bankers

With its (comparatively) gentle gradients and long, sweeping curves it is hardly surprising that the South Wales Direct line was soon used for testing locomotives and trains. It became a running-in line for locomotives off major repairs at Swindon factory. Locos on running-in turns frequently ran down via Bath and took the Bristol loop at North Somerset Junction. From there, they ran through Stapleton Road and up Filton Bank to Filton Junction and from there to Stoke Gifford. Then it was via Badminton and back to Swindon.

Twenty to twenty-five coaches were a common load for a test run. The steam loco would have a small shed-like structure built on the front buffer beam. This was an indicator shelter and, incredibly, a couple of engineers would crouch inside and take recordings from gauges. When a twenty-plus coach train was not used, a shorter train containing a dynamometer car was employed. The dynamometer could add load to the train, so that a five-coach train including a dynamometer car could be made to simulate the twenty-plus coach load. Some of

The BR Standard 2-6-0 2MT locos were introduced in 1952, with the first ten being allocated to the Western Region. This photo is undated, but 78001 looks brand new rather than off overhaul as it runs through Chipping Sodbury, so the year may be 1952–53. WILF STANLEY

1957 and recently restored 4-4-0 City of Truro is working a Swindon–Bristol stopping train as a running-in turn. It is seen heading into Chipping Sodbury Down platform. WILF STANLEY

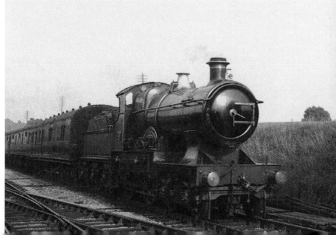

these tests were for the ex-LNER V2 2–6–2 locos. After nationalization, these locomotives had been fitted with blast-pipe modifications and self-cleaning smokebox apparatus and the opportunity was taken of testing them on the WR main lines between Reading and Stoke Gifford. These tests took place during March 1953 and included the ex-GWR dynamometer car No.W7W in the formation.

Leaving Stoke Gifford, a test train would face a long climb for 10 miles (16km) at 1 in 300. Once past the top of the climb at Badminton, the train would have ample opportunity to gain speed. It was this 'racing' stretch through Hullavington and Little Somerford where expresses would often reach 100mph (160km/h). Test trains did not often achieve this sort of speed, but 78–81mph (126–130km/h) was not unusual.

During the 1950s, test trains ran from Swindon to Stoke Gifford, where the locomotive would be signalled into the Down loop and another, waiting loco would back on and couple to the rear end. When the assisting loco was coupled up and the road set, the test train would set off slowly to Filton Junction. Here it would be signalled to Filton West and with the assisting loco now leading, would reverse to Filton West Junction. The test train would run on to the Down Avonmouth line and stand clear of the crossover. The junction would be reversed and the train would be signalled back to Stoke Gifford West, with the assisting loco once again at the rear. Back at Stoke Gifford and in the Up loop or reception line, the test train would come to a stand and the assisting engine would be uncoupled. The test train would then be ready to run back to Swindon. These tests were often made for the purpose of testing modified ex-GWR locos, such as the King Class when they had been fitted with double chimneys.

Later, new BR steam locos were tested; most BR Standard types were seen, including the unique Class 8P Pacific *Duke of Gloucester*. As steam was now being replaced by new forms of traction under the BR Modernisation Plan, so the new gas-turbine and diesel-hydraulic locos were tested along the South Wales Direct route.

Diesel Tests

The year 1957 was a busy year as regards locomotive tests on the South Wales Direct line. April was a particularly busy month, with diesel tests running both ways daily between Swindon and Stoke Gifford, or Dr Day's Sidings, Bristol. A 10.50 test would run from Swindon, arriving Stoke Gifford at 11.30 and returning to Swindon at 12.30. Sometimes this would be followed later by a further test that passed (or left) Stoke Gifford at 13.30, having run down the Bath line and then via Filton Bank.

The first diesel Warship Class loco, D600 Active, was tested on the Direct line. It is seen here passing through Coalpit Heath on its way back to Swindon Works. *WILF STANLEY*

It was not just diesels either; even the gas turbines 18000 and 18001 got in on the act, one being noted passing Winterbourne with a test special on the Up line at 13.08 on Thursday, 4 April 1957. Diesel multiple-units based at the new depot at Bristol St Philip's Marsh were also tested on the line.

During the week commencing 3 June 1957, a series of diesel test runs took place daily on the South Wales Direct line. A test train would run down from Swindon to Bristol Dr Day's Sidings, where the train would reverse and run back to Swindon, again via Badminton. Although the week started well, in the way of things with new technology, the tests were not always successful. The test train followed the 11.45 ex-Bristol Temple Meads. 'Is Line Clear?' for the test train was asked to Chipping Sodbury box by Wapley Common at 12.00, passed Wapley at 12.06 and cleared Badminton at 12.25, one minute slower than the express. No test ran on the Tuesday and on Wednesday, whilst the King-hauled 11.45 ran well and cleared Badminton at 12.17, the test was reported 'not off Stapleton Road' at 12.10. 'Is Line Clear?' was eventually asked for the test at 12.37. The test passed Sodbury at 12.42 and it cleared Badminton at 12.57 – fifteen minutes under clear signals. Clearly, all was not well with the test that day.

On Thursday, 6 June 1957 all was not well again. Chipping Sodbury signal box Train Register recorded 'Boxer [a box-to-box telephone message]: 8.0 a.m Neyland preceding 12.5 Dr Day's Diesel Test'. The Neyland passenger passed Chipping Sodbury at 13.13 and Wapley Common immediately asked 'Is Line Clear?' for the diesel test, which was described as '4 bells' – an express passenger train. Three minutes later, Wapley sent 'Train Entering Section' to Sodbury. A further three minutes later, the test train passed Sodbury at 13.19 and cleared Badminton at 13.24. The slow timings reflect the fact that the diesel test was unable to be given clear signals until the Neyland service had passed Badminton at 13.19, so rather than getting a clear run as desired, on this occasion the test had Distant checks all the way up the line.

No diesel test ran on the Friday. The following week, tests ran only on Wednesday and Thursday, again in the usual pattern of following the 11.45 ex-Bristol.

Judging by the Train Registers, the 1957 tests were, on the whole, fairly consistent and reliable. However, by 1961 things were a little different; rather than a box-to-box message being sent if the tests were *not* running, it became the norm for a message to be sent if they *were* running, as the following extracts from the Train Register at Winterbourne signal box demonstrate:

- Monday, 27 November 1961: 'Boxer: Cape [code for cancel] 10.35 Swindon test. 2.0pm will run.'
- Tuesday, 28 November 1961: No tests ran.
- Wednesday, 29 November 1961: 'Boxer: 10.35 diesel test will run. Rec'd & sent 10.43.'
- Thursday, 30 November 1961: 'Boxer: Both diesel tests will run. Rec'd and sent 09.40.'
- Friday, 1 December 1961: 'Boxer: 10.35 & 2.0pm tests will run.'

By February 1962, things had deteriorated to the point where one or both test runs were cancelled every day.

After the introduction of the 'Blue Pullman' diesel units, they were tested on the South Wales line. The Pullmans had only been in service for a couple of years when they were subjected to 'bogie test runs' along the Direct line, the rough riding of the bogies being a problem almost from the time the trains first entered service.

Testing of diesel-hydraulics continued through the 1960s, with the signal boxes being advised whether the train would run or not. Bearing in mind that the test train normally required a clear run down the line, there were still some dubious 'margin' workings to contend with. For example, on Tuesday, 19 April 1966, a message was passed down the line advising that the 10.35 test train would run. It did, following a slow freight train all the way! A fully fitted freight followed the test train. With loops available at Wootton Bassett, Little

The 'Blue Pullman' sets were introduced to the Western Region in 1960. Soon the sets underwent extensive testing, as they swiftly got a reputation for poor riding. One set is seen here, on the Up road at Coalpit Heath in 1964; it was booked to run 'empty stock' for 'bogie testing'.
WILF STANLEY

Somerford, Hullavington, Badminton and Chipping Sodbury, one would have thought that the slower freight could have been held back at one of those locations.

However, examination of the train moves at that time of the day shows that five minutes behind the fully fitted freight was the 10.00 Paddington–Swansea express. Behind that was another slow freight. Meanwhile, an out-of-gauge load from Gloucester to Stoke Gifford was heading south through Charfield, with another slow freight behind that. The out-of-gauge load passed Winterbourne at 12.17 and the Down 'South Wales Pullman' formed by a 'Blue Pullman' set was set to pass Westerleigh

eight minutes behind it and the second freight off the Gloucester line followed the Pullman. From this, it can be seen that control had a difficult job arranging a path for the test trains through all the daily traffic on the line.

After the line was upgraded in 1975 to allow trains to travel at 125mph (200km/h), the new HSTs were allocated to the new depot at Bristol St Philip's Marsh. During 1976 and 1977, these trains (including the prototype) were tested extensively on the South Wales Direct line.

Crew and maintenance training runs also took place, many at night. The latter were usually braking tests, whereby the train would run at the

The prototype HST was also tested on the 125 section of the Direct line between Wootton Bassett and Westerleigh Junction in 1976. Here, the prototype is seen standing at the (then) new depot at Bristol St Philip's Marsh in February 1977. P.D. RENDALL

In summer of 1978, HST set 253015 stands in Swindon station after a test run up the Direct line to trace a high-speed engine fault. Maintenance staff on the test run are (L–R) Electrician Steve Jones; Senior Technical Officer Andrew Sheppard; and Mechanical Fitter Chris Griffiths. P.D. RENDALL

line speed of 125mph and then the emergency brake would be activated. The group being trained rode in the rear cab. I travelled on several of these runs. The driver would be contacted by telephone before the brake test and once advised that the emergency brake was to be tested, the button was pushed. The deceleration was rapid as the brakes bit, but it would take over 1½ miles (2.4km) to stop a High Speed Train from 125mph.

It was not just staff training runs that took place. Often a fault would develop that could not be replicated on shed. In such circumstances, if it was deemed necessary, then a path for a test run would be negotiated with Control. Once clearance was given, the test (normally again at night, as fewer trains used the line at night) would creep off the depot and run via the Bristol Loop from North Somerset Junction to Dr Day's and up Filton Bank. From there, it would run via Bristol Parkway and Badminton to Swindon.

It was, perhaps, an echo of the days of steam, but instead of two engineers crouching in an indicator shelter on the front of a Castle or King, we had it a little easier, riding at 125mph sitting in the engine room on top of the Paxman diesel engine taking readings from a gauge.

28 September 1969 to 2 October 1969, Iron Ore Test Train From Llanwern steelworks to Swindon comprises:

- Locomotive
- Inspection coach
- Spacer wagon (platefit)
- 1 Test wagon
- Spacer wagon (platefit)
- 1 Test wagon
- Spacer wagon (platefit)
- Fully fitted brake van

Bankers

Owing to the steep incline into and out of the Severn Tunnel and the eastward climb from the bottom of the tunnel to Stoke Gifford and Badminton, assisting engines were required on most freight trains, plus some passenger trains from the early days of the line. Between the wars and to the end of steam on the BR Western Region, a couple of bank engines were kept at Pilning to assist trains.

Trains from South Wales that required assistance through the Severn Tunnel would stop at Severn Tunnel Junction, where the banking engine

The ubiquitous GWR 2-6-2 Prarie tank was used almost from its introduction into service in 1931. This photo, therefore, must date from the late 1930s judging by the lorry on Station Road. The tank is attached to the front of what looks like a boat train and the banker will work through to Badminton. Patchway Tunnel box is in the background. AUTHOR'S COLLECTION

would be attached to the front of the train. All trains requiring a banker had one attached to the front; no trains were permitted to be assisted through the tunnel by an engine in the rear. In GWR days, the train engine would have to be detached and the banker, or 'pilot', engine attached to the train and the train engine then coupled ahead of the banker. This practice was later discontinued. Trains were thus double-headed from Severn Tunnel Junction through the tunnel to Pilning Junction, where the train was put in the Up loop to allow the assisting loco to be uncoupled, crossed over and sent back to Severn Tunnel Junction when a gap in the traffic allowed.

One of the banking engines kept at Pilning would then be signalled into the loop and on to the rear of the train and from there would bank the train up to Patchway. The bankers were loose-coupled, which enabled them to drop off at Patchway station, having seen the train on its way on the level section. Ex-GWR Prairie tank No.4115 was one of the regular engines on the Pilning–Patchway banking duty. Some passenger trains were double-headed to Badminton, where the assisting engine

BR 'transition days' – a freight from South Wales draws to a stand in Pilning Up goods loop with the tunnel pilot on the front. This engine will cut off and return to Severn Tunnel Junction. One of the Pilning bankers will buffer up to the rear of the train and then it will be all systems go up to Patchway. The regulations at the time stated that steam locos should be coupled behind diesels to prevent cinders and so on finding their way into the diesel air intakes, but this tended to get lost in the 'normal way of things'.

The Western appears to have only ten parcels vans behind it, so perhaps It is running on one engine only, requiring 4115 to have a trip up to Badminton. Winterbourne, 1962.
WILF STANLEY

was detached. In such cases, the assisting loco was attached to the front of the train.

Having come to a stand at Patchway, the banker was then crossed over and returned 'light engine' to Pilning. It was always a problem getting bankers back from Patchway to Pilning, such was the density of traffic. Frequently, a signalman had to 'take a chance' and slip a banker (or several coupled together) in between two other trains and hope the light engine would 'get a move on' and cause minimum delay to following services. This

was where knowing the regular drivers came in handy, as they could be relied upon; an unfamiliar driver might take the opportunity to trickle down the line back to Pilning and thus cause delays. Signalmen like Stan Horn had spent most of their working life on the 'bottom end' of the Direct line and knew their drivers; as a result, delays were few. Two of the regular banker drivers were Bob Gale and Nathaniel Hart. Bob was a model engineer in his spare time and built live steam model locos.

The end of the climb is in sight! The banker is pushing for all it is worth to shove the train over the top of the climb at Patchway Tunnel box.
WILF STANLEY

A work-stained 4137 rests outside Patchway Station signal box whilst it waits for a gap in the traffic to run back to Pilning in 1962.
WILF STANLEY

It was permissible to attach a banker to a Down passenger train at Patchway in order to work it back to Pilning, but this was a rare occurrence. If it was anything but a 2–6–2 tank engine, then it must run chimney-first, the latter running bunker-first.

Some trains for Badminton or the Gloucester lines would be booked to run to Stoke Gifford yard to detach a banker. There were strict instructions for banking – banking engines were usually 2–6–2 Prairie tanks of 41XX and 51XX Class, although

Banking was still required in the 1980s, as the Didcot 'merry-go-round' coal trains were heavily loaded. Here, a Class 56 diesel pilots 47901 up over the summit at Patchway. The steepness of the climb can be appreciated in this shot. T.R. RENDALL

The 'merry-go-round' coal would run into the Up loop at Bristol Parkway and detach the pilot. Once the Class 56 had run clear into the spur, the train was able to make its way to Didcot unassisted. *P.D. RENDALL*

4–4–0, 4–6–0 and 2–6–0 tender engines that had coupled wheels of 5ft 8in diameter or above were allowed to assist passenger trains through the tunnel. Tender engines assisting passenger trains through the tunnel were only allowed to run chimney-first. In the case of a fish or perishables train that was fitted with vacuum brakes throughout, it was permissible to be assisted by a loco on the front from Severn Tunnel Junction to Patchway, where the train would have to stop to detach the banking engine.

In the 1980s, a 'merry-go-round' coal working from South Wales to Didcot power station would be double-headed by two diesels up to Stoke Gifford, where it would run into the Up loop and the leading loco would be uncoupled and run up into the spur. Once the signalman at Bristol had been advised that the banker was 'in clear', he would reset the points, clear the signals and the coal train could continue on its way to Didcot. Once the coal train was clear of the loop, the banking loco would be signalled back down the Up loop to the west end, where it would be sent back to South Wales when there was a gap in the traffic. The (then) unique Class 47, 47901, was a frequent performer on this working, which also regularly saw a Class 56 as the train engine.

Banking also happened between Hallen Marsh and Stoke Gifford. It took place regularly in steam days. Even in diesel days, some trains were assisted, although it was not necessarily a booked working; there was an occasion when I had a potash train for York at Hallen Marsh and also had a Class 45 diesel that was urgently required at Stoke Gifford. To wait until the York train had cleared the single line to Stoke Gifford before sending the light engine forwards would mean a delay of around twenty minutes. The obvious option was to attach the engine to the York train, but it could not go on the front as that would mean further delays detaching it at Stoke Gifford; it could go on the back, though ... I hastily scanned the signal box special instructions and the *Appendix to the Rule Book* to make certain that the plan was possible; there was nothing that said banking was no longer allowed. So the Class 45 was coupled to the rear of the York and the whole ensemble sent to Stoke Gifford. Having advised Bristol Panel Box of the move, they signalled the train into the Up loop at Stoke Gifford, where it paused briefly to detach the 'banker' and then went on its way.

Engineering Work and Single-Line Working

In order for the trains to run safely and at speed, regular maintenance of the track was needed. So that services were not disrupted too much, much of this work, carried out by the Civil Engineering Department, was done at night and at weekends, when the Engineers would take possession of sections of line. If it was necessary to work on both lines, the possession was 'absolute' over those lines and trains would be diverted or buses put on to replace the trains.

Should the work be on one line only, then 'single-line working' over one set of rails was brought in.

When the stations were open, single-line working involved the station masters at each end of the section of line involved. Each had to countersign the Single Line form carried by the pilotman and was effectively in overall charge of operations. Thus, single-line working between Chipping Sodbury and Badminton would involve both of those station masters, as well as a pilotman

---

Extract from BR Weekly Operating Notice December 1960

At or between	Lines affected	Remarks
45. WOOTTON BASSETT AND SEVERN TUNNEL JCT.		
SUNDAY, 18th DECEMBER		
Between Chipping Sodbury and Badminton.	Up. BLOCKED. Down.	6.0 a.m. to 5.0 p.m. Track renewal. 101¾ and 101 m.p. Trains to travel over the Down Line under Single Line Working arrangements. Wapley Common, Chipping Sodbury and Hullavington Signal Boxes open.

Extract from BR Weekly Operating Notice *for the week commencing 18 December 1960, showing that Single Line Working would be in operation over the Down line between Badminton and Chipping Sodbury.* AUTHOR'S COLLECTION

Viewed from Winterbourne signal box one Sunday in 1965. The permanent way gang is hard at work on the Down line and Single Line Working is in force over the Up line. A Stanier 2-8-0 trundles through 'wrong line', with a goods train 'off the Midland' at Westerleigh West. WILF STANLEY

(usually a senior relief signalman) and handsignalmen to clamp points and stand at signals with flags and detonators. The former jobs were often done by porters and the latter by signalmen.

Once the stations had closed, there were no station masters to take charge and the job was then carried out by district signalling inspectors, their assistants or senior relief signalmen. Later still, when panel signal boxes came in, the situation changed again; at first, a senior man was appointed to take charge and designated 'signalman's agent'. This was later done away with and the panel signalman became in charge. This was a sensible move, as only the panel man could see the overall picture. It was not unusual to have several sets of single-line working happening on one section of a panel; for example, between Chipping Sodbury and Westerleigh Junction (as it was renamed after the manual box closed), and between Westerleigh and Stoke Gifford East and between Patchway and Pilning. As this was all on the one section of Bristol Panel, the 'D-Position' or 'Stoke Panel', one signalman had overall control of all this work.

Being handsignalman could be a 'sod of a job'; standing at a signal for long periods of time if the weather was wet or cold was not fun. If the train service was sparse, the handsignalman could retire to the signal box for warmth, tea and company until required to trudge out to his signal. If the service was busy, he would stay at the signal for longer periods. The pilotman had his own advantages, being able to stay in the box until needed to travel on the footplate or 'send this one through', if more than one train travelling in the same direction needed to pass through the section before one could travel in the

opposite direction. If one was an enthusiast, there was the chance to travel on the footplate of different locomotives.

As a relief signalman, Wilf Stanley was often the pilotman between Chipping Sodbury and Westerleigh West during single-line working and recalled one memorable occasion in the 1950s when *City of Truro* was the train engine on a Down passenger. He rode on the footplate. Another loco Wilf rode on when pilotman was Britannia No.70026 *Polar Star*. Wilf knew that this was the engine which had been involved in a disaster at Milton, near Didcot, a few years before when the engine and its train had become derailed and crashed down an embankment into a field, with several fatalities. The driver was not aware of this until Wilf told him.

The following is a list of the trains piloted by Wilf Stanley during one twelve-hour shift (18.00–06.00) on Friday/Saturday, 18 November 1960, when he was pilotman between Chipping Sodbury and Westerleigh East over the Up line: 15.55 ex-Paddington (Down) and 17.45 ex-Bristol (Up); 19.15 ex-Swindon (Down) and 16.31 ex-Swansea (Up); 17.55 ex-Paddington (Down) and 14.30 ex-Neyland (Up); 18.55 ex-Paddington (Down) and

Britannia Class 70025 Western Star on a Paddington–Cardiff express, seen here passing Pilning. WILF STANLEY

15.50 ex-Whitland (Milk) (Up), followed by 19.40 ex-Carmarthen (Up); 00.45 ex-Paddington (Down) and 15.35 ex-Fishguard (Up); 16.13 ex-Grimsby (Down) and 17.20 ex-Milford Haven (Up), after which the engineer handed back the Down line for normal traffic and single-line working was withdrawn.

The locomotives that shift included: Britannia No.70026 *Polar Star* as mentioned above; Britannia No.70024 *Vulcan*; 9F 92220 *Evening Star*; Castle Class Nos 5048 *Earl of Devon*, 5006 *Tregenna Castle* and 5013 *Abergavenny Castle*; King Class No.6004 *King George 111*. In addition, there were various members of the Hall and County Classes, plus a BR Standard Class 5. All very Western Region/GWR-oriented.

Personal Experience as Pilotman

Although I was pilotman over the Direct line on several occasions during my time as a panel relief signalman in the 1980s, the job was never as demanding as it had been in the 1950s and 1960s. In 1987, I was pilotman one night between Westerleigh Junction and Stoke Gifford East. Single-line working was over the Up line, whilst rail grinding was in progress on the Down line. The locos I rode on were Class 46 and 47 and there were only about six trains all night, most having been diverted away from the work. The one 'consolation' was seeing the Speno rail grinder at work. From about a mile or more away, the showers of 'Catherine wheel' sparks from its grinders could be plainly seen in the darkness.

On the occasion of this photo, Single Line Working was in operation between Wapley Common and Chipping Sodbury signal boxes. The Up parcels train, double-headed by what appears to be a Castle and a Hall, has travelled up from Wapley Common over the Down line and is now crossing to the Up line. WILF STANLEY

The Speno rail grinder train, seen here at Bristol St Philip's Marsh sidings in February 1977. P.D. RENDALL

SINGLE-LINE WORKING SNAPSHOT – 18 JANUARY 1970

The Up branch line between Westerleigh West Up Branch Starting signal and Yate South Junction was under Engineering Department possession. single-line working was in force over the Down branch line. Hymek D7016, with headcode Z16, arrived at Westerleigh West. Marshalled behind the diesel were a crane, track-relaying gantries and a Drewery shunter, PWM 654. Another, unidentified Hymek was at the rear. The train pulled forwards and stopped on the Up main just beyond the box. A short while afterwards, an Up passenger train approached from the direction of Winterbourne and stopped at the Up Main Home and Up Main to Branch Home bracket signal.

A handsignalman appeared and strode up to the cab of the loco, which was D28. He instructed the driver to 'pass the signal at Danger' and to proceed on to the branch until the rear of his train was clear of the junction. The driver obeyed with a short blast on the loco horn.

Once the train was clear of the junction points, the signalman reversed the main-line crossover and 'clips' (large clamps) were fixed to the points and padlocked. This was a safeguard to prevent points being inadvertently moved under a train. A wave from the box indicated to the handsignalman that the train could back on to the Down main line. When the passenger stood clear of the crossover again, the clips were removed and the

crossover points were again reversed and clipped up again. The pilotman, wearing a red armband on his sleeve with the word 'PILOTMAN' embroidered on it, left the signal box and clambered into the loco cab.

The GWR issue Pilotman's armband worn during Single Line Working. P.D. RENDALL

A blast on the horn again and the train moved off slowly, 'wrong line' to Yate, where it would regain the right line again.

Other locos noted during this occupation by the engineer were D1731 and Hymeks D7060 and D7043, the latter arriving with a Permanent Way Department crane and several wagons of ballast.

Posing at Badminton during Single Line Working with Western D1014 *Western Leviathan* in 1962 are: (L–R) signalman Jack Griffiths (wearing Pilotman armband); the permanent way ganger and signalman Eddie Mann. WILF STANLEY

Mechanized Maintenance

By the time the Direct line had been uprated for 125mph (200km/h) trains, the majority of the work of lifting, packing of ballast and aligning the track was done by tamping machines. 'Tampers', as they were known, were not an innovation by then, having been around for years. Starting out as little more than a motorized trolley with packing 'blades', by the late 1970s the machines, now on bogies and carrying a lot of hydraulically operated machinery, were made by Plasser & Theurer. Tampers did away with the old-fashioned gang of men who packed ballast and gravel under sleepers. The long lengths of continuously welded rail with concrete sleepers and larger ballast needed the strength of a machine. By the 1980s, tampers had computers on board and were very sophisticated machines.

The South Wales Direct line was similar to all other lines in as much as it was now maintained under programmes of 'Mechanized Maintenance'. However, owing to the high speed of the line, the work of tamping, lining and keeping the super-elevation or cant that enabled the HST to travel at high speeds was carried out more often.

As, in those days, most engineering work was carried out over Saturday nights and into Sundays, the Civil Engineer would take complete occupation

B.R. 87215

Form referred to in Rules 175 clause (c), 183, clauses (f) and (g), 184 and 203)

BRITISH RAILWAYS

Western REGION.

(A supply of these Forms must be kept in each signal box.)

WRONG LINE ORDER FORM D.
SIGNALMAN TO DRIVER.

To Driver of Engine No. *D7005* ......working

Material .... train.

I authorise you to travel with your train on

the* *Down Main* line in the wrong direction to this signal box.

Catch points, spring or unworked trailing points exist

at...

Signed *J.E.Bush* Signalman.

at *Westerleigh West* signal box.

Date *10th Feb* 19.*66* Time issued *0900* m.

† Countersigned...

Signalman.

at...signal box.

* *Insert name of line, for example, Up or Down Main, Fast, Slow or Goods.*
† *If necessary.*

A Wrong Line Order form issued at Westerleigh West box on 10 February 1966, authorizing the driver of Hymek D7005, working an Engineers' train, to work 'wrong direction' back to the signal box on the Up main. AUTHOR'S COLLECTION

Squadron tamping: a line of four Plassermatic tamping machines is assembled in the Up reception siding at Stoke Gifford in September 1977. Sandwiched in the middle of the row is a blast-regulating machine. P.D. RENDALL

of the lines required, for example between Chipping Sodbury and Hullavington. During the preceding Friday, tamping machines would assemble at Stoke Gifford Up reception siding. Once the line was handed over to the engineering department, usually at around 22.30, the machines, now coupled together, would run under normal signalling to Westerleigh Junction, where they would be stopped at a red signal. On phoning the panel box, the driver would be advised to 'pass the signal at Danger and proceed to the protection at so-and-so'.

The tampers would proceed cautiously to the red lights and detonators placed on the line at the point where the Engineer's occupation began. Here, the protection would be lifted long enough for the machines to pass and they would be instructed by a handsignalman to proceed to the site of work. Once at the required site, they would uncouple and work separately. This was known as 'squadron tamping'.

On completion of their work, the machines would slowly make their way back to each other and recouple, then return to the protection, where they would be let back out on to the lines 'outside' the occupation, usually having been crossed over to the 'right line' at some convenient crossover within the occupation.

The Direct line is under Civil Engineering possession between Stoke Gifford East and Westerleigh Junction: a tamper is at work on the newly ballasted section at Winterbourne. Behind it can be seen the Automatic Ballast Cleaner and a line of ballast wagons. P.D. RENDALL

Problems – Personal Experience

Nine times out of ten all of the above would pass without incident, but occasionally a tamper would break down and have to be 'rescued' by another machine, thus meaning that the night's work was not completed and perhaps an emergency speed restriction would be in force until the following weekend, when another occupation would take place to finish the job.

One incident I recall nearly ended in trouble. I was working the Bristol Panel 'D' position one Saturday night. The Direct line was under occupation between Chipping Sodbury and Hullavington and squadron tamping was under way. A fleet of tampers was working somewhere in the occupied section. Late in the night I was advised by the Person in Charge of the Possession (PIP) that the tampers were coupled back together and would run back down the Up line to the protection, which was placed on the Badminton side of Chipping Sodbury loop.

I watched the track-circuit indications on the panel light up red as the machines trundled down the line. Then, to my horror, the indications between the spot where the protection was supposed to be and the loop also lit up; the machines were passing beyond the point at which they should have stopped and the handsignalman asked permission to let them out of the occupation. The indications behind the tampers went out, showing me that they were certainly still on the move. The indications in the loop and on the main line now lit up, a 'spread', and, to all intents and purposes, the tampers had become derailed at the entrance to the loop.

I called the supervisor over and we watched for a moment or two – the indications stayed lit. We now feared the worst. I picked up the phone and called the Permanent Way Office at Sodbury to get the protection man to go out and have a look, then call back to let me know what had happened. It did not take long for him to report that the tampers were safe in the loop and ready to move off back to Bristol's Marsh Junction, where they were based.

What had happened was this – the protection man, having been told by the PIP that the machines were on their way back to Sodbury, had walked out and picked up the detonators and red lights. The tampers ran down the line and into the loop without a problem. The track circuit 'spread' was caused because the move had passed the signal protecting the loop at Danger.

So all was well, but the protection man was given a piece of the supervisor's mind for failing to obey the rule book; he ought to have left the protection in place until the machines arrived, lifted it for them to pass and replaced it until the time that he was told by the PIP that the occupation was ended. There's always one!

CHAPTER 12

Accidents and Other Incidents

All railways are subject to accidents and other incidents. There was a time when only the major accidents were reported in the press, but it would seem that the twenty-first-century thirst for sensationalism sees almost anything getting large headlines. The GWR and its successor BR Western Region enjoyed the safest working record of all lines in the UK. However, the day-to-day running of a railway was not without incidents and the following happened one evening at Coalpit Heath.

Incident at Coalpit Heath

One fine, clear evening the Coalpit Heath signalman had a phone call from Stoke Gifford East box (Winterbourne box was switched out) to say that a freight train had passed the Stoke Gifford East Up Starting signal at Danger and was steaming up the line towards Coalpit Heath. There was already a train in the section and all signals were off. What could he do? Freight trains were quite slow in those days, so the Coalpit Heath signalman nervously waited for the legitimate freight to pass, sent 'Train Entering Section' to Westerleigh West and threw all his signals to Danger behind the train. Looking down the line he could see the approaching headlights of the 'runaway' freight approaching through the dusk. Thankfully, the 'runaway' was obviously slowing down, having seen the Coalpit Heath Up

Distant go back to Caution and the Home signal at Danger.

The train, obviously being under control and therefore just a 'simple' case of mistakenly passing a signal at Danger, the Stoke East and Coalpit signalmen decided to 'square' the incident to avoid getting the train crew into trouble. The Coalpit Heath man pulled off the Home signal slowly and the train crept into the station, the crew looking quizzically at the signal box, where the signalman found every excuse not to look out of the window. As soon as Westerleigh West gave 'Train Out of Section' for the previous freight, Coalpit Heath immediately asked 'Is Line Clear?' for the second freight, which was put 'on line' straight after. The starter and advanced starter were swiftly pulled off and the loco's exhaust sharpened as it proceeded on its (now legitimate) way. Stoke East and Coalpit Heath got on the phone to each other and agreed the train times for their Train Registers. Nobody ever found out what had happened.

Derailment at Chipping Sodbury

Another, much more serious, incident took place at Chipping Sodbury in diesel days, on the night of Tuesday, 20 September 1966. The sun was setting over the capital city as the 20.15 Kensington–Whitland Milk Train pulled slowly out of the sidings,

The softly lit interior of Chipping Sodbury signal box. WILF STANLEY

en route for West Wales. Coupled behind the diesel-hydraulic locomotive were forty-six discharged milk tankers with two parcels coaches marshalled as the rear vehicles. One of these coaches acted as the guard's van. The 6-wheeled milk tankers were not very steady runners at high speeds, so the train was limited to the maximum permitted speed of these vehicles – 50mph (80km/h).

Because of its comparatively slow speed, the train was often put on to slow lines and into goods loops to enable faster services to pass. Thus it was already running a little behind time as it headed west. By the time it arrived at Swindon, where it was booked to stop and change train crew, the Kensington–Whitland was well behind time.

At the Swindon stop, the London driver was replaced by a Swindon man, L.A. Lewis, and the guard by a Cardiff guard, W. Hale. Driver Lewis and Guard Hale would work the train as far as Cardiff, where they would be relieved by a Swansea crew, who would take the train on the remainder of its journey.[32]

It was getting close to 23.00 by the time the train was ready to leave. Driver Lewis opened the power handle steadily and was able to get the load under way with little difficulty. The train was booked to take one hour and fifty minutes to reach Cardiff. Lewis was sure he could recoup some of the lost time before then. Leaving Swindon, home

of the GWR, the old-fashioned 'semaphore" signals nodded Clear all down the line to Wootton Bassett Junction, where the train slowed to take the right-hand line for South Wales. There were still signal boxes every few miles in those days. As there was now little traffic at that time of night for the milk tankers to get in the way of, the signals were Clear right down the line from Wootton Bassett, through Badminton and Chipping Sodbury to Stoke Gifford.

In the softly lit interior of Chipping Sodbury signal box, relief signalman Harry Maidment, who was working the 22.00–06.00 night turn of duty, had 'accepted' the Whitland tanks from Badminton box and 'offered' it forwards to Westerleigh West signal box. Westerleigh 'accepted' the train and Harry Maidment was able to pull over his levers; the signals moved to Clear.

Next, Harry turned to his Train Register – the 'log' that every signal box kept for the purpose of recording all times that bell codes were received and sent, or when any other incident occurred – and he wrote in the times that he had been 'offered' the train and the times he had sent the bell code forwards. When, shortly afterwards, Badminton box sent the 'Train Entering Section' signal to him, Harry duly recorded that as well.

After passing Badminton, the line starts to descend steeply to the 4,444yd (4,064m)-long Chipping Sodbury Tunnel. In his van at the rear of the train, Guard Hale took out his journey log and wrote in the time that the train passed Badminton. His times showed that they had recovered five minutes of the lost time in the 16 miles (26km) from Wootton Bassett.

The train rattled through the dank tunnel and emerged into the night air, passing a Swindon-bound freight train on the opposite line as it did so. In Chipping Sodbury signal box, Harry Maidment heard the distant sound of the train and stood up. He leaned on his levers and watched the Distant lights of the locomotive grow nearer. Harry started to replace his signals to Danger as the train passed them. It was then that he noticed what appeared to be sparks flying from the wheels of the train. Suspecting an overheated axle box, Harry peered

Tuesday, 20 September 1966 – the wreckage of the Milk Train litters Chipping Sodbury station. View looking towards Westerleigh. Cutting from the Bristol Evening Post. BRISTOL UNITED PRESS

intently into the night, hoping to identify which vehicle was at fault so that he could advise his colleague in the next box along the line to 'stop and examine' the train.

Then, as the locomotive of the tank train passed the signal box, all hell broke loose. The ground shook violently, followed by a terrible crashing and smashing as the milk tankers became derailed. Wagons flew up in the air, hit the disused platforms and turned over amidst a cacophony of sound that Harry Maidment had not heard since the war. He ducked instinctively as something smashed through the box window, showering the levers with glass and striking him a glancing blow on the chin.

In less than a minute it was all over. All was suddenly quiet. Harry Maidment shook himself and reached out to his bells to send the 'Obstruction – Danger!' signal to Badminton and Westerleigh West boxes, thus preventing any other trains from approaching. Then he went to the box window to survey the scene. There were wagons scattered everywhere, blocking the four lines through the station and heaped up between the platforms. In all, fifteen of the empty milk tankers and the two bogie vans had jumped the rails. Rails had been bent and ripped up and sleepers smashed and dislodged. The two parcels vans were derailed, but stood upright in the ballast between the main line and the loop line. All four lines were blocked. Looking down the line, Harry could see no sign of the locomotive and wondered what had happened to it.

He got on the telephone and told the Control Office in Bristol of the accident. Soon, three ambulances rushed into the station yard, expecting casualties. There was only one; Guard Hale had been thrown roughly around in his van and was bruised and shaken. Signalman Maidment suffered only a scratch; he was a lucky man – the object which had struck him was later found at the rear of

Looking down on the station showing the tankers scattered between the platforms. Cutting from the Bristol Evening Post. *BRISTOL UNITED PRESS*

the signal box and was identified as a piece of metal from one of the tankers.

The locomotive driver was also unhurt. The loco had not been derailed in the darkness, as was feared. When the tanks had become derailed and had broken away, the vacuum brake pipe had 'strangled' itself, and the brake, instead of coming on hard, had instead leaked on, with the loco and twenty-nine tanks taking nearly ¾ mile (1,200m) to stop.

Soon, breakdown cranes were on their way to Chipping Sodbury from Swindon and Bristol and all trains that would normally use the blocked route were diverted via Chippenham and Box to Stoke Gifford. The re-railing crews worked all night and into the next day and by late afternoon, sixteen hours after the derailment, one line was able to be reopened. It was not until two days after the accident that all the lines through Chipping Sodbury were able to be reopened to normal traffic.

There was, naturally, an Inquiry. At the Inquiry, Driver Lewis stated that he had been travelling at about 48mph (77km/h) when the derailment occurred – within the maximum permitted speed of that type of train. However, the investigating officer, Colonel J.R.H. Robertson, disputed the driver's evidence. He said that examination of the signal box Train Registers had revealed that Lewis had been travelling at speeds in excess of 60mph (97km/h). Disciplinary action followed.

A further derailment blocked the line at Chipping Sodbury on 11 January 1967 when the 02.55 Acton–Margam freight was derailed. The line was reopened by 15.00, which was just as well because another incident had occurred on the Bath–Bristol line at Bristol East depot where a diverted London–Swansea service ran into the back of a London–Bristol train.

Derailment – Personal Experience

Another derailment occurred on Sunday, 8 July 1970 at Westerleigh West Junction. I was a witness to this incident and relate it in full, but the events recorded below must *not* be seen as typical of the way the railway was run in those days, although it may appear to be quite a comical affair to a non-railwayman, in spite of the serious side.

Being an aspiring signalman and having a spare afternoon I had decided to cycle to Westerleigh West box to see who was on duty. The regular signalman who would have been on duty, Ray Hicks, I knew to be on leave, but there was always the chance that his replacement might be one of the friendly relief signalmen whom I knew.

Approaching the twin bridges where the main and branch lines crossed the road to Yate, I glanced to the left and could see that the Up main to branch signal, no. 19, was in the 'off' position; something would shortly be passing on to the branch. I cycled under the bridges and swung left into the entrance to a field. A pathway led from here to the top of the embankment. Leaving my bike propped against the fence, I commenced the walk up the path. As I did so, I became aware of the hum of an approaching diesel loco and the clunking of a train over the junction, so I hurried towards the top. As I neared the top I noticed two lads standing there; both were looking towards the approaching train. An odd regular 'thumping' noise became evident. Suddenly, the two boys jumped and rushed away from the track and past me as if the Devil himself was after them. They said nothing as they ran past, so I carried on for a few yards.

The diesel loco, a Brush type 4 (Class 47) No.1651 was now passing slowly on to the branch and past the top of the path. Its train was a rake of ammonia tanks. The thumping grew louder as the rear of the train approached and suddenly, with the cold fear of understanding, I knew what it was – the last wagon was 'off the road'!

I stood, paralysed with fear as the wagon, with the last pair of wheels bouncing up and down on the sleepers, came towards me. The wheels smashed into the wooden foot crossing that led to the signal box and carried on, but the train was by now almost at a stand. Very soon it was stopped, with the offending vehicle almost on the bridge and its rear wheels partly buried in the ballast. From the signal box came the sound of levers crashing back in the frame and the 'Obstruction – Danger!' signal being sounded on the bells.

The driver, second man and guard were now making their way towards the derailed wagon and from their gestures and the fact that they were reaching under the wagon, I gathered that the brake rodding had become disconnected at the forwards end, fallen on to the ballast and, acting like a pivot, had thrown the wagon off the rails.

The rear window of the signal box slid open. I recognized the signalman as relief signalman Dave Mawle; a friendly chap, Dave (who was a Special Class relief signalman on Bristol East District) worked at the box on occasions. However, this time there was no chance of my spending any time in the box. 'I'd go down to the bottom and watch from there, if I was you,' he advised. 'Every bugger'll be here in a minute!' I took his advice and as I left the scene, so the train crew were making their way to the box, there to sign the Train Register and presumably have a cup of tea whilst they waited for the re-railing gang.

At the bottom of the bank, I met the two lads who had fled the scene. They explained that they had seen the wagon jump off the rails and just fled in panic. We stood at the bottom of the path and compared notes; I got a tatty notebook out of my saddlebag and started to make a record of the events as I had a feeling this could be interesting.

Very shortly after this, a car pulled up and out jumped a man whom I recognized as a Multiple Aspect Signalling (MAS) Inspector (the resignalling of Bristol was under way and this man was a relief signalman from the 'West' side of Bristol, who had been made up to 'Temporary MAS Inspector'). Without waiting for his companion, who was still getting out of the vehicle, the Inspector ran up the path towards the track. His colleague, Ted Barrett, Assistant Area Freight Manager, followed at a more sedate pace, carrying a small brown case. Both went up the steps into the signal box.

Another car arrived and a man wearing overall trousers and an old jacket got out. The fact that he was carrying a large spanner as he walked up the

The small signal box at Westerleigh West, seen here in 1969.
P.D. RENDALL

bank led me to believe that he must be a carriage and wagon examiner. He, too, went into the box, briefly, before leaving to walk down the track to have a look at the derailed wagon.

A further car drew up and a tall man wearing a dark uniform got out. He pulled an overloaded 'Doctor's bag' from the rear seat and then jammed a large peaked hat on his head. The hat was covered with gold braid. This was the District Signalling Inspector, Bob Yabsley. He stood and glared all round for a moment before ascending the pathway and going into the box.

Whilst the two boys and I looked on, two more cars arrived together. One was driven by the Area Freight Manager, Maurice Holmes, and the other, judging by his uniform, was a relief signalman, I did not recognize him. Presumably he was there to open single-line working. Both men went up into Westerleigh West box. The 23-lever box was, by now, bursting at the seams. Something had to be done, not just to get the trains moving again, but to reduce the amount of men in the box before it, too, became a casualty of the derailment.

I later learned that they decided to open up single-line working between Winterbourne and Yate South boxes, with Westerleigh West as the intermediate box. To this end, the relief signalman now left for Yate South to start distributing Single Line forms by giving a form to signalman Ron Tanner (who was on duty at Yate) and getting Ron to sign the pilotman's form.

From the box came the distant sound of two beats on the Winterbourne bell. I wondered what that could be for. Within ten minutes, a loco appeared in the distance, moving very slowly. Then I understood; the loco was examining the Up main line to ascertain just how far the track had been damaged by the derailment. Meanwhile, a lorry pulled up and disgorged a large detachment of permanent way staff, who cheerfully ambled up the path to see what they had to do to repair the track.

Then yet another car arrived with a permanent way inspector and another man. These two walked up the bank and along the track to the derailed wagon. The MAS Inspector now emerged from the box and dashed down the steps and along the line to join them. I crept a little way up the bank to see what they were up to. All three appeared to be doing something with three suitcases that they had got from somewhere. Whatever they intended to do, they apparently failed to achieve it, as all three of them then inspected the wagon's tail light. It was still there.

Ted Barrett left the box and wandered down the path, got into his car and left. The Inspector and the two other men now found a small bottle-jack from somewhere and set about an abortive attempt to lift the wagon by placing the jack under the rear buffer beam. With much effort, they managed to lift the wagon a little, but any further lift was sharply curtailed as the wagon slipped off the jack and fell back on to the ballast, much to the apparent delight of the watching permanent way gang, who got more overtime the longer the wagon was off the road.

By now, the loco that had examined the Up line from Winterbourne had arrived at no. 19 signal and stopped, blowing its horn. A handsignal was displayed from the box and the loco blew its horn again and began to slowly move forwards, passing the signal at Danger. A red flag was now held out from the box and the loco, another Brush 4, D1603, came slowly along the branch and stopped at the box. A rather large man climbed down from the cab

and went to the box, presumably to report the state of the track to the assembled group there.

The carriage and wagon re-railing gang now arrived in their lorry and whilst some remained behind to unload some jacks and wooden packing, the others trooped up the path and along the line to the derailment, where the MAS Inspector and his two colleagues were performing what looked like a highland fling around the wagon and, judging by their gesticulations, were attempting to re-rail it using some form of primitive ritual.

The sound of a loco horn now drew the attention of most people at the scene and they stood aside from the tracks. Coming towards Westerleigh West Junction was a Peak (Class 46) diesel hauling a rake of coaches. It was running 'wrong line' and stopped opposite the junction signals. Again, a handsignal was displayed from the box and, with a toot on the horn, the train moved slowly on to the branch and trundled past the derailment and off towards Yate, still 'wrong line'. I did not see the pilotman get off, so he must have stayed at Winterbourne and 'sent the train through' the section. This train was 1E21; I did not get the loco's number. As it passed, inquisitive passengers leaned out of carriage windows and gazed at the scene. By now, the MAS Inspector and his friends were sitting dejectedly on a couple of suitcases, magic having seemingly failed.

No sooner had this train passed than the carriage and wagon gang got to work. Oxyacetylene gear was fetched from their lorry and in no time at all they had burnt the coupling off the derailed wagon (this coupling had jammed and was stopping the wagon being lifted). A spare axle-bearing was produced, and, watched enviously by the Inspector and company, jacks were produced and the wagon was up in the air in no time at all. Soon they had the spare bearing fitted and the wagon was back down on the rails again. The brake rodding that had caused all the trouble was taken off. A quick inspection and the train was declared fit to proceed. The time was 16.30 – one and a half hours after the wagon had become derailed.

The examiner went up into the signal box and told the people there that the train could proceed.

single-line working was cancelled, the train crew ambled back to their train and, once Dave Mawle had 'got the road', the ammonia train was on its way northwards once more and the backlog of trains could start to be cleared.

To the obvious relief of the signalman, once the drama was over, his 'guests' started to disperse. D1603 was crossed over and sent 'right road' back to Winterbourne and one by one the various brass hats and overalls went back to their cars and lorries and left for home. Westerleigh West signal box had, at some time during the afternoon, been host to some twelve or thirteen men at the same time. They must have been standing on each other's toes and the teapot and kettle must have been worn out!

Surprisingly, the track was almost undamaged apart from a few splintered sleepers. The foot crossing would need a few boards replacing, but, all in all, the derailment had actually caused little damage and not much delay to traffic. In spite of what had seemed like a pantomime performance to those who were not railwaymen, everyone who needed to be there arrived within a short time of being called out and got the job done quickly. Can you imagine how that would have gone on the fragmented railway of the twenty-first century? By the time they had got the scene examined by people equipped with hi-visibility jackets and trousers, safety goggles and hard hats, got one company or another to admit responsibility and festooned the derailment with safety fences, established work zones, issued permits and the like, it would be hours and hours after the event that the wagon would have been lifted – and then probably by a road crane.

That is *if* anyone admitted responsibility; in my later experience of the privatized railway, responsibility was *never* admitted, even if the cause was plainly obvious. Technical research staff would then be sent for, causing the line to remain shut for hours, possibly even days, whilst they came from Derby or similar to examine the scene and make their judgement. All this at great cost, of course, involving overnight hotel stays and meals on expenses. Yes, it *did* happen!

Back in 1970, on the old, inefficient steam-age railway, long before business people and bankers got their hands on the system and divided it amongst themselves, the staff just got on with the job of running trains for the benefit of the passengers and freight, which, curiously enough, was exactly what the railway, and they, were there for.

Off the Road at Pilning

On 15 June 1970, a driver reported a 'bump' in the Severn Tunnel and a light diesel was despatched from the Welsh end to examine the tunnel (by this time, Newport Panel had taken over control of the entire tunnel, Severn Tunnel East and West boxes being closed). Following a successful examination of the track through the tunnel and nothing being found amiss, the diesel ran up to Pilning Junction box to cross over and run back to Severn Tunnel Junction.

The signalman on duty at the junction allowed the diesel to stand clear of the crossover. However, when he pulled the lever for the crossover points, it would not come fully over. He tried again, but still it would not come over. Something was stopping it, maybe a piece of ballast. The signalman advised his colleagues at the boxes either side and left the box to walk to the points, collecting a clip on the way. As he did so, up in the box, a phone rang out. What should he do? Answer the phone or ignore it? The loco driver heard the phone and called out for the signalman to give him the clip and he would move up to the points and drop off the clip. The signalman agreed, but advised the driver: 'Do not proceed any further than the points. Stop clear of the crossover.'

The driver moved off and as the signalman climbed the box steps so he heard a 'clunk-clunk-*thump*' as the diesel became derailed on the partially open points. The driver had ignored his instructions and was now 'off the road'. The approaches to the tunnel were still as important as they had been in the 1950s and soon all the phones were ringing as both lines were now blocked. Unfortunately, there had also been a derailment at Westerleigh

View from Pilning Junction signal box: the crossover where the diesel was derailed on 15 June 1980 was just opposite the brake van seen here. In this 1962 photo ex-GWR Hall No.4920 Dumbleton Hall passes through on a Portsmouth–Cardiff service. WILF STANLEY

Friday July 25th 1980   BRISTOL JOURNAL

'Miracle no-one died'

Rubble on road

A DAWN derailment sent tons of rubble crashing down on to a busy city road this week.

Derailed freight wagons smashed the parapet of the Gipsy Patch Lane bridge at Patchway.

And if the accident had happened just a few hours later the road would have been crowded with workers travelling to the Filton and Patchway factories.

Nobody was hurt in the 4.15 am crash which involved only the Cardiff to Didcot freight train.

"It was a miracle no-one got killed," said a railway worker at the scene of the accident.

Rush-hour traffic had to be diverted away from the area and tangled wreckage blocked the main Cardiff to London line.

British Rail will be holding an enquiry into why the freight wagons came off the tracks as the train came out of the Patchway tunnel.

The coal wagons were dragged a mile along the line badly damaging the track and spilling their load on to the road below.

Engineers hoped to get the line back into normal operation by the weekend.

London-bound trains had to be diverted via Gloucester and Swindon and British Rail laid on a special shuttle service between Parkway and Swindon.

Words: Maggie Armstrong
Pictures: Ian Newton

Extract from the Bristol Journal, *25 July 1980, showing the derailment at Patchway and the rubble from the bridge parapet lying in Gipsy Patch Lane.* AUTHOR'S COLLECTION

West, so trains to and from Gloucester, unable to reach Bristol via normal means (the Mangotsfield line had closed some months earlier) had already been diverted via Lydney, Chepstow and the Severn Tunnel, but were now subject to even more delay until the errant diesel was re-railed.

That derailment at Westerleigh West Junction mentioned above had occurred when part of a Down freight train of thirty-six wagons of sand jumped the rails whilst passing over the junction, with the result that both lines there were blocked. The last six wagons and brake van were derailed, the first ripping up track, point rodding and signal wires, and losing its wheels in the process; the next slid down the embankment and the last four and the brake van stayed upright with their wheels in the ballast. All lines at the junction being blocked, all trains to and from London via the Direct line were diverted via Bath and Filton, whilst all trains to and from the Gloucester line were diverted via Lydney, Chepstow and the Severn Tunnel until, of course, the derailment of the locomotive at Pilning.

Another derailment occurred at 04.15 on the morning of 25 July 1960, when an Up Cardiff to Didcot power station 'merry-go-round' coal train became derailed just before passing through the platforms at Patchway station. The wagons were dragged through the platforms and as they hit the junction, they became fully derailed and tipped over. One wagon hit the parapet of Gypsy Patch Lane underbridge sending masses of rubble crashing down into the road. Thankfully, the road was clear; if the accident had happened during rush hour there would have been serious injuries as the road would have been crowded with commuters heading for the nearby aero-engine works.

The 1991 Severn Tunnel Crash

The Severn Tunnel accident of 7 December 1991 has been the subject of much speculation. On the preceding Thursday, 5 December, there had been a failure of the remote electronic equipment. This had led the signalman at Newport Panel Box to switch to what was known as 'Through Routes'.

Through Routes enabled selected routes to be set and equipment in the area overseen by the selected route would operate automatically. This was standard practice and all signals in the area affected would be kept at Danger until a route was selected.

The signal protecting the tunnel on the Bristol side was N164. Owing to Through Routes working, the Newport signalman had no idea what the signal was showing; he had to rely on the automatic equipment to operate it. The equipment was 'fail safe' and reliable. However, the fault, which was in the equipment at the relay room at Severn Tunnel Junction, on the Welsh side of the tunnel, took longer to trace and it was during the afternoon of Friday, 6 December that a driver called Newport Panel Box from N164 to report that the signal was at Danger, when it should have been showing a Proceed aspect. It was ascertained that a failure of the axle counters through the tunnel had occurred.

In 1987, the track circuits through the tunnel had been removed as they were subject to failure owing to the wet conditions that are to be found in the tunnel. At their most basic, axle counters are devices that do much as their name suggests – an electronic device attached to the rail counts the axles of a train entering the tunnel and keeps the signal in the rear of the train at Danger. Another detector counts the axles when the train leaves the tunnel; if both counts are the same, the train is complete, the signal behind can be cleared again and no action is taken.

On the day in question, the axle counters had failed and whilst signal technicians were working to restore the equipment, trains were being stopped at signals either side of the tunnel and only allowed through the tunnel one at a time in either direction. Shortly after 10.00 on Saturday morning, an HST, 1B10, working the 08.30 Paddington–Cardiff service, had been stopped at signal N164 and the driver advised of the circumstances. The line ahead being clear, the driver was advised that he could pass N164 at Danger and proceed with caution through the tunnel. Following the HST was a Sprinter forming 1F08, the 07.00 Portsmouth–

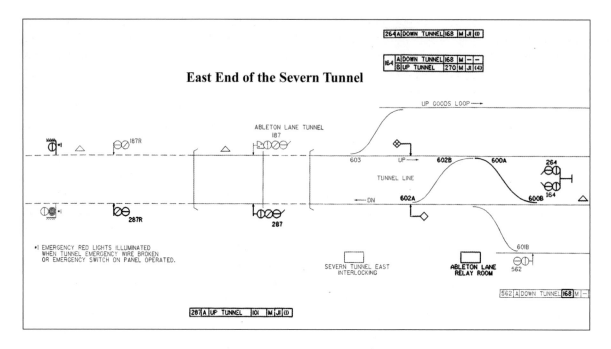

Diagram showing the signalled approaches to the Severn Tunnel as it was when the 1991 crash occurred. The tunnel is to the left, the lines from Pilning come from the right. Signal N164 is on the right of the diagram. (Based on an old BR resignalling notice.) AUTHOR'S COLLECTION

Cardiff service. This train approached signal N164 and in the evidence later given by the driver of the Sprinter, he saw the signal change to a Proceed aspect. He accelerated past the signal and into the tunnel, where his train collided with the rear of the HST, which was still moving slowly through the darkness.

Luckily, the Sprinter had not been able to pick up much speed and, although there was substantial damage to the Sprinter and to the rear of the HST, injuries were light and there were no fatalities. The driver of the Sprinter sustained a fractured skull and eye injuries. There were a total of 185 injuries on both trains; five, including the Sprinter driver, were of a serious nature.

In spite of various train crew and others calling the emergency services, it was more than two hours before rescue arrived. This was later found to be due to a mixture of mistaken location and failure of telephone equipment.[33]

The Investigation

As can be expected, once the damaged trains had been removed and normal working resumed, there was an immediate investigation, during which attention was focused on the actions of the signal technicians working on the axle counter equipment in the relay room at Severn Tunnel Junction. Had they inadvertently restored power to the equipment, causing signal N164 to change to a Proceed aspect? The driver of the Sprinter always maintained that the signal had changed to green as he approached it.

The Inquiry eventually decided that the collision had been caused by an 'unaccountable' error by the Sprinter driver, or by the S&T Technicians working in the Severn Tunnel Junction relay room, or possibly by a momentary or intermittent, undetectable and untraceable fault in the signalling equipment. In other words, there was nothing that could prove that an error, human or in the equipment, had occurred. The chances of an experienced train driver seeing a signal at Danger, slowing down, acknowledging the AWS warning and then accelerating past a red signal was something that the Inquiry acknowledged would be unprecedented.

However, there was one incident in the hours preceding the crash which set about the chain of events leading to the collision. As N164 was kept at Danger by the fault and by disconnection of the axle counters, a handsignalman was appointed to stand at the signal, displaying a red handsignal (lamp by night, flag by day) and maintaining a detonator on the line, in accordance with the Rule Book. At the Welsh end of the tunnel, at signal N168, another man was directed to report that every train which passed through the tunnel to Wales was complete with its tail lamp. Thus there were four preventative measures in place: red signal; red handsignal; audible detonator; and, at the other end of the tunnel, a person to report that the train had passed through the tunnel, was complete and that the tunnel was clear. The combination of the first three would have warned any driver who had inadvertently passed the signal at Danger that he had done so and he would bring his train to a stand immediately.[34]

The Handsignalmen

At the commencement of the day shift on that Saturday, the man at N168 was going off duty and there was nobody to replace him. Newport asked if Bristol could supply anyone.

Bristol agreed that it could, but, instead of sending an experienced signalman, the signal box supervisor decided to send a trainee signalman. Newport then realized that the day shift man rostered to be sent to N164 would be crossing the Severn Bridge to the Bristol side, whilst the Bristol man would be making a similar move in the Welsh direction. This seemed a waste of resources, so the Newport signalman arranged for the two men to change places, the Newport man going to N168 on the Welsh side, whilst the Bristol man went to N164 protecting the tunnel on the Bristol side.

However, the Bristol trainee signalman had never worked on the railway before being employed by BR, was not yet qualified and had little or no experience of the situation he found himself in when he reached N164. Nor did he have any of the correct equipment for the job. Nonetheless, he managed to pass a train or two before one train driver became concerned that there was no red flag or other equipment to be seen and reported the matter to Newport box when he got to the Welsh side of the tunnel. Newport relayed the information to Bristol where the day shift signalling supervisor withdrew the trainee. Shortly after the trainee left the signal, the Sprinter passed N164 and entered the tunnel to collide with the HST.

One of the conclusions reached by the Inquiry was that the decision to swap the two men around was 'improper', but well intentioned, and that once it was made it should have been observed 'to the letter of the Rule Book'.[35] Had I been the supervisor at the time, I would not have sent anyone who was not qualified or who was inexperienced; it was unfair to expect a trainee to know how to react in such a situation. In my opinion, sending a trainee was a decision that should never have been made. An experienced signalman should have been sent to that signal and my reasoning is this: had power been inadvertently restored to the disconnected axle counter circuit and N164 changed to a Proceed aspect, an experienced handsignalman would have recognized the 'click' as the lineside relay operated and would have looked up at the signal. Seeing it at green he would have kept his detonator on the line and his red handsignal displayed whilst he phoned the signal box to assure himself that normal working had been resumed, but that he had not been told. Should a train have approached and failed to see the handsignal, then the noise of the detonator exploding would have further served to warn him to stop.[36]

The Bristol day shift supervisor recognized that the trainee's presence at the signal was little more than a token gesture; to withdraw the trainee was the correct decision as that man did not have any equipment and would have been helpless to act should a train have passed N164 at Danger. There is no doubt in my mind that had an experienced signalman been sent to N164 by Bristol, the collision would probably never have happened.

Emergency Exercise

Names of places were often confusing to those who did not work on the railway. For example, in 1990 I was one of several supervisors who took part in an exercise with the Fire Brigade. The exercise took place in the Severn Tunnel one Saturday night and was to replicate what would happen if there was a collision in the tunnel.

I arrived at the tunnel mouth and parked my car in the large parking area at the top of the cutting. A permanent way man appeared and suggested I move the car out on to the road as when the Fire Brigade arrived, it would want to use the parking area. This was sound advice, as soon after the exercise began, around a dozen fire engines came tearing up the road, blue lights flashing, and filled the parking area. At such incidents, the emergency services open a series of Controls. Gold Control would be situated at a remote Control Room and the senior officer would be in overall control of the incident. Silver Control would again be at a site remote from the incident and this person's duties would be to act as Technical Commander, taking directions from Gold and passing them down to Bronze Control, who would be at the site of the incident. On this occasion, the local Bronze Control was to be in a fire service vehicle that was to be easily identified by the fact that it would be the only vehicle with the blue lights left flashing once all vehicles had arrived on site. Having the need to visit Bronze Control to pass on some information, I found that every fire tender in the vehicle park had left its blue lights on!

The main problem I found that night was that the brigade which was about to venture into the tunnel at Pilning in order to proceed to the 'crash' site radioed its colleagues at the Welsh end of the tunnel and said, 'We are about to enter the tunnel from the Severn Tunnel end'. I explained that this would cause confusion if said in a real incident, as to any railwayman involved this would indicate that the brigade was entering the tunnel from the Welsh end, i.e., from Severn Tunnel Junction direction. Of course, what the person on the radio meant was that they were entering the tunnel from the *east end* and not via the pumping shaft, but the choice of words could result in major confusion. I convinced him that it would make more sense if he said, 'from the Pilning or Eastern end'. I think the brigade eventually got the point, as the exercise was successful. Having related the above tale, I must add that any such vague wording played *no* part in the event of the 1991 crash.

Other Incidents

Thankfully, major incidents such as those relayed above have been few and far between, considering the concentration of traffic along the line over the years. But, any railway system has its fair share of minor incidents. Stoke Gifford was the site of several wagon derailments over the years, but the most spectacular derailment hardly caused any damage at all. The junction at Stoke Gifford West was quite an acute one and the diamond crossing was fitted with 'switch diamonds'. Rather than a solid diamond, the crossing joints could be moved to permit the flanges of trains to pass. This arrangement was known to the GWR as 'elbows'. On the occasion in question (the date cannot be recalled, but it was sometime in the 1950s) a pannier tank approaching the junction from Filton 'ran by the board'. The junction was set towards South Wales and therefore the 'elbows' set accordingly. Running into the junction points, the pannier hit the elbow points and jumped the track. But by some freak of nature it did not derail but miraculously came to a stand, all wheels still on the track, on the Down line.

Fatalities amongst staff working on the line were rare, but sadly there were a few and in this the Direct line was no different from most main lines. Steam locomotives made more noise than diesels and one would think that accidents due to not hearing a train approaching would rise once steam had gone, but this does not seem to have been the

A broken rail clamped to allow the passage of trains at walking pace. This one was at Cattybrook, on the Down line, in 1986. P.D. RENDALL

case. Once the High Speed Trains arrived, extra safety precautions and staff education kept trackside workers safe. However, steam-day fatalities happened and two incidents concerned the Coalpit Heath permanent way gang in the 1950s.

A gang of men was working just west of Coalpit Heath station on one occasion and was busy using screw-jacks to lift sleepers so that ballast could be packed under them. A train was signalled and there was no lookout man to warn the men. As the train approached, so one man was still struggling to get a jack out. He was hit by the locomotive buffer beam and thrown down the embankment. Sad to say, he suffered fatal injuries. The second incident was similar, in that a man failed to stand clear of a train quick enough and he, too, was hit by the loco and killed.

Broken rails are not unusual on the railway. In the past, when rails were 60ft (18m) lengths, a broken rail normally meant that the permanent way gang would liaise with the signalman to change the rail between trains. In modern times, when rails are in continuously welded long sections, replacing between trains is not possible. The first the signalman in his distant panel box or computer signalling centre knows about it is when he/she has a visual indication of a track-circuit failure.

The track circuit being disrputed, the indications will 'fail safe' and so the technicians are usually the first on the scene. Once a broken rail is discovered, the permanent way supervisor or on-call man is sent for and the rail break is examined in detail.

Often, the rail can be clamped and packed, with trains then allowed to pass over at walking pace; in such instances, the Civil Engineering Department would appoint a supervisor to watch each train move over the break. When a convenient occupation of the line could be arranged, the damaged section would be cut out and a new section welded in.

Should the break be so bad that it would be dangerous for trains to pass over it, all trains would be prohibited from passing over that section and either would use the opposite line where reversible working would be available, or would use a diversionary route until the rail had been replaced.

Floods

Flooding of the line in certain places was not uncommon. Regular spots were between 110 miles 30 chains (Badminton side) and 103 miles 48 chains (Sodbury side), which included the whole length of Chipping Sodbury Tunnel. Also affected was the stretch of line between 103 miles 48 chains and 104 miles 46 chains, including the water troughs. Landslips were an almost inevitable consequence of floods and there have been many examples of landslips necessitating closure of the line whilst the cuttings were stabilized and the tracks cleared.

One example of this happened on 5 November 1966, when, after a period of heavy rain, the line flooded near Chipping Sodbury Tunnel and there was also a landslip. The Engineer shut the line and trains had to be diverted via Bath for the rest of that day. Another example was in July 1968, when the Bristol area suffered an unusually heavy storm and floods affected not only Sodbury Tunnel, but Patchway Down Tunnels as well. In fact, so much flood water rushed down the cutting from the tunnels that at Cattybrook signal box the signalman feared that the embankment might be destabilized from all the water and the box – which stood on the embankment – might collapse! He shut the box and spent several hours sitting in the safety of his nearby car until the water subsided.

As can be expected, in the event of heavy rain the Civil Engineering Department Inspector would appoint staff from the permanent way gang to attend various locations at Chipping Sodbury Tunnel and watch for signs of flooding. Should the water level rise to 3–4in (75–100mm) above the sleepers, then the man would advise the Chipping Sodbury and Badminton station masters by telephone and they would arrange for handsignalmen to be called out. The handsignalmen would be equipped with red flags, lamps and detonators and one would be stationed outside of Chipping Sodbury signal box for the Up line, the other stationed approximately $1/8$ mile (200m) from the tunnel mouth on the Badminton side, for the Down line. Their duty was to stop each train when it approached, advising the driver and fireman of the flooding and instructing them to proceed with caution until clear of the flooded section (drivers of Down trains would also be cautioned by the Badminton signalman to stop at the handsignalman for instructions).

If the flood water continued to rise, the handsignalman at the Badminton end had instructions to walk back to Badminton signal box and station himself there. Trains would henceforth be stopped by signals at both stations and the handsignalmen would tell the drivers not to exceed 20mph (32km/h) through the affected section. Should the water rise to 5–6in (125–150mm) above the rail on the section between the Chipping Sodbury end of the tunnel and the station, trains were cautioned not to exceed 10mph (16km/h) through the affected section.

The Tunnel Flooded

During the latter part of November 1960 there had been a period of heavy rain. The water level in the 'cess' (as the lineside was known in railway terms)

Winter 1987 saw the tracks flooded at the west end of Chipping Sodbury Tunnel. All trains were diverted. The nearest 'bridge' is one of the many aqueducts that carry streams across the Direct line. P.D. RENDALL

was rising owing to the excess rainwater drain-ing off the surrounding farmland. On the night of Saturday, 26 November, signalman Ernie Hawkins, on duty in Chipping Sodbury box, was telephoned at 23.15 by the permanent way man who had been sta-tioned at the tunnel to keep an eye on the possibility of the water rising over the rails. He told Ernie that the water was rising quickly and that the ganger should be advised. There being no public phone in the signal box, Ernie closed the box and walked to the ganger's house in nearby Chipping Sodbury to call him out. The ganger inspected the rising flood and advised that a speed restriction of 15mph (24km/h) should be applied from 01.00. This proce-dure was carried out for all Up trains until 10.33 on the morning of Monday, 28 November, when, after another inspection, the ganger gave the 'all clear' for trains to run at normal speed, the floods having receded.

But the winter was a wet one and on Sunday, 4 December 1960, signalman Mike Goodrich was on the Saturday–Sunday nightshift turn of duty when he was told at 04.35 by the Badminton signalman that he had received advice that the tunnel was flooded at the Badminton end. Without further information, the Permanent Way Department was called out and the Up Bristol–Swindon stopping train was held in the Up loop until a decision was made about the state of the lines. The train was later cancelled.

At 07.00 after an inspection, the tunnel was declared closed and both main lines taken pos-session of by the Civil Engineering Department. A locomotive was requested for the purpose of exam-ining the tunnel and this arrived at Sodbury at 07.15. The day shift signalman, again Ernie Hawkins, issued a Wrong Line Order at 11.05, authorizing the loco with members of the permanent way on board to run through the tunnel in the Up direction but on the Down line as far as necessary to ascertain the state of the track. The loco returned on the Down line at 13.15, having run through to Badminton. The lines remained closed and five Up expresses were diverted via Bath. The 06.10 Bristol–Swindon stop-ping service ran as far as Sodbury, where it was crossed to the Down platform and started back to Bristol from there.

A further inspection with a light engine at 15.30 resulted in the lines being reopened with a speed restriction of 5mph (8km/h). All trains were to be

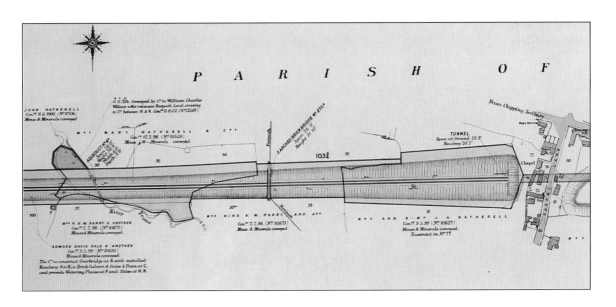

1903 plan of the west end of Chipping Sodbury Tunnel. WILTSHIRE HISTORY CENTRE

cautioned through the tunnel and over the water troughs. This situation continued until after another inspection of the tunnel on the morning of Tuesday, 6 December, when the speed restriction was raised to 15mph (24km/h). The restrictions were lifted completely at 11.05, the waters having receded.

In the days of steam locomotives, trains could be cautioned through the floods even if the water rose to 6in (150mm) above the rails. In this event, Up trains had to be stopped at Swindon and Down trains that would pass through the Severn Tunnel were stopped at Stoke Gifford, for the axle boxes to be examined in case the flood water had affected the oil lubrication.

In diesel days, however, this instruction changed. As before, trains were cautioned, but the instructions were amended as follows: diesel-electric locos, diesel multiple units, railcars and shunting locos on normal moves were prohibited to pass over a flooded section of track when the maximum water level reached 1in (25mm) below the head of the rail; emergency movements were allowed under these circumstances provided that

they were carried out at 3mph (5km/h) and that the water level did not exceed 4in (100mm) above the head of the rail. Diesel-hydraulic locos on normal services were prohibited as above, but in emergency could run at 3mph provided that the water level was not 6in (150mm) above the rail head; above that, trains were stopped from using the line. This was because diesel-electric locomotives have traction motors underneath and water entering a traction motor would damage the equipment. Diesel-hydraulic locos were not so badly affected, having hydraulic transmissions rather than traction motors.[37]

In 1986, the drains were modified in an attempt to stop or reduce the flooding. These attempts were only partially successful and flooding continues to affect the line whenever there is a period of heavy rain, with trains being frequently cancelled or diverted via Bath.

In 1991, the instructions were that trains would not be permitted to use the lines through the tunnel, nor would reversible working be permitted, should flood water be likely to rise above the rails.

CHAPTER 13

Signalling

Semaphore Signalling

From the opening of the line it was equipped with paraffin oil lit semaphore signals and GWR pattern Absolute Block signalling. Exceptions were the Up and Down goods loops at Stoke Gifford and between Pilning Junction and station and to Severn Tunnel East, and the Severn Tunnel itself, which was equipped with a Special Lock and Block arrangement using unique Tyer & Co. Lock and Block instruments – one in Severn Tunnel East and one in Severn Tunnel West signal boxes. There were no track circuits in the Severn Tunnel until the advent of Multiple Aspect Signalling in 1968. During World War II, Intermediate Block Signals were installed in the tunnel to allow more trains to use the line. As indicated earlier, these were removed after the war.

From information contained in records it would appear that experienced signalmen were moved on to the line when it opened for traffic and these moved from box to box as required until the vacancies created by the new boxes were filled permanently. For example, in 1903 signalman J. Raymond moved to Hullavington box from Dauntsey on the Wootton Bassett to Bath line. He moved on to Little Somerford in 1905. In September 1903, signalman C.J. Greenwood moved to Hullavington from Clifton Bridge box, on the

A fine example of a semaphore signal. Winterbourne Up Main Starting signal; a wooden GWR arm on a wooden GWR post.
WILF STANLEY

The interior of Severn Tunnel East signal box seen during the summer months of 1968. The large instrument on the right-hand side of the block shelf is the tunnel Lock and Block instrument. AUTHOR'S COLLECTION

until October 1903, when he moved to Pilning Junction box. Badminton also had several early moves: signalman E. Williams came there from Keynsham and then in November 1905 moved to Bristol as a reliefman; F. Giddings came from Risca, South Wales and later moved to Clifton Bridge box on the Bristol to Portishead line. R. Martin moved to Badminton from Patchway in October 1903 and moved on to Frome in March 1904. He was replaced by G.H. Osborne who came from Chipping Sodbury box. Other early moves were signalman A. Neal who moved from Bedminster to Badminton (date unknown) and S. Newman from Little Somerford (date unknown).

For the large part of its existence the 'new' section of the Direct line was operated by staff who came under the Bristol Divisional Superintendent. Signalling and other staff from and including Brinkworth (the next station down the line from Wootton Bassett) were supplied and governed by Bristol and came under the jurisdiction of the Bristol Signalling Inspector. This meant that although a signal box might have its regular signalmen, coverage for sickness, absence or annual leave (and rest days after these were introduced in the 1950s) could come from Bristol if local reliefmen were not available. For a Bristol signalman to travel to Little Somerford or Brinkworth in the days of mass motor-car ownership would not be a problem; in the days when a motorcycle was a

Bristol to Portishead line. He moved on to Chipping Sodbury box in February 1904. In the same month Signalman I.J. Mizen moved to Hullavington box from Pilning. August 1904 saw signalman A. Fellender move from Pilning box to Hullavington. He had been signalman at Wilton, near Salisbury,

A fine collection of GWR metal signals and posts seen at Stoke Gifford West in August 1968. R. CUFF/AUTHOR'S COLLECTION

luxury and almost all travel was by train and/or pushbike, it was quite an achievement.

If a signalman from the Bristol East relief district needed to cover a turn at Little Somerford or Brinkworth boxes, his usual method of travel would be as follows: the man would be booked on the Up 'Waker' (03.57 off Bristol Temple Meads, the previous evening's 20.45 ex-Penzance sleeping car train) as far as Chippenham. He would put his pushbike in the guard's compartment. From Chippenham he would have to cycle to Little Somerford or Brinkworth. The unfortunate thing was that by being booked to travel on the 'Waker', the only travelling time the man was able to book was the cycling time between Chippenham and the box, and back to Chippenham again. At the end of his shift he would have to pedal back to Chippenham station again and catch a train to Bristol. Not too bad, perhaps, on a lovely summer's day, but no fun at all in the depths of winter.

If local reliefmen were not available, it normally fell to Chipping Sodbury relief signalmen to cover turns as far as Brinkworth and Little Somerford. In the 1950s, some of these reliefmen were Harry Maidment, Jack Griffiths and Bernard Hicks. Maidment was a Sodbury reliefman until August 1955, when he became a Bristol East district reliefman. He lived in a railway cottage at Ram Hill, near Coalpit Heath station. Bernard Hicks was a Sodbury reliefman, until the signal boxes closed in the early 1970s. He was uncle to Ray Hicks, who had been a regular man at Chipping Sodbury for a while during the late 1960s after being made redundant from Westerleigh South box on the LMR main line, when that box and the goods yard closed in 1965. Ray later moved to Westerleigh West box and was there when it closed in May 1971. Both Hicks were related to Charlie Hicks, another Sodbury reliefman who lived near Malmesbury and is remembered for having a gauge 'O' model railway.

Not all Bristol East reliefmen had the opportunity to cover these far-flung parts of the Bristol Inspector's empire. Signalman Wilf Stanley, who lived in the Fishponds area of Bristol, was never rostered to go there. Wilf never worked beyond Badminton, but visited Brinkworth just after it closed. The box was intact, although all the signalling instruments had been removed. The nameplate was still on the front of the box. Chilston Frampton, who lived further away than Wilf, in Knowle, Bristol, went to Little Somerford several times.

By the 1960s, Pilning was still enjoying a busy period. In all, fifteen signalmen and two relief signalmen were allocated to the three Pilning boxes, Junction, Station and Branch (Low Level); Severn Tunnel East signal box and Cattybrook Siding box.

Margin Working

It was all 'margin working' (the art of letting a freight train or slow train proceed with sufficient time for it to be clear of a section or in a loop clear of the main line, without delaying a following train) on the Badminton line. Trains leaving Stoke Gifford yard had to have sufficient margin to get 'in clear' at Chipping Sodbury, Badminton, Hullavington or Little Somerford loops to avoid delaying more important trains. Chipping Sodbury, Badminton and Little Somerford loops were also platform lines and with the latter, the Up loop was often blocked by the Malmesbury branch train. Hullavington box generally worked out the margin to Wootton Bassett.

In steam days, there were long block sections on the 'upper' part of the line (from Wapley Common to Wootton Bassett) and with very long trains you had to be careful what you did. Once a 28XX 2-8-0 steam loco with forty-five wagons of coal got going, it was better to let it run, as the delays caused by stopping and shunting the train could be worse than letting it go. For example, owing to an Up express passenger train being considerably delayed by a preceding goods train on an occasion in May 1945, the Divisional Superintendent thought it necessary to advise all station masters and signalmen along the line of the required methods of working of express trains.

In order that the signalmen on the line should have the best possible information as to the running of expresses, it was emphasized that the

Long, slow goods trains spent lots of time in goods loops to allow faster trains to pass them. This goods, headed by an unidentified Hall Class, has been 'looped' at Chipping Sodbury to permit a Down express to pass it. WILF STANLEY

Pilning Junction signalman (or booking boy) was to advise both Stoke Gifford West and East boxes of the running of Up expresses. Stoke Gifford East box was to advise Badminton. It was up to the signalmen at Chipping Sodbury, Hullavington and Little Somerford to keep in touch with Badminton to ascertain whether trains were running to time or not.

This advice was reiterated in 1947 when the Great Western issued a notice to all staff concerning the method of advising others of train movements. In this, it was laid down that Badminton signal box should advise Patchway Station box when a Down passenger train passed Hullavington and in turn would be advised by Patchway when Up trains for the Badminton line passed Patchway Station. Patchway was also required to tell Severn Tunnel Junction Middle box of the passing times of all Down trains. Badminton also had to advise Wootton Bassett East box and Swindon Junction Telegraph Office of the passing times of Up trains. Pilning Junction box would

The rear of the train in the above picture; it will be seen from the length of this goods train that it would have to run to Stoke Gifford for the next goods loop big enough to accommodate it. WILF STANLEY

A GWR 28XX trundles its train slowly along the Up loop at Pilning Junction. WILF STANLEY

receive advice from Bristol Stapleton Road box Train Regulators when all Up trains, passenger or freight passed Stapleton Road station, with Pilning Junction advising Stapleton Road of the passing times of all Bristol-bound trains.

Westerleigh West junction signalman had to advise Bristol Temple Meads GWR Inspector of the passing times of trains for Bristol and beyond, whether they ran via Temple Meads or the relief lines through Bristol St Philip's Marsh. Stoke Gifford East box was advised by Newport Telegraph Office of the times that Up trains for the Badminton direction passed or departed from Newport station.

Margin working on the Down road was equally as important, as trains ran fast down from Wootton Bassett. Letting a freight train out when an express was imminent required cooperation between signalmen to get the train 'running', as Stoke Gifford loops were the next place the train could usually be put away if Wapley Common was switched out of circuit (Coalpit Heath could take short freights in its loop, but by the 1940s many freights were too long for Coalpit Heath to be of any use).

How this cooperation was essential is seen in the following example. One day in the 1950s, a Chipping Sodbury signalman had two Down freights to get rid of. He let one out behind a Down passenger train and let the second one trickle out to his Down Starting signal to wait for the road, which should not have been long coming, even though Westerleigh East and Wapley Common were both switched out. Time went on and the Sodbury signalman knew that a Down express was due and he had not yet had 'Train Out of Section' from Westerleigh West. He could not raise Westerleigh West on the box phone so rang Yate South box, on the LMR line. You could see the GW main line from Yate and the Sodbury man enquired of the Yate man if he could see if the freight was standing at Westerleigh, as it should have been past Coalpit Heath by then. The answer being in the negative, the Sodbury man tried Westerleigh again on the phone and this time got through. When asking where the freight was, he received the reply that the Westerleigh West signalman had 'forgotten to clear back'. This meant that the margin for both freights to run clear to Stoke

Gifford was now lost and the second Down freight delayed the express.

Sometimes when the line was very busy, an Up freight was 'looped' at Chipping Sodbury, only to be stuck there for a considerable time as it was not possible to get it out as far as the next loop. When the local passenger train, calling at Chipping Sodbury, was imminent, the freight had to be drawn out of the platform line and back-shunted on to the Up main to allow the passenger into the Up platform line. When the passenger had gone, the freight had to be pushed back outside the Up Home signal and then signalled back into the loop again. This only applied to very long freights, which would occupy both the Up platform/ Up goods lines.

Wilf Stanley was a relief signalman on the line during the 1960s and one day was on duty at Badminton box. An Up freight was signalled and passed along the line as far as Hullavington, where the signalman decided to signal it into the loop. Halfway into the loop the train failed, coming to a stand blocking the Up main. Close behind the freight came the Up 'South Wales Diesel Pullman', which had to be held at Badminton until it was decided to cross it over and send it back to Stoke Gifford, from where it took the Filton line and then travelled via Dr Day's and North Somerset Junction to regain the London line via Bath. Luckily, the crew knew the route.

Throughout their existence, the signal boxes on the Direct line went through a variety of changes, although these were mostly internal, such as lever alterations and so on. There were boxes that were replaced by new structures on different sites, such as Westerleigh East and Severn Tunnel East; boxes that were extended, such as Pilning Station (internal and external extensions to accommodate extra levers), Stoke Gifford West (internal only, extra levers added without extending the box); and new boxes altogether, such as Wapley Common, Westerleigh North and East, and Patchway Tunnel. Hullavington had a longer frame when its refuge sidings were converted to loops and Little Somerford also had a new frame when its loops were lengthened.

Signal Box Closures and Multiple Aspect Signalling

Signal box closures did not necessarily match those of the stations, which are given in the section on stations above. The first signal box on the Direct line to be closed was Westerleigh North (GWR), which was, of course, part of, although not actually on, the Direct line. Having opened in May 1903 and been temporarily closed between February 1907 and May 1908, it closed again in December 1916, the east curve being taken out of use and the block section becoming Westerleigh West to Yate South

British Railways notice from January 1949 regarding the taking out of use of Westerleigh North signal box. The box was not, at this stage, officially closed, just 'out of use'. AUTHOR'S COLLECTION

It may have two modern diesel locos pulling it, but this long coal train passing Patchway is still a Class 8 and would take a long time to reach Swindon. R. CUFF/AUTHOR'S COLLECTION

Junction (MR). The North box and east curve reopened in February 1918, but closed again in July 1927. This time both the box and the east curve were removed. The strategic needs of World War II saw a new Westerleigh North opened on the same site along with new tracks on the east curve. Both box and curve were finally closed in January 1950, except for the brief reprieve for a royal train mentioned earlier. The box was removed after lying derelict for a while. The site could still be discerned as late as 1970.

As also mentioned earlier, the first Westerleigh East box closed and was removed in July 1927 when the east curve was taken out of use, the new East box being built in 1942. The third box closed was Severn Tunnel East, which was replaced by a wartime box in May 1942, as mentioned above.

Fourth to be closed was Brinkworth, on 15 March 1959. Coalpit Heath signal box closed on 24 May 1964 and its loops were taken out of use, being recovered in August the same year. Patchway Tunnel box closed on 19 January 1965 and was soon followed later the same year by the wartime Wapley Common, which had a short life of twenty-three years, closing on 18 July 1965. There were no more closures until the Swindon resignalling works closed Little Somerford on 18 June 1967, the new Swindon Panel Box working to Hullavington.

Hullavington then controlled a layout of all-electric points and colour-light signals until it, too, closed on 24 March 1968. Wootton Bassett having lost both its signal boxes to progress in March 1968, Swindon Panel Box was then working to Badminton. Train description between Badminton–Swindon and vice versa was by a rotating counter-train describer.

After the closure of Little Somerford box, a new crossover was brought into use and was controlled by a ground frame released from Swindon Panel Box. This ground frame was sited approximately ½ mile (800m) nearer to Swindon. Its purpose was to be used during engineering works and single-line working.

Little Somerford possessed two of the longest loops on the line and it was always a puzzle to many why these loops (which had better access by road) were not retained instead of Hullavington's loops, which were staggered and with no access to the Up loop from the road. It must be remembered that although the introduction of Multiple Aspect Signalling was modern in 1968, the general thinking of the railways and the speed of many freight trains was still steam age. Most freights were at that time still Class 7, 8 or 9; that is, still partially, or not at all, fitted with the continuous vacuum brake. Speeds therefore were slow. For a slow Up freight train leaving the Chipping Sodbury–Badminton section and entering the area controlled by Swindon Panel, the time taken to reach Little Somerford would be approximately fifteen minutes longer than it would take to reach Hullavington loop. Should a passenger train be following, albeit at a 'respectful' distance, it would inevitably catch the freight and be delayed.

It must also be remembered that although Badminton still had loops at the time of Swindon Panel's opening, these would be lost when Bristol took over the control of the western half of the line and trains would have to run between Hullavington and Chipping Sodbury loops. So, keeping the loops at Hullavington made better sense with regard to train regulation.

The march of colour-light progress was advancing from the west as well; Newport Panel Box took over control of the Severn Tunnel from 6 July 1969, Severn Tunnel East box closing the same weekend.

Next box to go was Winterbourne, which closed under Stage 2 of the Bristol resignalling scheme on 7 June 1970; it was replaced by colour-light automatic signals supervised from Westerleigh West and Stoke Gifford East boxes. Stage 6 of the

Bristol resignalling on 21 February 1971 saw Filton Junction, Patchway Station, Cattybrook Siding, Stoke Gifford West and East signal boxes closed and Bristol Panel Box working to Westerleigh West and Pilning Junction boxes.

A month later, on 15 March 1971, Pilning Junction and Station boxes were closed and Bristol Panel worked to Newport Panel. With the closure of Westerleigh West and East, Chipping Sodbury and Badminton boxes on 10 May 1971, Bristol Panel worked through to Swindon Panel on the Badminton line and colour-light signalling and continuous track-circuiting was in use right along the Direct line.

Standby generators that would automatically come on line in the event of a mains power failure and thus keep all points and signals in operation, were located at: Westerleigh Junction (covering the area from the approaches to Hullavington to Coalpit Heath); Stoke Gifford (covering the area from Coalpit Heath to Cattybrook and Filton Lunction, Filton West and the Patchway chord line); and Pilning (covereing from Cattybrook to the east end of the Severn Tunnel).

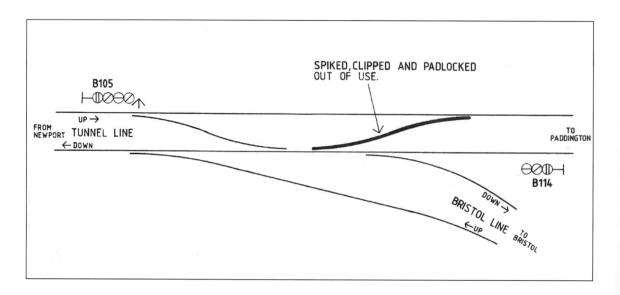

British Rail plan of the modified Patchway Junction. AUTHOR'S COLLECTION

Layout Alterations

With all these closures and resignalling came track alterations as well. The lower section of the Down goods loop at Severn Tunnel East had been removed in February 1968, the remaining connection from Down loop to Down main being now controlled from Pilning Station box. Control of the entrance points to the Up goods loop between Severn Tunnel East and Pilning Station was transferred to Newport Panel Box. The Up loop between Pilning Station and Junction boxes was removed in May 1969. With the closure of the Pilning signal boxes, control of the exit from the Down goods loop passed to Newport Panel Box.

Patchway, already a shadow of its former steam-age self, had only the rarely used Up refuge siding to lose; this had been officially 'taken out of use' and recovered in May 1968, but in reality was just not used any more after that date and was eventually recovered when the box closed. The rest of the layout had gone by 1967, leaving just the junction. With the resignalling of 1971 came the new chord line between Patchway and Filton West on the Avonmouth line. This chord was a single line and the junction for it consisted of a facing crossover between the Up and Down tunnel lines, followed by the single lead on to the chord. Using this chord obviated the need for Avonmouth traffic to and from South Wales to reverse at Stoke Gifford. The junction with the Bristol line was later modified when the diamond crossing was removed and replaced by a facing crossover and a single lead on to the Down Bristol line to Filton Junction. This was further modified when on 24 March 1980 a trailing connection was laid in between the Up and Down tunnel lines and between the existing facing crossover and the facing connection to the Down Bristol line. This new crossover was to be for reversible working and was fixed out of use for the time being.

At Stoke Gifford, little changed. A new ground frame was brought into use to control the connections from the Down yard and most of the Up sidings were recovered to make room for the car

A lone Class 56 passes the site of Westerleigh East box in 1980. In the background is a bracket with main and reversible working signals on it. It was later replaced by a standard four-aspect signal on a single post. P.D. RENDALL

park for the new station. Otherwise, the control of all points passed to Bristol Panel Box.

There was no crossover or siding between Stoke Gifford and Westerleigh West Junction. The latter lost its 'west' title, being now known as 'Westerleigh Junction'. Reversible working was brought in between Yate and Westerleigh on the Down branch line, allowing trains to be signalled in the Up direction over the Down branch to permit following trains to pass. The sidings at Westerleigh East – all that remained of the wartime Wapley yard – were removed.

Chipping Sodbury lost its Down loop, the Up loop being signalled for working in both directions, with a new crossover being installed at the west end of the layout to permit Down trains in the loop to regain the Down main line. The Up sidings remained, access from the Up loop to the sidings being controlled by two new ground frames, 'east' and 'west', which were both released by Bristol Panel.

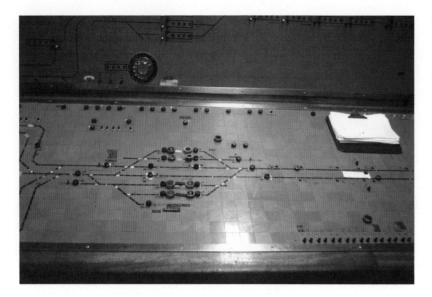

Bristol Panel signal box 'D' position seen in November 1985. Stoke Gifford West Junction is on the right side of the photo, Bristol Parkway in the middle. P.D. RENDALL

At Badminton, all sidings and loops were removed. Two new crossovers sited a short distance to the east of the old layout were brought into use. These crossovers, one facing, one trailing, were controlled from a ground frame released by Bristol Panel Box. Their function was the same as those at Little Somerford.

The Up and Down main lines between Wootton Bassett and Stoke Gifford West Junctions were renamed 'Up and Down Badminton' lines. The lines between Severn Tunnel West and Patchway Junctions were renamed the 'Up and Down Tunnel' lines.

Working the line from the panel boxes was a lot simpler. The signalman could see the entire section of line under his control and it was easier to work out margins. Although the Badminton lines from Alderton Tunnel through to Stoke Gifford and then the tunnel lines as far as the eastern end of the Severn Tunnel were all on one panel at Bristol, they were on a separate panel within the box. This was the 'D' position, better known as the 'Stoke Panel', and was set at 90 degrees to the main signalling panel. Working the Stoke Panel was like working in your own signal box, as the signalman had the entire Direct line between Alderton and Pilning under his control.

Trains passed from the 'C' position of Bristol main panel on to the 'D' position at Ashley Hill; no acceptance was needed, as train description was taken forwards automatically. It was usual, though, for the 'C' signalman to call out the train description to his colleague to ensure smooth working. Train descriptions from Newport were again automatically transmitted to Bristol, but the Bristol signalman had the choice of accepting the train up the loop or main line as applicable, Newport having control over the entrance to the Up loop. Likewise, Newport would accept a train 'main line' or 'loop' as necessary.

The description of Down trains from Swindon would be transmitted forwards to Bristol when the train passed Hullavington; Up trains would be described to Swindon when passing Chipping Sodbury.

Westerleigh Junction was realigned and the diamond crossing replaced by movable 'switch diamonds', or, to give them the old name, 'elbows'; 'elbows' they had been and 'elbows' they remained, whatever new name was given to them. Reversible working was brought in over the Up branch from Yate to Westerleigh.

At Stoke Gifford, there was the new station of Bristol Parkway; the station staff were advised of the approach of trains calling there by means of a telephone on the 'D' position desk. Stoke Gifford kept the Up goods loop and Up reception siding, along with a siding for crippled wagons. The Down No.1 and No.2 goods loops were also retained, along with many of the Down sidings. From 1985, the Up reception was regularly used by the (then) Avon County waste train, which would run from its last pick-up at Bath Goods to Stoke Gifford, where the loaded containers would be left on the Up reception and the train would proceed to Yate, where it would run round and proceed down the old LMR line to Westerleigh sidings. There, the train would leave the empty containers and collect the loaded ones, afterwards running back to Stoke Gifford for marshalling with the other loaded containers and then 'right away' to Swindon. The official title for this train was the 'Binliner', but it was always known to Bristol railway staff by no other name than 'Dustybins'.

As mentioned above, Chipping Sodbury kept the Up loop and sidings. During the 1990s, the sidings were used for a short period for repairs and maintenance to Procor stone wagons, a shunter travelling up from Stoke Gifford on the loco when shunts were required.

Filton Junction was modified and a new, faster crossover laid in. The coal concentration depot was still able to be accessed by means of a ground frame from the goods loop. Following the 1984 rationalization of the four-track section between Bristol, Dr Day's Junction and Filton, Filton Junction was changed by means of just removing the Down and Up relief lines beyond the crossovers, rather than redesigning the junction. This made for a bit of an operating nightmare that the signalmen had to cope with; rationalization to save money does not always work.

High Speed

Much has already been written about the upgrading of the Direct line to take 125mph (200km/h) trains, so there is no need to go into too much detail here. The Class 253 High Speed Trains being built by British Rail in the early 1970s were to be allocated first to the Western Region, where they would take over the Bristol to Paddington and South Wales

Superpower! Four Class 25 diesels find themselves at the head of a ballast train on the Up main line at Westerleigh Junction during the preparation of the line for 125mph speeds, July 1975. Also seen is the new bracket signal for the reversible working that was never brought into use. P.D. RENDALL

to Paddington services. It was decided that in order to make full use of the 125mph trains, the Direct line between Wootton Bassett Junction and Stoke Gifford (Bristol Parkway) would be upgraded for high-speed running. Accordingly, in May 1975 the line from Wootton Bassett as far as Westerleigh Junction was closed to all except Civil Engineering trains.

Over the next five months, all track was lifted and the ballast removed. New polythene membranes were laid in, new drains installed and new ballast laid. Continuously welded track was laid on the new ballast and the track brought up to 125mph speed except where passing through Alderton Tunnel, where speed was to be restricted to 110mph (177km/h) as there were no ventilation shafts to prevent a build-up of air pressure when a train entered the tunnel – the combined pressure of two trains passing in the tunnel at 125mph was thought to be capable of dislocating carriage windows.

The whole period of work went smoothly and there were no real incidents of note. Train crews working the Engineers' trains on the 'dead' line were ferried to the agreed crew changeover locations by the Bristol Bath Road diesel depot minibus. Tales were often related of how the minibus drivers were suddenly confronted with unfamiliar names and places and how the minibus would frequently be driving up and down narrow country lanes in the dead of night whilst the driver peered into the dark trying to work out where he was. The east end of Chipping Sodbury Tunnel was one such location – difficult enough to find in daylight, it was next to impossible in the dark.

Reversible Signalling

At the same time as the track was being renewed, so BR installed new signalling along the line. Although less than five years old, the existing Multiple Aspect Signalling was based on the old principles of 'Up trains for Up lines and Down trains for Down lines'. Quite naturally, BR wanted to maximize the use of its new trains and track and the new signalling was to enable trains to run in either direction on either line – 'reversible signalling'.

Reversible signalling was not new; it had been used elsewhere to good effect and was being progressively installed down the main lines from Didcot, although was not yet in use. BR could see that the new service to be brought in with the introduction of the new trains would have the ability to transform the region's InterCity services, in terms of both speed and frequency. There was an old and accepted notion that Sundays were the days when services were disrupted and diverted owing to the Civil Engineers taking partial or complete possession of lines in order to carry out essential maintenance.

Whilst possessions would still happen, it would not be possible to gain maximum use of the new trains all year round unless these old practices were to be changed. This would mean that the current practice of single-line working by pilotman would have to go; it was effective in as much as it kept trains running when one line was blocked, but it was also labour-intensive and time-consuming. With reversible signalling, the engineers could work on one line and trains could be run in both directions over the other line with no extra staff being involved. It was BR's wish that by introducing reversible signalling on most of the lines between London and Bristol, Sunday services could be operated to within eight minutes of normal weekday services without disrupting engineering work. Speed would not be 125mph (200km/h) in the 'wrong' direction, but was expected to be able to be up to 100mph (160km/h). The new signalling being installed between Wootton Bassett and Stoke Gifford was still at that time planned to adhere to the old principles, so the management set about negotiating with the trade unions to bring in reversible working.

Negotiations with the local trade unions had opened in March 1974; representatives from the National Union of Railwaymen (NUR) and the Associated Society of Locomotive Engineers and Firemen (ASLEF) being invited to attend a Joint Consultation meeting held at the Transport and General Workers' Union premises at Transport

House, Victoria Street, Bristol. At that meeting, the representatives were told that it was proposed to install the new signalling in many places on BR and to divide the lines into 10-mile (16km) sections, at each end of which would be a pair of facing and trailing crossovers, over which trains could cross from one line to the other at 40mph (64km/h). On more intensely used lines, such as the section of line between Didcot and Wootton Bassett, the sections would be 6 miles (10km) long. It was intended to signal the wrong direction moves with two-aspect signals. Where trains would cross from wrong line to the correct line, the signals would be three- or four-aspect to reflect the aspects shown on the normal running line.

Not only would the new signalling be used during engineering works, but it was intended also to use it in instances where a train may have failed and following trains would be able to bypass the obstruction, when for regulation purposes a slower train could be 'overtaken' by a faster service.

The BR management thought that the biggest safety problem to encounter would be the problem of how to ensure the safety of permanent way track patrolmen going about their inspection of the line. How would they know from which direction the next train would be approaching? Early thoughts were that each patrolman would have to be accompanied by a lookout man.[38]

The staff representatives were then told that there would be some necessary alterations to staffing levels as a result of the introduction of reversible working. These would be at Bristol, where three posts of signalman ('panel pool' – handsignalmen who were ex-signalmen and employed almost entirely on handsignalling work) would be lost, while throughout the area an extra six permanent way lookout jobs would be created. The 'panel pool'

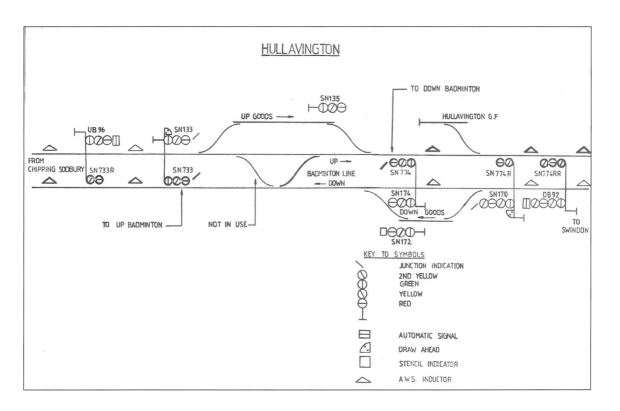

British Rail diagram showing the reversible working at Hullavington, which was brought into use on Sunday, 6 July 1980. AUTHOR'S COLLECTION

was a relief signalman's post, lower graded than the panel box jobs. These men worked with the Civil Engineers, mainly at night, where they would be employed as handsignalmen or pilotmen for single-line working. Reversible working would, naturally, make their jobs redundant.

From this meeting, the Union men went back to their members (drivers, secondmen, guards, permanent way staff and signalmen) and advised them of the contents of the meeting. Diagrams of the new signalling had been provided for the Union reps to show staff what was planned. A further meeting was to be held on 18 April 1974. It was at this meeting that the management could explain how the proposals would benefit BR. It was explained that many passengers who did not travel by train on a weekday, did so on Sundays. Currently the standards of Sunday services were much lower than those of weekday services; Sunday trains were affected by engineering works and were thus slower overall, for example the Paddington–Bristol Sunday service was up to forty to fifty minutes slower than on weekdays. If the High Speed Trains were to be fully exploited, then something had to be done to avoid these delays – the answer was reversible signalling.

The system had received the funding and had been given preliminary approval by the Chief Inspecting Officer of Railways. It was expected that the new signalling would be commissioned throughout between Didcot Foxhall Junction and Bristol Stoke Gifford West, by October 1976. It was hoped that the section between Swindon and Bourton (east of Swindon) would be in operation by the end of 1974.[39]

It was claimed that the reversible signalling would only be used by High Speed Trains on Sundays during planned engineering work, or on weekdays during an emergency. Then the managers went on to tell staff that weekday use would be 'confined to either bypassing a failed train or a broken rail, or during weekday nights to enable tamping machines to operate'. And: 'it will be likely, however, that on some routes, the reversible working facility would be used to enable slower

freight trains to be bypassed, i.e., the opposite line would be used as a "long goods loop" '.[40]

In fact, the management even admitted, in answer to a question from the Bristol Bath Road diesel depot representative, that certain trains would be timetabled to run over reversible sections in the wrong direction, 'probably at night', in order to make sure that the equipment was regularly used. So rather than being for use during engineering work or emergencies, in fact the reversible signalling would actually be available for use at all times.

Staff Concerns

Quite naturally, the staff were not happy with the situation. They were most concerned with the safety of men working on or about the lines with trains not only soon to be running at 125mph, but up to 100mph in the wrong direction. No solid answers to this problem were available, they were told. There were thought to be several methods of protecting staff that could be used, including the possibility of locking wrong direction signals at Danger by means of a key at the signal post, or the already mentioned option of every track patrolman being accompanied by a lookout man.

Another staff question centred on the future provision of proper footpaths at the side of the lines concerned. This was not a frivolous question; in steam days, footpaths alongside the tracks were always present and kept in excellent condition. Men used them to walk on, or even cycle along to and from work. Modernization had not only reduced the staffing levels needed to keep such paths in good condition, but modern ballasting covered many lineside pathways, rendering them useless. If, with the advent of HST and reversible signalling, staff were to move about the track safely, they once again needed good walkways. No problem, said the managers, this has already been ruled necessary by the Chief Inspecting Officer and was currently being progressed.

In progress it may have been, but the problem of blocking lineside paths was a big one. No matter how neat and tidy you made a pathway, someone would unload a heap of concrete sleepers on to it, or a pile of rails. Inevitably, most engineering jobs take place during the night and with staffing levels less than they had been ten years earlier, owing to economies, it was quite usual for a material train to move slowly along a line at night, unloading materials into the lineside 'cess'. These would be used during the occupation of the line that night or on future occasions, so would often be left where they had been unloaded. Staff were quite aware of this and could envisage what had become a bit of an obstacle course turning deadly once the new working was introduced, even more so when the management confirmed that reversible working would be used during periods of fog and reduced visibility.[41] Sadly, the question of the standard of lineside pathways was to become both a physical and metaphorical stumbling block to reversible working over the next few years.

BR hoped that once the high-speed section of the Direct line was opened, the new reversible signalling would soon be brought into use. New signals and signal gantries were erected and new cabling laid in. Testing began and as the trackwork was completed, so the new signalling was ready to use. The signals appertaining to the reversible working remained out of use and were covered up. Prior to the reopening of the Badminton line in October 1975, BR's Western Region issued a 'Notice to Trainmen' and other staff announcing the introduction of new signalling between Swindon (Wootton Bassett) and Bristol (Westerleigh Junction) on the reopening of the line to all traffic on 6 October that year.

The Line Reopens

On the ground, there had been changes to layouts during the five-month closure. At Wootton Bassett West two new crossovers had been laid in, one facing and one trailing, and the former connection into the Up main from the British Lely private siding had been removed. The crossovers at Little Somerford, Hullavington and Badminton had been removed and a new pair of facing and trailing

crossovers laid in at Hullavington. The crossovers at Wootton Bassett West and Hullavington would, for a while, be hand-operated where necessary for use during emergency working or planned engineering work.

The new signalling consisted of three- and four-aspect colour-light signals, many of which were now on overtrack gantries. The whole line was now signalled for trains travelling up to a quarter as fast again as previous services; thus there were more signals and better sighting. Eighteen new signals, most of them four-aspect, replaced eight existing three-aspect and two-aspect signals on the Up road. Seventeen new four-aspect signals replaced nine existing three- and two-aspect signals on the Down road. Of these new signals, fourteen on each road were automatic signals. There was a new four-aspect signal, DB102, inside Chipping Sodbury Tunnel on the Down line and this was preceded with 'countdown' markers at 300yd (275m) intervals that would only be illuminated when DB102 stood at Danger. In this way, HST drivers had more frequent and better reminders of a signal's aspect; necessary when travelling at over 2 miles (3.2km) a minute.

As is well known, the InterCity 125 services commenced in 1976 to great acclaim and soon became a success story for BR and the Western Region. HSTs were also brought into use on the East Coast main line. But what of the reversible signalling? On the face of it, this was a technological advance and one that makes a great deal of sense today. Sadly, the approach to introducing the new signalling must have gone awry with regards to getting the staff to accept it. Whilst the trade unions had accepted reversible signalling at national level, the BR Western Region managers failed to convey their excitement with it to the staff at local level. Local union representatives became bogged down with trivial matters; it was not just obstructed walkways that became an issue, but even the type of vandal-proof lineside telephones to be installed developed into an obstacle to reversible signalling.

It was not just mere intransigence on the part of the unions; it must also be taken into account that, almost to a man, all the signalling staff from both Bristol and Swindon Panel Boxes and just about everyone else involved in other grades were long-serving railwaymen. To expect them to get their heads round the fact that trains would not only be running at 125mph in the right direction, but would also be able to run at up to 100mph in the *wrong* direction was going to be difficult. The staff required educating in the new methods, rather than just being told that it was going to happen. Eventually, reversible signalling familiarization courses *were* held, but they were for trainmen only, of one day's duration and were held in the early months of 1978.

By then, BR was intent on commissioning reversible signalling, but it would be between Didcot Foxhall Junction and Wantage Road, and would be restricted to use only where planned engineering work had been notified in the weekly Operating Notice. The future extension of the work would be reviewed at six-monthly intervals.

Eventually, reversible signalling was brought into use all the way to Hullavington[42] and then through Chipping Sodbury Tunnel to the Up/Down loop, where it stopped. By now, the non-commissioned signals were showing signs of decay, with the gantries beginning to rust where paint had flaked off. The signals were removed and, in due course, so were the unused gantries. The South Wales Direct line remained, on the whole, conventionally signalled.

Patrolman's Lockout

In the 1980s, a 'Patrolman's Lockout' device was installed at key locations along the line. This was a device for use by the permanent way track patrol-

Travelling at 110mph (177km/h), a Down Paddington–Swansea HST passes the site of Badminton station, summer 1982. The old goods shed is still standing. P.D. RENDALL

man (or other key staff who needed to work on, or walk along, the line), whereby a switch was operated and this locked the reversible signalling, ensuring that trains could only run in the 'normal' direction.

Before operating the switch, the patrolman had to phone the controlling panel signal box and ask if it was in order to operate the switch. If it was, he would turn the device to 'Protected' and carry out his duties, phoning in again when his patrol (or work) was complete. Permission to use the device was only granted by the panel signalman on condition that the patrolman or other person was in possession of an issued radio paging device so that he could be contacted if the need to use reversible working arose. If the section required to be patrolled was overseen by both Bristol and Swindon Panel Boxes, for example, both signalmen concerned had to be contacted and their respective permissions obtained.

Computer Future

On 4 January 2010, a new signalling centre was opened at Newport. Named the 'South Wales Control Centre' (SWCC), this took over the South Wales lines between Patchway and the Severn Tunnel, previously operated by Bristol and Newport Panel Boxes. Controls in the new SWCC are computers and visual display units (VDUs). The area now controlled by the SWCC commences on the Down line at the Patchway end of the lines from Avonmouth, Filton and Stoke Gifford and includes the whole of the junction at Patchway. Track circuits have been replaced by axle counters from a point at the Bristol end of Patchway Long Tunnel right through the Severn Tunnel. On the Up line, the SWCC controls all track and signalling as far as the approaches to Patchway station. Axle counters have replaced track circuits on the Up tunnel line as far as a farm underbridge known as 'Virgos Farm Lane Bridge', just east of Pilning station. Many new signals, mostly equipped with single- or double-lens light-emitting diode (LED) lights, have replaced the old colour lights.

Network Rail plans to replace Swindon and Bristol Panel Boxes with a new signalling centre to be known as the 'Thames Valley Signalling Centre'. This is to be sited at Didcot and will, in due course, control all the lines between Paddington and Penzance. It will be one of just fourteen such computer signalling centres controlling the whole of Britain's railway network. Thus the South Wales Direct line will come under the control of just two 'signal boxes' – one at Didcot and one at Newport, South Wales.

CHAPTER 14

The Future of the Line

Although the line has been a high-speed 125mph (200km/h) line since 1975, it has still seen a lot of freight traffic and continues to do so. As mentioned above, most of the freight movements have been on the section of line between Westerleigh Junction and Stoke Gifford. But fast freight traffic has been able to use the 125 section. This traffic consists of Freightliner trains and other fast bulk traffic.

Stone traffic has played an important part in the line's life, mostly from the reopened Thornbury branch between Yate South, on the line to Gloucester and the Midlands, and the Tytherington quarry of Amey Roadstone Construction (ARC). This rail link provided much traffic for the line, with empty stone trains moving between Stoke Gifford sidings and the quarry and the loaded traffic returning to Stoke Gifford. From Stoke Gifford, the trains would be moved to their destinations, often via Badminton.

This traffic was predominant for years, but has slowed considerably during the years of the twenty-first century as quarry output has all but ceased. The 'merry-go-round' coal traffic from South Wales to Didcot power station has also ended since the power station's closure.

As the only high-speed route to South Wales from London, the future existence of the line is in no doubt. On 23 July 2009, the then Labour Transport Secretary announced the electrification of the whole of the old Great Western main line between London Paddington and Swansea, via Bath to Bristol and via Badminton. Faster and more economical trains will

The line was much used for stone traffic during the 1970s and 1980s – a Class 52 shunts stone tipplers at Stoke Gifford in 1977. P.D. RENDALL

An Up train of loaded ARC Procor stone hoppers passes Coalpit Heath in 1984. Note that the goods shed is still standing here, too. T.R. RENDALL

use the line; these are planned to be built in Japan by Hitachi and will be SET (Super Express Trains). Hybrid, or Bi-Mode, versions of these trains are also planned, consisting of SETs with a diesel generator vehicle at one end of the formation and an electric transformer vehicle at the other end. These trains will enable the SET to operate beyond the stations where the electrification will end, thus ensuring that services that are timetabled to go beyond the end of the electrified sections can continue without passengers having to change trains.[43] It has also been announced that there will be a new maintenance depot built on the site of the tip sidings near Stoke Gifford. The depot, which will be constructed in the triangle formed by the Avonmouth lines and the lines to Patchway and from Filton, will have connections to the main lines at both the Bristol Parkway and Patchway ends. At the time of writing, work to level the site has begun.[44]

The first SET trains are expected to reach these shores in 2015 for testing and the first SET is expected to enter service on the Paddington–South Wales route in 2017. The 1970s HST will most likely be retired from service, as its main function in the West will cease to exist.

The electric trains will collect their 25kV current from overhead catenary wires; huge challenges will be faced on the Direct line installing the wires through Alderton, Chipping Sodbury and Patchway Tunnels and, of course, through the 7,688yd

A Down HST powers under the 'Ha'penny Bridge' at Coalpit Heath in 1982. P.D. RENDALL

Road closure notice on the Fosse Way in Wiltshire for bridge replacement in connection with pre-electrification works.

P.D. RENDALL

(7,030m) of the Severn Tunnel, with its notoriously wet interior. The wires have to be no closer than 11in or 12in (275mm or 300mm) from any earthed structure and so the installation of the wires will also involve the rebuilding or raising of over 110 bridges along both the Bath and Badminton lines. Undoubtedly, the appearance of the line will change, as overbridges will be rebuilt with higher parapets and more secure fencing will be needed to keep people away from the wires.

This has already been seen at Badminton, where the road overbridge, famous in the photographs and paintings of George Heiron, has been replaced. At the east end of the Badminton station site an occupation overbridge has already been replaced. At the time of writing, Bridge No.261B, a skew girder bridge of 34ft 10in (10.6m) width that carries the Fosse Way, a minor road between the villages of Grittleton and Sherston, over the railway is due for replacement during the period August–November 2013. Between Badminton and Chipping Sodbury, there have been planning applications submitted for the purpose of raising the height of the parapets on several other overbridges.

In order to cause as little disruption as possible to normal rail traffic, Network Rail plans to carry out most of the electrification work during night-time engineering possessions, where piling trains will operate within a possession, drilling holes for and installing mast bases, whilst a following train will place masts on the bases ready for the wiring train.

The scheme is expected to cost over £1 billion. The lines to Bristol are expected to be electrified by 2016 and the lines to Swansea by 2017.

Specials

The line has seen many steam-hauled specials. After the end of steam traction on British Rail in 1968, the BR Board put a blanket ban on steam locomotives running on BR metals. Steam was said to be 'old-fashioned' and 'out of date' and had no place on a clean, modern and efficient railway. This situation lasted for three long years, until the BR Board had a change of heart in 1971. How fitting it was, then, that the ban was temporarily lifted to allow a steam excursion, hauled by an ex-Great Western loco to run on the South Wales Direct line. The engine itself was very appropriately No.6000 *King George V* and hauled a rake of Pullman coaches from its base at Hereford, to Tyseley, Birmingham, via Didcot. The train returned to Hereford three days later, again via the Severn Tunnel. It was watched on both journeys by hundreds of people. I went to a derelict Westerleigh East box on the first journey to watch it pass. There were dozens of people on the site of the old Up sidings; they had all turned out to see this 'old-fashioned' loco – the King was in spotless condition and did not disappoint the watchers.

This change of heart by BR was said not to be a case of returning to steam-hauled trains, but that the BR Board was looking at the possibility of running steam-hauled excursion trains on the network if they could be made to be economically viable.

As anyone will know, the ban was lifted and steam excursions are a common sight on the Direct line nowadays. *King George V* was the loco of choice used to run the 'Brunel Pullman' between Bristol and South Wales on 12 June 1983; the train ran to

Driven by Bristol Bath Road driver Gordon Barge, King George V *passes Cattybrook with the 'Brunel Pullman' on 12 June 1983. P.D. RENDALL*

Newport with a Bristol crew, before being used on the 'Welsh Marches Specials'. *King George V* is not the only King to have used the line; classmate *King Edward I* has been used on excursions, as have several Castle Class locos.

But the most notable steam excursion to date must surely be the April 2010 'Bristolian' run from Paddington to Bristol via Bath and back via the Direct line. The excursion, which took place on 17 April, was hauled both ways by Castle Class No.5043 *Earl of Mount Edgcumbe* – magnificently restored at Tyseley – and achieved 75mph (120km/h) at Hullavington on the return journey. Since then, the *Earl* has made several visits to the Direct line, the most recent being on 25 May 2013, when it ran down from Birmingham to Bristol, joining the Badminton line at Westerleigh Junction.

A year or two ago, I went to Badminton to see the passing of newly restored Britannia Class loco No.70013 *Oliver Cromwell.* There was a small crowd of people on Bridge 272B to watch the train.

Not having witnessed a main-line steam excursion for many years, I was expecting the train to pass at a modest speed. Its approach was indicated by a rapid 'tif-tif-tiff' of exhaust before *Cromwell* hurtled

Nameplate of No.5043 Earl of Mount Edgcumbe – a regular performer on railtours on the Direct line during the twenty-first century. Picture taken when the loco was in BR service. WILF STANLEY

King Edward I *seen here near Badminton on a railtour soon after restoration.* WILF STANLEY

31005 and 31019 run over the reversible Up Branch in the Down direction from Yate up to Westerleigh Junction with the 'Farewell to Toffee Apples' railtour in October 1977. P.D. RENDALL

through Badminton at a speed that would not have disgraced the 'Capitals United Express' of days gone by. It was a really magnificent sight and sound experience.

But diesels, too, are used on excursions. During the 1980s, when diesel loco classes were starting to become thinned by scrapping, enthusiasts ran specials headed by diesels. The South Wales Direct line saw pairs of Class 40 and Class 20 locos on excursions. In October 1977, a pair of Class 31/0 (nicknamed 'Toffee Apples' after the shape of the control handle) was used to run a 'Farewell Special' before being withdrawn for scrap. The locomotives concerned were 31005 and 31019. Both diesels were in immaculate condition.

Westerns and Deltics have also been seen on enthusiasts' specials on the line, both during their time in BR service and in preservation. At the time of writing, the most recent of these was Deltic D9009 *Alycidon*, which headed an excursion from the LMR line to Bristol and beyond in lieu of D1015, whose overhaul was not yet complete. With the approach of electrification, who knows what 'specials' might be seen on the line? Would it be too

Deltic 55002 King's Own Yorkshire Light Infantry *at Bristol Parkway during the harsh winter of 1982.* WILF STANLEY

much to hope that in the future we might see the faithful and long-serving HST in preservation and once again running on the route it made famous in the 1970s?

Hopefully, the electrification of the South Wales Direct line will be yet further guarantee of its continuing future and will enable trains to speed along the line at higher speeds than they do today; but I hope that this will not prevent steam-hauled (and even preserved diesel) excursions from using the line, thus continuing that link between the old and the new.

Class 40 double act: the Devon Quarryman *headed by 40086 and 40118 pauses in the Down loop at Bristol Parkway for a crew change on 24 November 1984.* P.D. RENDALL

Appendix

Weedspraying and Brushwood Spraying Programme, 1982

Western Region Weedspraying will, this year, be undertaken exclusively by Chipman Chemical Co. during the period 27 April to 15 June 1982, using a conventional fully fitted vacuum brake train.

Formation: Machinery coach (incl Guard's brake*), Mess Van, five water tanks, Chemical storage van/s.
*Guard may alternatively travel in rear cab of loco.

Speed: Running light 45mph, Normal spraying 40mph, Brushwood spraying 20mph. (Those locations at which Brushwood Spraying is undertaken will be included in the timings schedule and in addition will be advised to train crew by Civil Engineering Department representative.)

This train is authorized to run with a locomotive coupled to each end between points specified on this Notice. The driver of the trailing locomotive in the direction of travel must NOT apply power.

It is essential that at those locations where more than one running line is available for trains running in the same direction, the train runs over the line shown in the timings. Attention is also drawn to the necessity for trains to run through loops as indicated in the timing. It is NOT possible to spray loops from the main line.

AREA MANAGERS to arrange for Signal Boxes and Ground Frames to be manned as necessary. Local Freight trains to be kept clear.

Notes: F = Run via loop and also spray main line. PR = Propel. RR = Run Round.

Friday 4th June 1982   6Z07
Ashton Gate Engineers depot: depart 08.16
Bristol Temple Meads: 08.31–08.33
Chippenham: 09.35
Swindon: 10.03–10.24 (run-round)
Chippenham: 10.52
North Somerset Junction: 12.02
Dr Day's Junction: 12.04
Filton Junction: 12.18–12.21
Stoke Gifford Up side: 12.24
Westerleigh Junction: 12.34
Chipping Sodbury: 12.40 F 12.50
Hullavington: 13.10 F 13.21
Wootton Bassett West: Goods Loop F
Wootton Bassett Junction: 13.42
Swindon: 13.53 (run-round)
Wootton Bassett Junction: 14.26
Hullavington: 14.47– 15.08
Westerleigh Junction: 15.35
Stoke Gifford Down side: 15.45–15.50
Filton Junction: 15.53
Ashton Gate Engineers depot: arrive 16.23

Weedkilling in 1959; a Class 3MT 2-6-2 tank loco heads a weedkilling train through Coalpit Heath station. WILF STANLEY

References

Kelly's local directories, various, Wiltshire area.

British Railways Working Timetables of Passenger Trains, 1960, 1969, 1970.

Great Western Railway Rule Book, 1936.

Bristol Journal, 25 July 1980.

Bristol Evening Post, Tuesday, 6 April 1970.

Station Log Book from Chipping Sodbury station, commencing 1903.

Various signal box Train Registers from boxes along the line, from 1948 to 1966.

Bristol Panel signal box 'Special Instructions to Signalmen', 1992 (now obsolete).

Starting Something New at Bristol – The Story of the 1970 Bristol Resignalling, P.D. Rendall, Past-Track Publications, 2007.

'Classification of Station and Yard Masters and Goods Agents'. GWR, 1920s, www.ancestry.co.uk

1903 plans of the South Wales Direct line supplied by the Wiltshire Records Office, Chippenham.

First Great Western website: firstgreatwestern. co.uk

Strategic Rail Authority website (no longer in existence; the SRA was abolished in 2005).

Further information has been gleaned from the notes, notices and diagrams that were compiled by the Bristol District Signalling Inspectors in the period between the 1950s and the 1980s and which are held by the author.

Notes

1   W.J. Robinson, *West Country Churches*, Vols 1 & 2, Bristol Times and Mirror Ltd, 1914.

2   *Chipping Sodbury Station Log Book, 1903*, Author's Collection.

3   *Classification of Signal Boxes and Relief Signalmen's Posts*, Great Western Railway, March 1925.

4   *Classification of Station and Yard Masters and Goods Agents*, GWR, 1920.

5   *Sectional Appendix to the Working Timetable and Books of Rules and Regulations*. British Railways Western Region, 1 October 1960.

6   www.ancestry.co.uk, *Register of Clerks, GWR*.

7   *Sectional Appendix to the Book of Rules and Regulations*, British Railways, 1960.

8   *Railway Magazine*, August 1968. Transport & Technical Publications Ltd.

9   *Chipping Sodbury Station Log Book*, 1903, Author's Collection.

10 *Correspondence between Charles Kislingbury and Frederick Savage*, March 1905, Author's Collection.

11 *1962 Note in Chipping Sodbury Station Log Book*, Author's Collection.

12 *General Appendix to the Working Timetable and Books of Rules and Regulations*, British Railways Western Region, 1 October 1960.

13 *Chipping Sodbury Station Log Book, 1921*, Author's Collection.

14 South Gloucestershire Mines Research Group

and Yate & District Heritage Centre/South Gloucestershire Council, *Frog Lane Colliery 60 Years On*, Lightmoor Press, 2009.

15 R.A. Cooke, *Track Layout Diagrams of the Great Western Railway: Section 19B*, privately published, 1996.

16 *Ibid.*

17 www.ancestry.co.uk, *1911 UK Census.*

18 *Sectional Appendix to the Working Timetable and Books of Rules and Regulations*, British Railways Western Region, 1 October 1960.

19 *Bristol Evening Post*, 6 April 1971.

20 *Report of Visit of Institute of Transport to Wapley Common Sorting Depot June 1945, Port of Bristol Authority, Document PBA/F/Stat/7*, Bristol Records Office.

21 *Ibid.*

22 Anderson, Captain Barry; USAF, *Army Air Forces Stations*, Research Division, USAF Historical Research Center, January 1985, www.afhra.af.mil/shared

23 *Bristol Division News* (last issue), Summer 1963, Vol. 4, No. 15, British Railways (WR).

24 R.A. Cooke, *Track Layout Diagrams of the Great Western Railway: Section 19B*, privately published, 1996.

25 *Sectional Appendix to the Rule Book*, Great Western Railway, August 1936.

26 *Working Time Table of Passenger Trains, Bristol District: Section B.* British Railways, June–September 1960.

27 Cecil J. Allen in *Railway World*, Ian Allan, May 1964.

28 BR publicity leaflet *Revised Through Express Services*, May 1961.

29 *Ibid.*

30 George's photo can be seen in his book *Roaming the Western Rails*, Ian Allan, 1980.

31 Great Western Railway: 'NOTICE shewing the Arrangements for the Diversion of THROUGH trains to Alternative Routes in cases of EMERGENCY', June 1940, Author's Collection.

32 HM Railway Inspectorate, *Report on Railway Accident at Chipping Sodbury, 1967*, HM Stationery Office.

33 HM Railway Inspectorate, *Railway Accident in the Severn Tunnel: Report on the Collision that Occurred on 7th December 1991*, HM Stationery Office.

34 *Ibid.*

35 *Ibid.*

36 I can vouch that this worked; I was once hand-signalman in the Limpley Stoke Valley at a signal that was disconnected and maintained at Danger. I was displaying a red handsignal in the form of a flag and had a detonator on the rail. An approaching Sprinter failed to heed the AWS warning, failed to see the red signal and failed to see my red handsignal. He passed the signal at Danger at normal speed and ran over the detonator. A full emergency brake application followed as the noise of the 'shot' brought the driver to his senses. He stopped the train about a ¼-mile (400m) along the line. An Inquiry followed.

37 *Regional Appendix to the Working Timetable and Books of Rules and Regulations*, British Railways Western Region, 1 October 1960.

38 From *Minutes of Joint Consultation Meetings between BR (WR) Management and Representatives from the National Union of Railwaymen (NUR) and the Associated Society of Locomotive Engineers and Firemen (ASLEF); held at the Transport and General Workers Premises at Transport House, Victoria Street, Bristol, between March and April 1974*, Author's Collection.

39 *Ibid.*

40 *Ibid.*

41 *Ibid.*

42 *Supplementary Notice of Signalling Alterations etc., Swindon Panel–Hullavington, Sunday 6th July 1980.* British Rail.

43 'Expansion Plans Unveiled in Great Western ITT', *Rail News*, Issue 186, August 2012, p12, Railnews Ltd.

44 R. Clark in 'GW gets SET for IEP', *Modern Railways*, August 2013, pp. 62–65, Key Publishing Ltd.

Index